The Naturalist in Vancouver Island and British Columbia.

John Keast Lord

PRESS
SHELF
N°

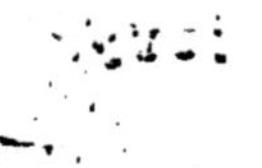

A GROUP OF SPOKAN INDIANS

(Drawn from a Photograph).

THE NATURALIST

IN

VANCOUVER ISLAND AND BRITISH COLUMBIA.

BY

JOHN KEAST LORD, F.Z.S.

NATURALIST TO THE BRITISH NORTH AMERICAN BOUNDARY COMMISSION

THE 'KETTLE' FALLS: A SALMON LEAP ON THE UPPER COLUMBIA

IN TWO VOLUMES—VOL. I.

LONDON:

RICHARD BENTLEY, NEW BURLINGTON STREET,

PUBLISHER IN ORDINARY TO HER MAJESTY.

1866.

PREFACE.

Many interesting and useful works have been already published relating to the Colonies of Vancouver Island and British Columbia, which, however, contain little if any information on the subject of their Natural History.

This missing link I venture in some measure to supply. But 'The Naturalist in Vancouver Island and British Columbia' is not intended to be a book on Natural History merely; neither does the Author desire to weary his reader with tedious descriptions of genera and species. Comparative anatomy and physiology can be acquired at home, but *habits* are only discoverable by those who devote themselves to the rough though pleasant life of a wanderer, or by the actual observation of a careful investigator.

In the following pages, the Author has purposely avoided any definite system of arrangement, preferring a pleasant gossip, chatting, as it were, by the fireside about North-Western Wilds.

A detailed list of the Zoological collection made whilst Naturalist to the Government Commission will be found in the Appendix.

JOHN KEAST LORD.

LONDON: *May* 28, 1866.

INTRODUCTION.

BEFORE setting sail from Southampton, it may perhaps be as well to devote a few pages explanatory of the early history and discovery of Vancouver Island; why we are going there; and the object of the Commission to which I belong.

In the year 1587, we learn, that a Captain Cavendish, in order to repair his shattered fortunes, fitted out three ships for the purpose of plundering on the high seas. After many unsuccessful raids, we next hear of him lurking in his ship behind a spit of land, Cape St. Lucas, on the Californian coast (a prominent rocky bluff, not unlike 'the Needles,'), waiting for the 'St. Anna,' a galleon freighted with rich merchandise and a hundred and twenty-two thousand Spanish dollars. She heaves in sight, little dreaming of her danger; is pounced upon, boarded, and taken, her treasure transferred to the hold of the buccaneer; the crew rowed ashore, and their ship set on fire. Death seemed inevitable, when a breeze, which soon increased to a gale, drifting the burning hull on the rocks providentially proved a means of escape, for a raft was made, and launched. Upon this the men stood out to sea.

After enduring frightful privations, a friendly ship picked them up, and they eventually reached Europe in safety. Amongst the sailors rescued from the raft was a Greek, Apostolos Valerianos, who for some reason was nick-named by his shipmates Juan de Fuca. Nine years after his escape from the raft we hear of him in Venice.

In 1596 Mr. Locke, a merchant, and his friend John Douglas, a sea-captain, were residing in Venice, and nightly smoked their pipes at a snug wine-shop, the resort of sea-faring men. A constant visitor at this house of entertainment was a pilot on the Greek seas, who had attracted Douglas's attention by the wonderful stories he related; so much so that he induced his friend, Mr. Locke, to listen to the old man's adventures.*

* For full narrative of Apostolos Valerianos, see Samuel Purchase His Pilgrims.

The story of the raft we already know. The remainder was to the effect that he entered into the service of the Viceroy of Mexico, by whom he was sent, in a small *caraval*, to explore the Californian coast. He managed to reach lat. 47° N., and finding the coast inclined towards the N. & NE., and that a wide expanse of sea opened out between 47° lat., his position, and 48°, he entered the Strait, and sailed through it for twenty days. Finding the land still tended to NE. & NW. and also E. & SE., he proceeded, passing through groups of beautiful islands, and so sailed on until he came into the North Sea; but being quite unarmed, and finding the natives very hostile, he made his way back, and reported his discovery of the entrance to what he believed the North-West Passage.

But the Viceroy was not impressed with the value of the old man's report, and paid him nothing for it. Disgusted with the government and all belonging to it, he worked his way back to the Mediterranean, and we next meet with him as a pilot on the Adriatic.

Master Locke at once wrote to Sir Walter Raleigh, Master Hakluyt, and to Lord Cecil, asking for 100*l.* to bring over the mariner who possessed such a knowledge of the north-west coast. All thought the information invaluable, but no one felt disposed to pay the money. Time wore on; the old storm-worn pilot, growing feeble, left for his native island. Locke again and again urged his request. At last the long-coveted means came, but too late, the old sailor was no more.

This strange story was current in England long after he who told it was dead and forgotten. A few believed it, but the many thought it an entire fabrication.

In 1776, Captain Cook missed the entrance to the Straits, and, mistaking the west side of Vancouver Island for the mainland, reported the story to be a fiction as told by the old sailor. It will suffice for explanation to skip a crowd of events, and take up the narrative of the discovery of the island in 1792, when Captain Vancouver was sent to Nootka Sound, for what purpose does not matter now. Coasting southwards, he entered the Straits, and eventually came out at Queen Charlotte Sound: which settled the question. The Island bears the name of its discoverer (Vancouver Island), the Straits that of the old sailor (Juan de Fuca).

By the treaty of Washington, the 49th pl. of lat. N. was to be the recognised *Boundary Line*, the course through the sea to be the centre of the Gulf of Georgia, and thence southward through the *Channel* which separates the continent from Vancouver Island, to the Straits of Juan de Fuca.

The duties of our Commission were to mark the Boundary line from the coast to the eastern slope of the Rocky Mountains.

May 1866.

CONTENTS

OF

THE FIRST VOLUME.

CHAPTER VIII.

CHAPTER IX.

CHAPTER X.

CHAPTER XI.

CHAPTER XII.

CHAPTER XIII.

ILLUSTRATIONS

FOR

THE FIRST VOLUME.

ERRATA IN VOL. I.

Page 88, line 19, *for* blubbering *read* blubbery
,, 105, ,, 20, *for* within *read* in
,, 157, ,, 2, *for* scenery on my left. The *read* scenery. On my left the
,, 158, ,, 23, *for* Nimkis *read* Nimkish
,, 164, ,, 9, *for* this cannon *read* these cannons
,, 177, ,, 13, *for* cauiare *read* caviare
,, 179, ,, 9, *for* are *read* is; and line 16, *for* fourteen *read* seven
,, 195, ,, 9, *for* three *read* one
,, 232, ,, 8, *for* pack and equipment *read* pack equipment
,, 268, ,, 5, heading to chapter, *for* The Desert Prong-horned *read* The Desert—Prong-horned
,, 296, ,, 8, *for* Reiney *read* Reiner
,, 349, ,, 12 for *Actomys* read *Arctomys*

VANCOUVER ISLAND

AND

BRITISH COLUMBIA.

CHAPTER I.

THE VOYAGE.

WHETHER Good Friday was more unlucky than Fridays usually are, in the estimation of sea-going men, I know not, but from England to St. Thomas we encountered a succession of head-winds and terrific seas. Of course it was the regular typical storm: 'waves running mountains high, threatening instantaneously to engulph the struggling ship in a watery abyss; rent sails, creaking timbers, men lashed to the wheel (real tarry Ixions); screaming mothers, and remarkably sick papas and passengers,'—that ended in our case, as it usually does in all sensation sea-voyages. St. Thomas was arrived at in perfect safety, some few days after time.

Amongst the passengers was a lady, fat beyond anything I have ever seen (of the human kind) outside a show. From the time of her appearance in the morning until her bedtime, she invariably sat in one place—her throne a small sofa, behind the cabin-door. Flying-fish were constantly driven on the deck of the steamer, or flung up into the sponsons by the paddlewheels; and being most anxious to preserve some of these curious tenants of the ocean, I tried every means to procure them; but the 'stout party,' by resorting to most unjustifiable bribing, so enslaved the sordid mind of the steward, that he got hold of the fish in spite of me, and actually had the delicate beauties cooked, and ignominiously fried at the galley-fire, for that terrible old lady to eat. With regret and indignation I have watched her munching them up, and wickedly longed to see her prostrated by that terrible leveller seasickness, or the victim of dyspepsia—evil wishes of no avail: she ate on, in healthful hungry defiance of wind and waves, and the wrath of an injured naturalist.

The first peep one gets of the little Danish town of St. Thomas, too well known to need more than a casual notice, is picturesque and pretty. Built on the scarp of a steep hill, its houses arranged in terraces, and all painted with bright and gaudy colours; its feathery groves of tamarind-trees; gay gardens decked with flowers, possessing a brilliancy and magnitude seen only in a hot climate; together with the showy dresses of the natives, it becomes the more impressive as contrasted with the sombre island so recently left behind.

Scarcely had the 'Parana' steamed into the harbour—much more, by the way, like a stagnant cesspool than a rocky inlet, filled with pure sea-water—when boats of all sizes, and far too numerous to count, crowded round us. Everyone, seeming at once to forget seasickness and rough weather, scrambled into this medley fleet, and with all speed were rowed ashore—there to remain, during the transference of the mails and baggage from the English steamer to the other vessels waiting to take their departure.

It has often puzzled me to imagine, why travellers in steamboats and sailing-ships invariably do the same thing. Take this very case as an instance of what I mean. Though yellow-fever was raging like a plague, still the greater number of the passengers made straight for the hotel, and there and then devoured a heavy breakfast composed of bad fish, raw vegetables (libellously called salad), unripe fruits, followed by a brown substance, in size, shape, and texture, vastly like to the heel of a boot floating in hot oil, which we are informed by the polite waiter is 'bef steek à la Anglais'—the whole washed down with copious libations of intensely sour claret iced to the freezing-point.

The next thing in the programme is the exploration of the town, during which all sorts of things are purchased at fabulous prices, that can never, by any possibility, be required. Such unusual exercise in a hilly place, exposed to the scorching heat of the sun, soon begets a feverish thirst, necessitating copious draughts of iced-water dashed with cognac, unlimited cobblers, or more cold sour poison. Raw vegetables, acid wine, cobblers, cognac, cocoanut, and other 'comestibles' soon produce disagreeable admonitory twinges: dread of yellow-fever immediately suggests itself—bang goes the signal-gun! A hasty scamper for the boats dispelling further alarm, all rush on board, there to compare notes, groan over their pains and stupidity, and go through precisely the same performance at the next place of landing.

At St. Thomas we exchanged the commodious steamer 'Parana' for the 'Trent,' much more famous for getting into trouble than for getting out of it. The run from the island across the Caribbean Sea to Santa Marta, after the tumblings and buffetings that would have been good training for an acrobat, endured betwixt England and St. Thomas, seemed to me the very perfection of sea-travelling. Although a most enjoyable passage, still it became monotonous: one tires of old threadbare jokes and yarns, and wearies even of gazing day after day into the clear blue sea, each day appearing the very counterpart of the other.

Sluggish lump-fish, with their uncouth heads and misshapen bodies, continually wriggle slowly and idly along with us; sun-fish, in their particoloured armour, float by, ever performing eccentric undulations. Now a stiff black fin cleaves the water suspiciously, leaving a wake behind, as would a miniature ship—the danger-signal of a greedy shark; huge leaves of kelp, wrack, and sea-tangle drift by, rafts to myriads of crustaceans and minute zoophytes; the rudder creaks and groans to the music of its iron chains, clanking over the friction-rollers, as the helmsman turns the wheel; sea-birds peep at us, then wheel away to be seen no more; whilst ever following are the 'Chickens of Mother Carey,' dipping, but never resting, on the ripple at the stern.

I had both heard and read of a formidable fortress that once guarded the entrance to the snug harbour, on one side of which stands the neat little town of Santa Marta, embowered amidst the trees. We sighted the land before it was dark, but the captain deemed it expedient to lay-off and await the daylight, ere venturing through the narrow entrance between the rock on which stands the remains of the fortress and the mainland. Issuing strict orders, coupled with a silver refresher, to my cabin-boy to call me before daylight, I turned in, and was soon in dreamland; my dreams were dispelled by a sudden shake, and the voice of the faithful darkie boy screaming into my ear, 'Hi, massa, him no see fort if him no tumble out and tumble up pretty quick.' Lightly clad and hardly awake, I rush, glass in hand, on deck, and quietly seat myself in the bow of the steamer. It was just in the grey of the morning; not a sound disturbed the deathlike silence, save the 'splash-splash' of the slowly-revolving paddle-wheels. I could discern on my right a dim line of trees, that looked as if they grew from out the water; on my left the dark rock, crowned with its ruined fort, that, as the light increased and the rays of the rising sun slanted down upon it, looked like a mass of frosted silver—so brilliant was the contrast to the dark water and darker woods, still in shadow, behind and around it.

Delighted with the singular beauty of the scene, and wandering, in imagination, far away into the vistas of the past, recalling scenes of frightful atrocity once enacted within the dreaded gates of the buccaneers' stronghold—wondering too if gems and gold, plunder wrenched from many a rich argosy, still lay hidden amidst the dust of its crumbling walls—a sudden flash, and a jerk that sent me sprawling on the deck, at once recalled my thoughts from the past to the present. Utterly oblivious of what had happened, as I scrambled on my legs, a stifled laugh induced me to look round. 'Wish I may never taste rum again, Cap'en, if I ever see you a-sittin on the signal-gun,' said a sly-looking rascal in sailor's dress. There was a roguish leer in his eye that revealed the whole secret. Seeing me seated on the signal-carronade, loaded to announce our arrival, was too tempting a chance to indulge in a practical joke for Jack to resist; so he quietly touched off the gun, without giving me any notice. No doubt he has had many a hearty laugh at my expense since then, when telling the 'yarn' in far-away latitudes. Our stay in the harbour was very brief; the mails and a passenger or two landed, away we steamed again.

At Carthagena we only lay-off a short time, to land the mails, and take on board the strangest assemblage of natives I ever saw. They were bound for Colon, to sell the various products of their farms, gardens, and native forests. We were about half a mile from the beach; a good rolling swell broke, in small waves, against the ship's sides, and spread its foam far up the shingle inshore. Up to their waists might be seen the dusky forms of the natives, launching long, ugly, shallow canoes, dug from out the solid wood. Soon a perfect fleet of them neared us, each striving to be first alongside; as they converged, and steadily packed together, into a confused mass, the yelling, screaming, and swearing in bad Spanish, mixed with some unknown tongue, baffled all description. Bad as the hubbub was when some distance from the steamer, it was ten times worse as they literally fought and struggled to get on board. Those who were to be passengers, in dread of being left behind, dashed from canoe to canoe, reckless of the rage of those intent only on selling their wares. Here one held up a poor little drenched and shivering monkey, another a screaming parroquet, a third a squirrel; others fruits, strings of beads, vegetables, bunches of bananas, and cocoanuts—all shrieking at the very top of their voices, but what they said no living soul could tell. Soon the deck forward was filled with its live and dead freight. The first turn of the paddlewheel sent the queer-looking assemblage scudding out of the way, to ply back again, with their unsold wares, to dingy old Carthagena.

As we steamed quietly along, I had time to examine the new arrivals. Squatted in little groups or families, each group had all its property, piled or stowed in some fashion, amidst them, consisting of bundles of all shapes and sizes, crockery, parrots and parroquets, quantities of eggs and live poultry, fruits such as are usually consumed in tropical countries; bananas, mangoes, cocoanuts, water-melons, bad oranges, and vegetables; but what was most valued and cared for, clearly the grand object of the visit, were numbers of gamecocks, all *trimmed*, according to the most approved fashion, and tied by the leg, either to the bedding or, failing anything else, to the person of the owner. These Carthagenian blacks are evidently of mixed descent; most likely a sprinkling of Spanish blood flows through their veins. The men, of small stature, are lithe, sinewy, and extremely active; the women have a decided tendency to become fat; one or two of them had attained to such a state of obesity, that walking was next to an impossibility. The children are the most singular little frights imaginable; guiltless of garments, they seemed all eyes and stomach, arms and legs being merely trifling unessential appendages; a singularity of form that may, I presume, be traced to the habit of consuming such vast quantities of innutritious vegetable food.

We reached Colon (or Aspinwall, as the Americans have named it) in due course, and landed about midday. The outfit being enormously heavy, some time had necessarily to be occupied in landing; and as the afternoon train was about to start, it was deemed the wiser course to send the men and officers at once to Panama, where Her Majesty's ship 'Havannah' was waiting to take us to Vancouver Island—the Commissioner and myself remaining at Colon, with a sergeant and small working-party, to bring on the baggage. All the attendant miseries of unshipping such a heterogeneous medley of packages as we had on board was finished at last, and our equipment safely stowed away in the goods-vans of the Panama Railway Company.

An invitation from the manager of the railway to the Commissioner to sleep at their messhouse was by him gladly accepted; a favour not extended to myself, so I had to take up my quarters at the 'Howard House.' Now the 'Howard House' was managed precisely on the same plan as a travelling wild-beast show; the entire attraction was on the outside. The bar-room, brilliantly lighted, and glittering with gilt, glass, and gaudy ornaments, was open to the street; an array of rocking-chairs, before the pillars supporting the verandah, enabled the luxurious lounger to sit with his heels higher than his head, and in smoky abstraction contemplate his toes. The barman, all studs and shirt-front, hardly deigned to answer my request for a bed, but, pointing to the entry-book, said, 'Waal, you'd better sign.' My name duly inscribed on the page of a huge and particularly soiled book, a key was handed me, adorned with a brass label, attached to a chain of like material, with No. 10 on it. 'Guess, stranger, I want a dollar—and you jist look here: there are two beds, so if anyone comes along, he'll jist have to room with you.' This I decidedly objected to. 'Waal, can't help it nohow; thar ain't no other room.' 'If I pay for both beds,' I replied, 'surely I can have it all to myself?' This was at length agreed to, the money paid, and at an early hour I turned in, to enjoy a good sound sleep ashore.

Excepting two miserable, hard, curtainless beds, an old rickety chest of drawers, and a couple of chairs, the room was destitute of furniture; but spite of all discomfort, mosquitos, and other pests, *felt* if not seen or heard, I fell fast asleep, soon to be roused again by a loud knocking at my door, the sound of numerous feet scuffling hurriedly up and down the passage, and a very Babel of voices. Hardly awake, my ideas were in a jumbled sort of chaos as to the cause. Fire, burglars, riots, a house-fight, were all mixed in strange confusion, until an angry voice, that appeared to come through the speaker's nose, yelled, rather than spoke, 'Say, ar you agwine to open this door? Our women want them beds for a lay-out, and jist mean to havin em, anyhow.' 'Ah!' thought I, 'they want the spare bed I have paid for.' Of course I refused—who would not?—and, dragging the old chest of drawers against the door, defied them to do their worst.

In the angry parley that ensued, I discovered that a steamer had just arrived from New York, en route to the new gold-diggings in British Columbia, with 1,500 passengers, who, rowdy-like, demanded everything. Threats of administering the summary law of Judge Lynch—of firing their six-shooters through the door, and riddling me like a rat in a hole—together with sundry hard names (it is better to imagine than mention), were heaped profusely on my devoted head. As it appeared to me quite as unsafe to surrender as to remain in my fortress, I determined on holding out to the last.

Fortunately, daylight soon came, and with it the shrill whistle and clanging bell, announcing the departure of a railway-train. Peeping cautiously through the window, I saw, to my intense delight, a long train specially put on, and the rowdies just ready to start. I watched them scrambling in, and as the engine with its freight dashed into the tropical jungle, I emerged from my room and the 'Howard House' with all possible speed, completed my toilet at the barber's shop, breakfasted with the Commissioner at the Company's messroom, and thus ended my night in Colon.

The agency and mess establishment of the

Panama Railway Company are really delightful residences, overshadowed by cocoanut trees, and surrounded by perfect bijous of gardens entirely reclaimed from the swamps: the papaw, the banana, blossoming creeping plants, fruit-bearing vines, and curious orchids, all growing together, a wild tangle of loveliness, yielding beauty, fruits, and shade. The cool verandah, and cane-chairs from China, together with the comfortably-furnished interior, gave ample proof that the products of a tropical country may be used to good account, as additions to our northern ideas of a substantial home.

One of the most singular flowers growing in this pretty garden was an orchid, called by the natives 'Flor del Espiritu Santo,' or the 'Flower of the Holy Ghost.' The blossom, white as Parian-marble, somewhat resembles the tulip in form; its perfume is not unlike that of the magnolia, but more intense; neither its beauty nor fragrance begat for it the high reverence in which it is held, but the image of a dove placed in its centre. Gathering the freshly-opened flower, and pulling apart its alabaster petals, there sits the dove; its slender pinions droop listlessly by its side, the head inclining gently forward, as if bowed in humble submission, brings the delicate beak, just blushed with carmine, in contact with the snowy breast. Meekness and innocence seem embodied in this singular freak of nature; and who can marvel that crafty priests, ever watchful for any phenomenon convertible into the miraculous, should have knelt before this wondrous flower, and trained the minds of the superstitious natives to accept the title the 'Flower of the Holy Ghost,' to gaze upon with awe and reverence, sanctifying even the rotten wood from which it springs, and the air laden with its exquisite perfume? But it is the flower alone I fear they worship; their minds ascend not from 'nature up to nature's God;' the image only is bowed down to, not He who made it. The stalks of the plant are jointed, and attain a height of from six to seven feet, and from each joint spring two lanceolate leaves; the time of flowering is in June and July.

We were to have a special train (the cost of crossing the isthmus was something enormous—the actual amount I do not now remember); and as we were most desirous to see as much of the country as possible, an open goods-truck was appropriated to our use, in which we could stand, and have a full peep at everything as we steamed along. Whilst the train was getting ready, I took a turn over the Company's wharf and round the town.

The Wharf, built on piles driven into the coral reef, extends about a thousand feet in length, and forty in width, with a depth of water at its landing-end sufficient to float the largest ship. The piles are from the forests of Maine, and have to be coppered above high-water-mark, to resist the destroying power of a boring worm (*Teredo fimbriata*), that would otherwise destroy them in a very few months. The Freight Department is a handsome stone structure, three hundred feet long by eighty wide, through the arched entrance to which is a triple line of rails.

Man, it is said, differs from all other animals, in being 'a tool and a road-making animal,' the truth of which was well exemplified in the curious assemblage of products collected from all parts of the world, and stowed in this huge house, brought by man's ocean highways, and awaiting removal by his iron roads and horses.

Ceroons of cochineal and indigo from Guatemala and San Salvador, cocoa from Eçuador, sarsaparilla from Nicaragua, coffee from Costa Rica, hides from the North and South Pacific coasts, copper-ore from Bolivia, linen goods from the French and English markets, beef, pork, hard bread, cheese from the States, and silks from China.

The town of Colon, as everybody perhaps does not know, stands on a small island called Manzanilla, cut off from the mainland by a narrow frith; the entire island being about one square mile in extent, composed of coral reefs, and only raised a few feet above highwater-level. It has no supply of fresh water but what is obtained during the heavy rains; this, collected in immense iron tanks, that hold over four thousand gallons, supplies the inhabitants during the dry seasons.

The most conspicuous objects one meets with in this dismal place are flocks of turkey-buzzards (useful inspectors or nuisances, as they do their own work of removal), pigs, naked dirty little children in legions, blear-eyed mangy curs that do nothing but growl and sleep; together with peddling darkies, bummers, and loafers (I know no other names so expressive of this species of idler as these Transatlantic ones), that employ their time much in the same fashion as the curs. A line of shops faces the sea, and at a little distance is the 'mingillo,' or native marketplace, a spot no one would be disposed to linger in or visit a second time, unless the nose could be dispensed with. 'Noses have they but they smell not,' must surely apply to the dwellers in the marketplace; the air is *literally* (and not in figure of speech only) *laden* with the mingled fragrance of past and present victims, an odour far more potent than pleasant. Surely ladies never go to market in Colon!

The train was by this time ready to take us to Panama, and, with a parting scream, the iron horse rushed into the tropical wilderness. On leaving Colon, the line winds its way through a deep cutting across a morass, and along the right bank of the Rio Chagres; glimpses are caught of the river from amidst the tangled and twisted foliage that shuts it in on either side like dense walls. From out this leafy chaos rise the gaunt trunks of the mango, cocoa-nut, plane, cieba, and stately palm. Plantains, too, spread their green succulent leaves—sunshades of nature's own contriving—to protect the tender growths that love to live beneath them. Every tree seemed strangling in the coils of trailing vines and climbers; real ropes, pendents, and streamers of brilliant blossoms, fit resting-places for the birds and butterflies, themselves like living flowers. Wondrous orchids, grotesque in form and colouring, grew everywhere, springing alike from the living and the dead; for amidst this flood of vegetable life, decay and beauty, like twin sisters, walk hand-in-hand.

We stopped at Gatun for a short time, the station being close to the little village of bamboo huts thatched with palmetto-leaves, and only remarkable as being the place where the 'bongoes' (or native boats) used to stop for the travellers to refresh themselves ere the railroad was. From here the line skirts the bases of an irregular series of hills to cross the Rio Gatun, tributary to the Rio Chagres, on a well-made truss girder-bridge of seventy feet span; passed Frijoli, where the fields of golden maize were decked with what looked, at a distance, like immense bouquets of scarlet flowers; and along the banks of the Rio Chagres, which are here very deep, to cross it at Barbacous on a wrought-iron bridge, six hundred and twenty-five feet in length, eighteen in breadth, and forty feet above the surface of the water. There are six spans, each over a hundred feet; iron floor girders, three feet apart, support the rails—the entire structure resting on five piers and two abutments.

After crossing the river, the country becomes open, and large patches of rich land are seen under a rude kind of cultivation, until the native town of Gorgona is reached, where, in old days, boats were exchanged for horses and mules, on the overland route.

Leaving the course of the river, the line passes through deep clay banks and rocky cuttings, suddenly emerging on the green meadow-lands surrounding Matuchin. I never gazed on a more exquisite panorama. Dotting the foreground was a pretty native village; to the left the Chagres, and its tributary the Rio Obispo; on the right a group of conical hills, so clothed with vegetation that it was impossible to imagine what the land would look like if the trees were cut away. During our stay at this station we were regularly beset; numerous vendors of native merchandise crowded into and round about the open van; grey-haired old men, and women, pushed trays under our very noses, covered with filthy pastry, gingerbread, sweetstuff, and other like abominations; whilst little black urchins sat like imps on the rails of the truck, each with some live captive for sale—monkey, squirrel, parrot, or other bright-plumaged bird.

Following the valley of the Obispo, which

river is crossed twice within a mile on iron bridges, we ascend gradually (the gradient being about sixty feet in the mile) to reach the water-shed, over which the descent commences to the Pacific. About a mile from the summit the line winds through a huge pile of basaltic columns, that look as if some Titan force had hurled them into the air, and let them fall again one over the other, like a mass of driftwood piles itself in a North American river. Below, the Rio Grande may be seen, a mere brawling burn; a short distance through thick woods, and we are at Paraiso; as unlike one's ideal of paradise as Cremorne Gardens or Ratcliff Highway. Again we reach the swampy low-lands with their dense growths; ahead, and looming high in the glowing atmosphere, stands Mount Ancon, whose southern base is bathed by the blue waters of the Pacific; on the left, Cerro-de-los-Buccaneros, or the Hill of the Buc-caneers, from whose summit the terrible Morgan first looked on old Panama in the year 1670. We rattle past San Pedro Miguel and Caimi-tillo, small tidal tributaries to the Rio Grande, scream through the Rio Grande Station, sweep round the base of Mount Ancon; and before us are the tall spires of the cathedral, the long metal roofing of the terminus, and the quiet waters of the Pacific.

Captain Harvey, R.N., then in command of Her Majesty's ship 'Havannah,' met us at the terminus; the ship's boats were in waiting to take both men and baggage on board, so that I saw but little of Panama. My old foes (that waged war against me at Colon), the gold-seekers, were assembled on the wharf, awaiting the small tugboat to take them off to the larger steamer anchored in the offing. To judge from appearances, there were amongst them a goodly sprinkling that would have deemed lynching or riddling a Britisher, a capital joke.

A tropical sun soon makes one thirsty. I wanted 'a drink,' and for the first time tasted iced cocoanut-milk; never in my life have I ever drunk anything half as delicious. Don't imagine that, in the least degree, it resembles the small teacupful of sweet insipid stuff dribbled out from the cocoanut as we buy it here in England. What we eat as kernel is liquid in the young nut, and the outer husk soft enough to push your thumb through. Surely the cocoanut palm must have been specially designed for the dwellers in the tropical world! It supplies everything uncivilised man can possibly need, to build his ships, rig, paddle, and sail them; from its products, too, he can make his houses, and obtain food, drink, clothing, and culinary utensils. Strictly littoral in its habits, the cocoa-palm loves to loll over the sea, and let the frothy ripple wash its rootlets. .This also looks like another link in the chain of Divine intentions. The nuts necessarily fall into the sea—winds and currents carry them to coral reefs, or strand them on desert shores, there to grow, and, by a sequence of wondrously-ordered events, in time make it habitable for man. The 'Havannah' dropped down to the beautiful island of Tobago, to take in water ere she sailed for Vancouver Island.

As we crossed the Bay of Panama (which is, I believe, about 135 miles wide, running inland 120), pelicans, far too numerous to count, were floating high in the air, some of them mere specks. The species *Pelecanus fuscus* (the brown pelican) is a permanent resident on the southern coasts of America, frequenting in great numbers the shores of the Gulf of Mexico, California, the Bay of Panama, and other sheltered inlets. They frequently build in the trees, although the nest is quite as often placed on the ground, even when the former are close at hand. My acquaintance with the pelicans in the Zoological Gardens in the Regent's Park had given me an idea of clumsiness, and to see them *spooning* the fish from out their pond is certainly no indication of being adepts at fishing. I know no prettier sight than to watch the brown pelican fishing in the Bay of Panama; no awkwardness there, every movement easy and graceful. Soaring high in the lurid atmosphere, to the eye little more than a tiny dark spot, suddenly down comes the bird as if hurled from the clouds; plunging in head-first, its sharp beak cleaves the water like a wedge; a fish seized is at once pouched; and, rising without any apparent effort from the sea, it soars off again, to look out for another chance. Should the fish be missed, an event that does not often happen, the bird sits quietly on the water, and stares round in stupid astonishment.

We remained several days at Tobago; and as we rode at anchor in the deep roadstead, I could have easily pitched a penny into the groves of tamarind and orange-trees, that grew on the very beach. From the sea-line to the summit of the island, which is quite a thousand feet in altitude, the hills rise in terraces, but so densely clothed with cocoa-nut, banana, tamarind, orange, and other tropical trees, that one hardly credits the existence of terraces, or that hill and valley are hid beneath the unbroken surface of green. A little village lies hid in a palm-grove at the base of the hill, and in the ravine behind it bubbles up the spring of pure fresh water, that never fails, and from which all vessels touching at Panama obtain their supply.

Mr. Baurman, a geologist, accompanied me on a ramble through its woods and along the sea-coast. We did nothing to distinguish ourselves save getting frightfully hot, being wellnigh famished with thirst (for we were far away from the water), and although I fired at the cocoanuts in the hope of bringing one down, only succeeded in making holes in them and letting out the much-coveted milk, that fell on us like a shower of rain; shooting a few doves amongst the pineapples, and a turkey-buzzard on the summit —a frightful crime in Tobago, of which, at the time, I was in happy ignorance; but, fortunately for me, Baurman carried the bird, and was deemed, for his good nature, the greater culprit. The most singular sight we stumbled on was a bull, saddled and bridled in equine fashion, with a black man riding on his back. Tauro might have been a good hack, but he certainly did not look so as he waddled lazily along with his sable rider.

The inhabitants, with few exceptions, are blacks. There was one girl (the property of as repulsive an old demon as one could well see) perfectly blonde, fair even to paleness, with soft blue eyes and long golden hair, that hung in wavy ripples down to her waist—her feet and hands delicately small, and a figure Venus might have envied. Where she came from no one knew: one might have supposed her the descendant of some Viking, if Vikings had ever cruised in the Pacific. Perhaps her owner was a 'Black Pirate,' who stole the damsel, and knifed her friends; not bad material for a *sensation* story—'The Fair Captive of Tobago.'

The view from the summit was exceedingly lovely. Behind, and to the right and left, the dark-green slope looked as if one could have slid into the vessels at their anchorage; before, a vertical wall of rock a thousand feet from the sea. It looked to me as if the island had been broken in two in the centre, and that one-half had sunk into the water and disappeared; the air quivered even at this height, as it does over a limekiln; not a leaf stirred—

the intensely blue sea was unrippled far as eye could reach; the very birds and insects, too hot to fly, sat panting under the shadow of the leaves. We gathered a pineapple, but it tasted hot, as if half-roasted.

I am not favourably impressed with the honesty of the islanders that do the washing, or rather that do not do it. Following the example of the officers of the 'Havannah,' I delivered my bag of clothes, the accumulation since leaving England, to the washer, who promised, as only a black washerman will promise, to have it on board before we sailed: he kept his word, for he came when the ship was under weigh, had his money, and with bows, and prayers for my welfare in this world, vanished over the side. We were well out to sea when I looked at my bag; imagine my wrath at finding everything just as I had given it. It was lucky for the rascal he was out of reach, and perhaps quite as well for me; a dollar (4*s.*) a dozen to carry one's clothes ashore, most likely to wear, and bring back again dirtier than it went, would enrage the meekest saint!

The voyage in the 'Havannah' from Panama to Vancouver Island was a long and wearisome one. We left Tobago on June 4, and entered the Straits of Juan de Feuca on July 12. Reference to the track-chart shows how we idled and idled along on the sea, sauntering, rather than sailing; with a blazing sun right over the masthead, the heat was intolerable, and attended with a depressing languor, that forbade all energy, and fairly melted one in body and mind. The only land sighted was a very distant view of the Gallopagos Islands, a mere black-looking spot on an interminable surface of blue. This group of volcanic islands, so strangely isolated, might have been a monster fish, a phantom ship, or even the great sea-serpent, for anything that could be definitely made out, even aided by a ship's telescope.

We caught great numbers of dolphins (*Coryphæna hippuris*), which are far more lovely to the eye than agreeable to the palate, in my estimation. This fish, usually from four to five feet in length, is built for rapid passage through the water: the tail, forked like horns, together with the long dorsal fin, reaching from head to tail, enables it to turn with an ease and celerity during even its swiftest transit through the sea. All who have written (in prose or poetry) about the dolphin have attempted a description of its marvellous colouring: to convey, by word-painting, the slightest idea of the changing, flashing, glowing radiance that plays around and upon this fish, when fresh from the ocean, is as impossible as to describe the colours of the Aurora, or the phosphorescence of the tropical seas; it must be witnessed to be realised in all its magnificence. Flying-fish are its favourite food, and these the dolphins course as greyhounds course hares; what is called 'flying' being merely an extended leap, aided by the immensely-elongated pectoral fins, made in sheer desperation to escape the voracious sea-hounds so hotly pursuing them.

In reference to these same flying-fish, the species washed on board the 'Parana' by the waves of the turbulent Atlantic, and that found their way into the stomach of a dolphin of terrestrial habits, was *Exocetus exiliens.* I could see nothing of its movements, as the sea simply washed it into the sponsons, or left it floundering on the deck. Its general appearance was exactly like a newly-caught herring: the scales, thin and rounded, easily detached, and adhered to the hand; the back a light steel-blue, with greenish reflections, shading into silvery whiteness on the sides; the pectoral fins reached quite to the tail, and were shaped like the wings of a swift; the dorsal and anal fins are opposite each other, and placed near the tail, which is deeply but unevenly forked—the lower limb being much the longer; the ventral fins, which are posterior to the middle of the body, are unusually long and strongly rayed.

But in the uncomfortably calm Pacific, where I watched the flying-fish every day, and often all day long, I had ample opportunity to observe its so-called 'flying.' The species that tenant the two oceans are very nearly allied, *Exocetus volitans* being the one common to the Pacific; but it is of habits I wish to treat, not of minute specific distinctions—that can be settled in the studio. It seems to me that the distance traversed when the fish leaps from the sea, and the length of time it remains out of the water, are much overestimated in books on Natural History. Ten or twelve seconds may be taken as the average time of its flight, and eighty yards the maximum distance traversed when the water is perfectly tranquil; if aided by a breeze of wind, or propelled from the crest of a breaker, the distance accomplished would necessarily be greater; but the fins have no power to raise the fish a single inch above the level of its leap, and simply aid in its support, as the extended skin of the flying-squirrel bears it up in its spring from bough to bough. I have never seen the fins vibrated or flapped, as all wings invariably are, but, stiff and rigid, are extended and still, until the fish plunges into the sea. Numbers, beyond all computation, were constantly seen by us in the air together, when chased by predatory fish. The flying-fish, as a rule, is about twelve inches in length.

We caught several sharks, and an immense hammerhead (*Zygæna vulgaris*), that we could not catch, followed us for a very long time. As I looked at him sailing along under the stern of the ship, I was at a loss to imagine for what purpose such a head was given to it; exactly like an immense caulking-hammer, with an eye in each end; in every other detail of shape, and in habits of voracity too, as far as I know, it resembles the ordinary sharks. That it is so constructed to serve some special purpose in its economy there can be no doubt, but what that may be, remains to be discovered. We fished for albatross with marked success, to be devoured by both men and officers, stuffed as a goose; the rag from off the bung of a cask of whale-oil, rubbed with an onion and chewed, would be mildly flavoured as compared to the flesh of this sea-bird. Petrels were ever with us, like flights of martins round the habitations of man; always on the wing, never resting, or roosting either, as far as I could see; watch them in their easy graceful flight, till the last lingering ray of light sank away beneath the watery horizon; and, as night wrapped them in her sable mantle, they were still on the wing. Be on deck as the first blush of early dawn crept drowsily over the sleeping sea, and with the rosy light came the petrels, still flying, as they had vanished in the darkness. We tried to catch them by loosing long threads over the stern, and tangling them, like human spiders; we did trap one, but the sailors were mutinous at such unheard-of barbarity; injuring the chickens of 'Mother Carey' was an offence not to be tolerated, even in a zealous naturalist; so, at the captain's request, the cotton webs were abandoned. The one taken was the black stormy petrel, *Thalassidroma melania* (C. Buonaparte): upper plumage entirely black (as are the wing-coverts), below feluginous; tail deeply forked, and very short.

It is a well-marked species, and readily distinguished from all its kindred by the absence of white on the rump and wing-coverts. We caught a huge turtle with a hook and line: a number of lines were hanging from the bow, the ship almost still, when there was a tremendous hue-and-cry that a turtle was hooked. To hold him with the line would have been an utter impossibility—he could have smashed it like pack-thread. The barbed trident called 'a grains' was brought into immediate requisition, and from the 'dolphin-striker' an experienced hand sent it crashing through the turtle's armour-plates; a boat was lowered, tackle rigged, and the ponderous reptile safely deposited on the deck. The species I was unable to determine, for I had barely time to seize the sucking-fish (*Remora*) that were clinging to its shell in clusters, and observe the curious beings, parasitic and others, that evidently used the turtle as a living raft, on which to cruise about, ere the remorseless cook, armed with knife, axe, and saw, hewed and hacked the monster, I could have devoted days to examine, into junks for the pot. The harvest gleaned from his shell I shall speak of in the chapter on Fishes.

All our fresh provisions had long been expended, and water reduced to a very small supply per diem, when on the 11th of July, the seventieth day at sea, 'land on the starboard bow' was an announcement welcome to all. Being near dark, it was deemed advisable to stand off until morning, and enter the Straits of Juan de Feuca with a good light. It appeared a longer night than I ever remember, so impatient was I once more to see and tread on *terra firma*; what in the mist and distance seemed but a dark undefined shadow, was in reality the lighthouse, standing grey and lonely on the wild wave-lashed rocks of Cape Flattery. The wind was dead aft, and blowing freshly, as we dashed up the straits, faster far than we had ever gone during the long tedious voyage.

Nowhere is this curious inlet more than twelve miles in width: on the right, seen over an ocean of dark-green forest, sloping to the shore, were the snowy summits of the Olympian range of mountains; on the left the more rounded and lower metamorphic hills, quite as densely timbered, but broken along the coast-line into open glades and grassy slopes, like well-kept lawns, reaching to the water-line. About sixty miles from the entrance we round the dreaded 'race rocks,' and with scarce time for even a hasty look at the new land, glide round a rocky point, on which is a house, and people anxiously watching our movements. The sails are clewed up;

orders are rapidly given, and as quickly executed. A heavy plunging splash and the rattle of the massive cable, as it crashes through the hawse-holes, proclaim our anchorage in Esquimalt Harbour, and safe arrival at Vancouver Island.

CHAPTER II.

VICTORIA—THE SALMON: ITS HAUNTS AND HABITS.

WE were landed, soon after our arrival, on a rocky point of land with a snug sheltered bay on each side; an easy slope led up to the frame of a house, destined to be our headquarters; a pretty spot, very Englishlike in its general features, but in the rough clothing of uncultivated nature. Tents were pitched, the baggage carried safely up and stowed away, and the first camp of the Boundary Commission established in this new land of promise.

Our first walk to Victoria, now the thriving capital of Vancouver Island, was made on the evening of our landing. The gold-fever was just beginning to rage fast and furiously, and all classes, from every country, were pouring in —a very torrent of gold-hunters. Not that *gold-hunter* means only he that digs and washes the yellow ore from out Nature's treasury, but includes a herd of parasites, that sap the gains of the honest digger; tempting him to gamble, drink poison (miscalled whisky), and purchase trashy trumpery, made, like Pindar's razors, only to sell; and thus fool away his wealth; 'earned like a horse, squandered like an ass!' Both species were well represented, in what could not, in any sense of the word, as yet be called a town.

The old trading-post of the Hudson's Bay Company, the governor's house, and a few scattered residences of the chief traders and other employés of the Company, alone represented the permanent dwellings. But in all directions were canvas tents, from the white strip stretched over a ridge-pole, and pegged to the ground (affording just room enough for two to crawl in and sleep), to the great canvas store, a blaze of light, redolent of cigars, smashes, cobblers, and cocktails. The rattle of the dice-box, the droning invitation of the keepers of the monte-tables, the discordant sounds of badly-played instruments, angry words, oaths too terrible to name, roystering songs with noisy refrains, were all signs significant of the golden talisman that met me on every side, as I elbowed my way amidst the unkempt throng, that were awaiting means of conveyance to take them to the auriferous bars of the far-famed Fraser river. Along the side of the harbour, wherever advantageous water-sites were obtainable, the noise of busy industry sounded pleasantly in contrast to the mingled hubbub I had just left. Higher up the slope, substantial stores were being rapidly built. Out of these germs grew the present town the capital of the island, that we shall often have to visit in the course of this narrative.

With the island, and its history as a colony, I have but little to do. Other and more able writers have said all that need or can be told about its commerce, agriculture, politics, and progress. The prairie, forest, lake, river, sea, estuary, and rocky inlet are my domains; to their tenants I have to introduce you, guide you to their homes and haunts, and bring you face to face, in imagination, with the zoological colony of the Far North-west.

First, of the island. Vancouver Island is situated between the parallels of 48° 20″ and 51° N. lat., and in from 123° to 128° W. long—its shape, oblong; length, 300 miles; its breadth, varying at different points, may be taken at an average of from 35 to 50 miles. The island may be characterised as an isolated ridge of mountains, which attain, at their greatest elevation, an altitude of about 6,000 feet. There are no navigable rivers, but numerous mountain-streams, that, as a rule, have a rapid descent, and empty into inlets or arms of the sea, everywhere intersecting the coast-line, east and west of the watershed. Lakes, large and small, are common, from the summit of the hills to the flat gravel lands near the coast; dense pine-forests clothe these hills to their very tops. On the open lands, misnamed prairies, the scrub-oak (*Quercus garryana*) grows so gnarled and contorted that stock, branch, twig, and even the very leaves look as if they suffered from perpetual cramp. Alder, willow, black birch, and cottonwood fill the hollows.

The climate of the island is milder and more equable than it is on the adjoining continent, and closely approximates to that of Great Britain.

The shortest road to an Englishman's heart, says the adage, is down his throat; and being a road a good deal travelled, is it to be wondered at if fish (especially such as are welcome travellers down this same 'red lane') should have been the first objects of practical Natural History to which the naturalist, fresh from the 'old country' and seventy-two days' imprisonment on board-ship, turned his attention? The first fish I saw and tasted was salmon; and to the Salmon and its haunts I at once introduce you.

SALMO QUINNAT.

Richardson, F. B. A., 'Fishes,' p. 219; Common Salmon, Lewis and Clark. INDIAN NAMES: at Chinook Point, mouth of the Columbia, *Quinnat*; at the Kettle Falls, *See-met-leek*; by the Nesquallys, *Satsup*.

SPECIFIC CHARACTERS.—Head, just one-fourth of the entire length, measured from the tip of the nose to where the scales terminate at the tail; the operculum very much rounded, and usually with several spiny projections on the outer margin; preoperculum rounded much the same, but wanting the serrated margin; branchial rays, fourteen. Cleft of the mouth posterior to the eye, which is a dark copper-colour in the freshly-caught fish. The teeth are large and strong in both jaws, but they vary in number according to the age, sex, and condition of the salmon; about ten in each limb of the jaws may be taken as the usual average in an adult fish. Those on the tongue are smaller, and placed in two rows, six in each row. The vomerine and palatine teeth are again much smaller and weaker than any of the others, corresponding to such as stud the gullet.

Fresh from the water, the colours in a healthy fish are particularly marked and bright, but change rapidly after death. The back, through its entire length, is a light steel-blue; shading off on the sides to a lighter tint, that merges by imperceptible gradations through grey to silvery-white on the belly; blushed over with pink, that disappears soon after death. Back, above the well-defined lateral line, thickly spotted with black, the spots being like stars with rays of irregular length; but I have very often seen the spots extending beyond the lateral line, and even on the white of the belly. Opercula, all the fins and the tail more or less spotted, and of a pinkish hue, the anal and pectoral fins tipped with black. The general appearance of this salmon is that of being very thick for its length, the dorsal outline slightly arched, forming almost a notch with the tail.

Soon after our commencing work, I was encamped for many months on the banks of the Chilukweyuk river, a tributary to the Fraser, having a short but rapid course through a rocky valley.

In June and July salmon ascend this stream in incredible numbers, filing off as they work upcurrent into every rivulet, filling even pools left on the prairies and flats by the receding floods.

About a mile from my camp was a large patch of pebbly ground, dry even at the highest floods, through which a shallow stream found its way into the larger river. Though barely of sufficient depth to cover an ordinary-sized salmon, yet I have seen that stream so filled, that fish pushed one another out of the water high-and-dry upon the pebbles. Each, with its head up-stream, struggled, fought, and scuffled for precedence. With one's hands only, or, more easily, by employing a gaff or a crook-stick, tons of salmon could have been procured by the simple process of hooking them out.

It seems to me that thousands of the salmon ascending these small mountain-streams never can spawn from sheer want of room, or, if they do, it must be under most unfavourable circumstances. At the end of the pebble-stream was a waterfall, beyond which no fish could by any possibility pass. Having arrived at this barrier to all farther progress, there they obstinately remained. Weeks were spent in watching them, but I never, in a single instance, saw one turn back and endeavour to seek a more congenial watercourse; but, crowded from behind by fresh arrivals, they died by the score, and, drifting slowly along, in time reached the larger stream. It was a strange and novel sight to see three moving lines of fish—the dead and dying in the eddies and slack-water along the banks, the living, breasting the current in the centre, blindly pressing on to perish like their kindred.

Even in streams where a successful deposition of the ova has been accomplished, there never appears, as far as my observations have gone, any disposition in the parent-fish to return to the sea. Their instinct still prompts them to keep swimming up-stream, until you often find them with their noses worn quite off, their heads bruised and battered, fins and tail ragged and torn, bodies emaciated, thin, and flabby; the bright silvery tints dull and leaden in hue, a livid red streak extending along each side from head to tail, in which large ulcerous sores have eaten into the very vitals.

The Indians say all the salmon that come up to spawn die; but if all do not die, I have no hesitation in saying that very few spring-salmon ever reach the saltwater after ascending the rivers to spawn. Why there should be this marvellous waste of salmon in the rivers of the North-west I am somewhat puzzled to imagine. The distance the fish have to travel from the sea up-stream, or the obstacles they may have to overcome, have clearly nothing to do with their dying. In the Chilukweyuk river the distance from the sea is not over 200 miles, and that clear from any kind of hindrance; and yet they die in thousands. In the Columbia they ascend a thousand miles to the Kettle Falls, and they have been caught many hundred miles above that; still they die just the same as in the shorter streams. Up the Snake river they push their way to the great Shoshonee Falls, over a thousand miles against a rocky stream, but perish there just as they do in the Sumass and Chilukweyuk rivers, which are close to the sea.

Unlike the salmon in our own streams, the spring-salmon in North-western waters spawn in midsummer, when the water is at its lowest temperature and greatest flood-height, from the melting snow. As there is no impediment or hindrance to prevent them returning to the sea, why do they die in N.W. waters ? In my opinion, from sheer starvation. Careful observations, made at various Indian fishing-stations and extending over a long space of time, have quite convinced me that salmon (I more particularly allude to the spring-fish) never feed after leaving saltwater. My reasons for thus thinking are, first, no salmon (as far as I know) has ever been tempted to take a bait of any kind in the fresh water above the tideway. The Indians all say that salmon never *eat* when in the *rivers*; and I could never discover that they had any recorded instance, or even tradition, of a salmon being taken with bait.

I tried every lure I could think of, to tempt these lordly salmon. The most killing salmon-flies of Scotch, Irish, and English ties, thrown in the most approved fashion, were trailed close to their noses; such flies as would have coaxed any old experienced salmon in the civilised world of waters to forget his caution. Hooks, cunningly baited with live fish, aquatic larvæ, and winged insects, were scorned, and not even honoured with a sniff. Others of the Commission also tried their powers of fascination, but with equally unsuccessful results.

I have opened a very large number of salmon at various Indian fishing-stations, on their first arrival, and during every stage of their wasting vitality, and after death had ended their sufferings; and not in a solitary instance did I ever discover the trace of food in the stomach or intestinal canal. But in every case where a salmon was taken in the tideway or saltwater,

I invariably found the remains of small fish and marine animals in its stomach; and in the estuaries and long inland canals that so strangely intersect the coast-line of British Columbia, salmon are readily and easily caught with hook and line; clearly showing to my mind, that whilst in salt and brackish water the North-western spring-salmon feed and fatten, but, after quitting their ocean-haunts for the cold fresh-water, they starve, waste, and die, as a lamp goes out from sheer want of oil. Surely, where hundreds of salmon are split in a day, as at the Kettle Falls, it is fair to assume that if they took any food, by chance a fish would be caught immediately after its meal, with enough evidence in the stomach to prove the fact of having broken its fast; but such proof is never discoverable. Digestion would scarcely be more rapid in the rivers than it is in the ocean and estuary, where we know they eat. Open a salmon and examine its stomach at any time, caught either in nets or with hook and line, and food in various stages of digestion will be invariably found.

Another proof that they undergo a rigid and persistent lent is found in the rapid wasting of all the tissues that goes on during their sojourn in fresh-water. Allowing for the consumption of material requisite for the purposes of reproduction, and the wear-and-tear consequent on making their way up stiff currents, leaping falls, and laboriously toiling up rocky *canions*—still I contend, if only a partial equivalent was resupplied in the shape of food, waste would not go on to the actual death of the muscles, that slough away in large pieces, as the exhausted fish makes feeble efforts to struggle on; dying at last a loathsome mass of rotting animal matter.

Sores, in both male and female fish, often arise from injuries inflicted by the teeth of a jealous adversary; but these wounds are utterly different from the sloughing ulcer, arising, as I believe, from sheer lack of vital force. These salmon veritably consume themselves, and perish, when life's stove burns out, for want of fuel to keep it alight.

In August the Chilukweyuk river became perfectly unendurable from the quantities of dead fish floating down. I had with me a splendid retriever, that, to my disgust and annoyance, used to amuse himself, during my absence from the tent, by swimming in after the floating salmon, bringing them ashore, and safely storing them in my canvas dwelling; and on my return I used to discover a heap of fish, the stench from which was beyond human endurance. If fastened out from the tent, he piled them up at the door: all the lessons bestowed on him failed to convince him of his folly; he stuck to his disagreeable habit with a perseverance worthy of a better cause.

Arriving a little later than the preceding, is a smaller fish, which I believe to be the *Salmo paucidens* (Weak-Toothed Salmon) of Sir J. Richardson, F. B. A., p. 223; the *red charr* of Lewis and Clark, but the red they allude to is a colour every one of the different species acquire after being a short time in the rivers.

This fish seldom attains a weight over from three to five pounds, and is called by the Indians, at the salmon-leap at Colville on the Columbia, *stzoin*; it is a very handsome fish, back nearly straight, a light sea-greenish colour; sides and belly silvery-white, tail very forked, fins and tail devoid of any spots; the teeth are wide apart, and not strongly implanted. I was disposed at first to think they were the *young* of some other species; but the Indians are positive they are not, and they spawn much as the others do. In a small stream or tributary to the Chilukweyuk river, a mountain-torrent on the west side of the Cascades flowing into the Fraser, on the banks of which I was for a long time encamped, and up which the salmon come in great numbers, I amused myself watching this species of salmon (*Salmo paucidens*) deposit their spawn. It was in August, the water clear as crystal, the bottom a fine brown gravel. A trench, that looked about three or four inches deep and three feet long, was muzzled out by the noses of the females. A female fish poised herself over the trench, head up-stream, and by a rapid vibration of her fins kept herself nearly still; this lasted about a minute and a half or two minutes, during which time a quantity of ova were deposited. She then darted off like an arrow; four males at once took her place over the spawn-bed, and remained, just as the female had done, about two minutes. On their leaving two females came, and were followed by the males, as before. The water was about four feet deep. I am quite sure, from often watching these streams, that one spawning-bed is used by a great many males and females: it was both curious and interesting to watch the extreme regularity with which the sexes succeeded each other.

The question as to what becomes of the young

salmon after leaving the egg, is a query more easily asked than answered. There are no snug breeding-ponds, no cosy little aquariums or water-nurseries, where the baby-salmon may be watched and carefully tended until, honoured with a badge, it is sent away to travel through pelagic meadows, deep-sea forests, and ocean gardens, where, growing rapidly, bigger if not wiser, it returns to tell how long it has been away, and how rapidly it has grown. Assistance such as this falls not to the lot of the hunter-naturalist, who with prying eye peers, searches, and grubs about on the banks and into the depths of the lakes and mountain-torrents, in this far-western wilderness. Had he the eyes of Argus, he could only register a few hasty observations, and generalise on their value: he has no opportunities for investigations, such as they have, who at home can watch the egg in their very parlours, gradually shaping itself into the quaint little salmon; see it come from out the egg-case with its haversack of provender, wonderfully provided to supply its wants, until able to live by its own teeth and industry; track its growth and habits through its youthful days; then, marking it with a leaden medal, send it off to sea, to welcome it back after its wanderings a full-grown salmon.

It may be that Creative wisdom has implanted the same instinct in the North-western salmon, prompting it to obey similar laws, and follow the same routine as to the exodus seaward, and return to fresh-water, as directs it in our native streams: my own impression is, that the fish spawned in midsummer or autumn remain up in the lakes and deep still river-pools until the following summer freshets, when they take their departure for the sea as the fresh-run salmon come. I think so, because in the Sumass and Chilukweyuk lakes, already spoken of; along the banks of the Fraser river, and in the Osoyoos lakes and tributaries to the Columbia river, I have in September and October observed large shoals of what I believed to be young salmon, that disappear when the snow begins to melt during June and July in the following summer. I suspect the first flood carries them down and out to sea; but, after all, this is but surmise, and of little practical value.

I never caught salmon-fry whilst fishing for trout, as we could so easily do in our streams; and it is just possible that the rapid rise (unlike anything we know of in our streams) that takes place in every river, brook, and rivulet during midsummer, when the snow melts on the hills, reducing the temperature of the water down to freezing-point, may send the young salmon-fry into the saltwater at a very early period of its life. 'At three days old he is nearly two grains in weight; at 16 months old he has increased to two ounces, or 480 times its first weight; at 20 months old, after the smolt has been a few months in the sea, it becomes a grilse of 8½ lbs., having increased 68 times in three or four months; at 2⅔ years old it becomes a salmon of from 12 to 15 lbs. weight, after which its increased rate of growth has not been ascertained; but by the time it becomes 30 lbs. in weight, it has increased 115,200 times the weight it was at first."* These smolts that I have seen in shoals were about half an ounce in weight, the produce of the summer's spawning. As I have stated, they disappear when the floods set in; and nothing more is seen of them until they return salmon of various sizes, from 2 lbs. to 75 lbs., or, as I believe, the Quinnat and Stzoin.

The next salmon in importance, as affording food to the Indians, is called by them at the Kettle Falls *cha-cha-lool*, and arrives with the quinnat. This is unquestionably a fully-matured fish, and a distinct species, answering in many par-

* Buckland's Manual, 'Salmon Hatching,' page 24.

ticulars to the *Salmo Gairdneri* of Sir J. Richardson, F. B. A., 'Fishes,' p. 221; it will be as well to retain that name. It may be readily distinguished from the quinnat by its rounded blunt-looking nose, shorter and much thicker head, straighter back, and more slender figure—the tail not nearly as much forked. The entire colour of the back is much lighter, and thickly freckled, as are the fins and tail, with oval black spots. The average weight of the *cha-cha-lool* is from 8 to 11 lbs. This salmon is common in the Fraser, Chilukweyuk, and Sumass rivers, and in every stream along the mainland and island coasts up which salmon ascend. When they first arrive the flesh is most delicious—fat, pink, and firm withal, and to my palate finer than that of the mammoth quinnat. The Indians also prize these salmon, and pack them when dried in bales apart from the others.

Salmo Gairdneri and *S. quinnat* are the spring salmon, but the autumn has also its supply of 'swimming silver,' quite equal to that of spring in point of numbers, but inferior in quality. Up the Columbia in October to the Kettle Falls, and somewhat earlier in the Fraser and rivers north of it, comes an ugly, unprepossessing, hook-nosed, dingy-looking salmon, called by the Colville Indians *Keasoo*, by the Chinooks *Ekewan*, by the Clallams *Kutch-kutch* — the *Hooked Snout* of the fur-traders, *Salmo lycaodon* of Pallas, *Zoog. Russ. Asiat.*

When fresh-run, this fish in colour is of a silvery-grey lustre; back, overshot with a greenish hue; belly, silvery-white; no spots on either the back or sides. The hooked nose, said to be peculiar to the male fish after spawning, is a well-marked, constant, and specific character in every fresh-run fish, the females having at all times symmetrical jaws. I found, from carefully observing great numbers of these fresh-run males, that the hooked state of the snout differs very materially in fish arriving at the same period; and I am quite convinced that large numbers of these salmon do get back again to the saltwater after spawning, and that the strange change that takes place in the hooking over of the snout and growth of the teeth, during their sojourn in the rivers, remains a permanent mark; and the vast difference observable in the males, at the time of arrival, is simply attributable to the fact, that those having the large fanglike teeth and tremendously crooked snout are such as have been up the rivers perhaps the year before, or, it may be, long prior to that period.

In every stream and rill, where they can by any possibility work a passage, you find these salmon; they remain until January and February in the succeeding year, becoming fearfully emaciated and worn, from a long and tedious abstinence; for I believe these salmon feed sparely, if at all, after leaving the sea. The fish in January is of a pale dirty-yellow colour; the sides, showing a bright purplish stripe (sure sign of waning vitality), are flattened and compressed; the back is straight until near its posterior third, when it dips down suddenly, and rises again at the tail just as if you had cut a notch out. The belly, instead of being silvery-white, is rusty yellow, and hangs pendulous and flabby; the eye is dull and sunken.

But the most curious change is in the head of the male fish: the nose becomes enormously elongated, and hooks down like a gaff-hook over the under-jaw, and the under-jaw bends up at the point into a kind of spike that fits into a regular sheath or hole in the upper jaw, just where it begins bending into the hook-like point; the teeth become regular fangs, sticking out round the jaws at irregular distances, and having a yellow bonelike appearance. I have often seen the teeth more than half an inch in length. It is quite clear that these teeth grow during the time the fish remain in fresh-water; no shrinking of the gums could account for such a length of tooth; and their use, I believe, is for fighting.

My own observations lead me to assume that at least there are eight or ten males to every female; and as one spawning-bed is used by many females, terrible battles ensue between the males as to which shall impregnate the ova; and it would appear, reasoning from analogy, that the same law holds good with fish as with gregarious mammals and birds—the stronger and more able male always begets the offspring. I hardly think the ova of a female fresh-run salmon, impregnated by the milt of an old and spent male fish, would produce as strong and healthy an offspring as the male fat, fresh, vigorous, and healthy. I cannot help thinking there must have been some purpose—as antlers are given to the deer tribes, spurs to the males of gregarious birds, and like examples—in giving such formidable weapons to these salmon during their breeding-time; and why not the reason above stated?

Quoting from Dr. Scouler: 'Observatory Inlet (which I should imagine to be just such an inlet as Puget's Sound) was frequented at the time by such myriads of the salmon, that a stone could not have reached the bottom without touching several individuals—their abundance surpassing imagination to conceive.' He goes on to say, that in a little brook they killed sixty with their boarding-pikes. Then, he says, the hump before the dorsal fin consists of fat, and appears to be peculiar to the males, who acquire it after spawning-time, when their snouts become elongated and arched.

The Fall-salmon (*Salmo lycaodon*) differ most extraordinarily at different periods of their growth—so much so, that I quite believed the adult, middle-aged, and young were three distinct and well-marked species; but Dr. A. Günther has very kindly investigated the matter, and knocked my three species into one.

Indians take the young of this salmon in large numbers in the bays, harbours, and fiord-like inlets surrounding the island, and along the British Columbian and Oregon coasts; also in the Sumass, Chilukweyuk, and Sweltza rivers, and indeed in all inland lakes that are accessible to fish from the sea. These handsome, troutlike young salmon are easily caught with bait of any kind; they rise readily to a gaudy fly, and seize even a piece of their brethren if carefully tied round a hook; from six ounces to a pound is about the average size. When they go to sea again from the lakes I had no opportunity of proving, but I imagine they go down with the floods, as the spring salmon come up.

The second form in which I mistook it for a distinct species is that of the Humpbacked Salmon (*Salmo proteus*, Pallas; *Salmo gibber*, Suckley; '*gerbuscha*,' Kamtschatka; '*hud-do*' of the Nesqually Indians; '*hun-num*' of the Fraser river Indians). In its general outline it differs altogether from the Hook-nosed Salmon. The back is much more arched; nose curved, but not nearly as much as in the mature *Salmo lycaodon*, and the under-jaw turns up and terminates in a protuberance or knob; teeth much more numerous, sharper, and smaller; tail deeply notched, and thickly spotted with dark oval-shaped marks. The most conspicuous feature is a large hump of adipose material situated on the shoulders, a little anterior to the dorsal fin, and only found in the male fish. It has generally been stated that this hump grows upon the male fish after entering the fresh-water: this is a mistake, for I have seen them again and again taken in the sea, before going up into the rivers, with this hump well developed. On cutting it open, it appears to be a sort of cellular membrane, filled with an oily, semifluid kind of material. The use of this deposit, there can be no doubt, is to supply the male with this material in some mysterious way during the spawning-time, for, after that period has passed, the hump entirely disappears. They arrive about the same time as the older fish, but only in very large runs every second year—have the same range, and die in thousands.

At Fort Hope, on the Fraser river, in the month of September, I was going trout-fishing in a beautiful stream, the Qua-que-alla, that comes thundering and dancing down the Cascade Mountains, cold and clear as crystal; these salmon were then toiling up in thousands, and were so thick in the ford that I had great trouble to ride my horse through; the salmon were in such numbers about his legs as to impede his progress, and frightened him so, that he plunged viciously and very nearly had me off. They are never at any time good eating; the flesh, in fresh-run fish, is white, soft, and tasteless. The Indians only eat them when they are unable to obtain anything else. These salmon work up to the very heads of the tributaries, and

I have often seen them where the water was so shallow as to leave their backs uncovered.

The *Salmo canis* of Suckley (Dog-Salmon, Spotted Salmon, 'Natural History of Washington Territory,' p. 341), which he says arrives at Puget's Sound in September and October, I believe to be only the old males of the *Salmo lycaodon* (Hook-nosed Salmon), that have had a turn in the rivers perhaps a year or two before, and have got safely back again to the sea, recruited their wasted energies, and returned again for another perilous cruise up the streams. The large fanglike teeth, from which they derive the name of dog-salmon, are the large teeth grown and developed, as I have previously described them, whilst spawning in the fresh water.

Salmon is of the most vital importance to the Indians; deprived or by any means cut off from obtaining it, starve to death they must; and were we at war with the Redskins, we need only cut them off from their salmon-fisheries to have them completely at our mercy. If salmon-fisheries—well managed, and conducted by persons who thoroughly understood salting, barreling, and curing salmon—were established on some of the tributaries to the Fraser and Columbia rivers, I am quite convinced they would pay handsomely.

Some few attempts have been made by speculators, but always failed for want of capital and proper management. The Hudson's Bay Company, in some of their inland and northern posts, feed their *employés* on dried salmon during the winter. At Fort Langley, on the Fraser river, the Company generally *salt in* several hundred casks of salmon, and these principally go to the Sandwich Islands or to China. There was one large salmon-curing establishment at the mouth of the Puyallup river, but I have been told it did not pay; the fish, being badly put up and carelessly packed, often spoiled before reaching the markets for which they were destined. In Victoria, salmon is now a very important article both of food and commerce.

CHAPTER III.

FISH HARVESTING.

The systems adopted by the Indians for capturing salmon vary in accordance with the localities chosen for fishing. Besides the stages or baskets in use on the Columbia river, they construct weirs reaching from one side of a stream to the other, with skilfully-contrived openings, allowing fish to pass easily through them into large lateral stores made of closely-woven wicker, where they are kept prisoners until required.

They have rather a clever contrivance for catching salmon in the bays and harbours, using a sort of gill-net (a net about forty feet long and eight feet wide), with large meshes; the upper edge is buoyed by bits of dry cedar-wood, that act as floats, and the net kept tight by small pebbles slung at four-foot distances along the lower margin. This kind of net the Indians stretch across the mouth of a small bay or inlet, and sit in their canoes a short distance off, quietly watching it. These small bays, or saltwater aquariums, are the lurking-places and strongholds for shoals of anchovies and herrings. Often tempted to wander and make excursions beyond the gateway of their rocky home, they are at once spied by predatory piratical salmon; seeking safety in flight, they dash headlong for their hiding-place, hotly pursued by their dreaded foe, and shooting easily through the cordy snare, laugh to see Master Salmon 'run his head into the net;' bob-bob go the floats beneath the surface, up paddles redskin, hauls up his net, clutches the silvery pirate, and with a short heavy club gives him a blow on the head, drops him into the canoe, lets go his net, and waits for the next.

With this kind of net immense numbers of spring and fall salmon are taken. All their nets are made of cord, spun from native hemp, that grows abundantly along the banks of the Fraser and other streams. Squaws gather the plant about a week before the flowering-time; first soak, then beat it into fibre; this, arranged in regular lengths, is handed to the Indian, who, seated on the ground, twists the bundles of tiffled hemp into cord—a cord as regular and symmetrical as the handiwork of a practised ropemaker—using neither tools nor machinery, but simply the hand and naked thigh.

The first salmon entering the Columbia are taken at Chinook Point, a short distance above Cape Disappointment, near the mouth of the river. These are known as 'Chinook salmon,' and are celebrated, not only in the immediate neighbourhood but in the markets of San Francisco, as the fattest and finest-flavoured salmon taken on the coast; they are large, ranging from 35lbs. to 70lbs. in weight.

In June the grand army arrives. We need not linger at the old fishery of the Chinook Indians, so prosperous fifty years ago. The Indians have disappeared; but the salmon army marches on, with little interruption, until they have arrived at the Cascades.

Here we must remain awhile, and see for ourselves how the red man harvests his salmon. Salmon is quite as essential to the Indians residing inland as grain to us, or bananas and plantains to the residents in the tropics: gleaning the regular supply of fish, the Indian literally harvests and garners it as we reap our grain-crops. It cannot be by mere chance that fish are prompted, by an unalterable instinct, to thread their way into the farthest recesses of the mountains—fish too that are fat and oily, and best adapted to supply heat and the elements of nutrition.

The winters are long and intensely cold, often 30° Fahr. below zero, the snow lying deep for at least six months. Birds migrate, most of the rodents and the bears hybernate, and such animals as remain to brave the biting cold, retire where it is very difficult and often impossible to hunt or trap them. In a small lodge, made of hides or rushes, as far from windproof as a sieve would be; wrapped in miserable mantles (simply skins sewn together, or ragged blankets, bought of the Hudson's Bay Company), cowering and shivering over the smouldering logs, are a family of savages. The nipping blasts and icy cold forbid their venturing in pursuit of food; flesh they could not cure during the summer, for they have not salt, and sun-drying is insufficient to preserve it. A miserable death, starved alike by cold and hunger, must be the fate of this, and of all Indian families away from the seaboard, but for salmon: sun-dried, it preserves its heat and flesh-yielding qualities unimpaired; uncooked, they chew it all day long, and frequently grow fat during their quasi-hybernation. The waterways are thus made available for the transport of coals and provisions necessary to keep the life-stove burning, floated free of freight up to the very doors of the Indian's wigwam. The way he harvests this store, and preserves it for winter use, we shall see as we follow the course of the salmon in their ascent of the Columbia river.

The Cascades, where the salmon first meet with a hindrance to their upward course, is a lovely spot. The vast river here breaks its way through the Cascade Mountains, a mountain-gap unequalled, I should say, in depth and extent, by any in the world. Some parts are massive walls of rock, and others wooded slopes like to a narrow valley. One can hardly imagine the possibility of so great a change in climate, and consequently vegetation, as there is betwixt this place and the Dalles, only a few miles farther up the river. I have left the Dalles when the ground was covered with snow, and within a distance of forty miles entered this gap, and found the climate to be that of summer. The sloping forests brightly green, shrubs of various sorts, tropical in appearance, immense ferns, the emerald moss clothing the rocks, over which dozens of waterfalls, unbroken for a thousand feet, tumble from the hills into the river

—all together make up a scene of beauty and rich luxuriance, unlike any other part of the river.

From the Dalles to the Cascades the river has scarcely a perceptible current, either side being bounded by perpendicular walls of mountains. Tradition says, that once the river had a uniformly swift course the entire way, and that where the Cascades now are, the water passed at that time under a huge arch that reached from side to side. Afterwards an earthquake tumbled it down, the ruins of the arch still existing as a chain of islands across the head of the rapids; the river, having gradually carried away the fragments, forming now the long rapid. The river, thus suddenly thrown back, flooded the forests up to the Dalles, and to this day stumps of trees are to be seen sticking out of the water many hundred yards from the shore.

Below the Cascades, before reaching the flat district about Fort Vancouver, the scenery is bold and massive; immense hills densely wooded, bold promontories, and grassy glades are passed successively as the steamer dashes on her downward trip. At the Cascades there is now a railway, over which goods and passengers are conveyed to the steamers above the rapids, which are so swift that canoes plied by experienced Indians dare not venture to run them.

Wandering along by this foaming rush of water, one sees numberless scaffoldings erected amongst the boulders—rude clumsy contrivances, constructed of poles jammed between large stones, and lashed with ropes of bark to other poles, that cross each other to form stages. Indian lodges, pitched in the most picturesque and lovely spots imaginable, are dotted along from one end of the rapids to the other. Indians from long distances and of several tribes have come here to await the arrival of the salmon.

Leaning against the trees, or supported by the lodges, are numbers of small round nets (like we catch shrimps with in rocky pools), fastened to handles forty and fifty feet in length. Hollow places are cunningly enclosed, with low walls of boulders, on the river-side of each stage.

It is early in June; the salmon have arrived, and a busy scene it is. On every stage plying their nets are Indian fishers, guiltless of garments save a piece of cloth tied round the waist. Ascending the rapids, salmon seek the slack-waters at the edges of the current, and are fond of lingering in the wake of a rock or any convenient hollow; the rock-basins constructed by the sides of the stages are just the places for idling and resting. This the crafty fisher turns to good account, and skilfully catches the loiterer by plunging his net into the pool at its head, and letting the current sweep it down, thus *hooping* salmon after salmon, with a certainty astounding to a looker-on. Thirty salmon an hour is not an unusual take for two skilled Indians to land on a stage. As soon as one gets tired, another takes his place, so that the nets are never idle during the 'run.'

The instant a fish reaches the stage, a heavy blow on the head stops its flapping; boys and girls are waiting to seize and carry it ashore, to be split and cured—a process I can better describe when at the salmon-falls. As there is at the Cascades simply hindrance to the salmon's ascent, of course vast numbers escape the redskins' nets.

Forty miles above this fishery is another obstruction, the Dalles; where the river forces its way through a mass of basaltic rocks in numerous channels, some of them appearing as if hewn by human hands. Another portage has to be made here, a neat little town having grown up in consequence of the transhipment. The journey from steamer to steamer is accomplished in stages, the heavy goods being hauled by mule and ox-teams. The road lies over a steep ridge of hills to the junction of the Des Chutes, or 'Fall river,' with the Columbia. Fishing at the Dalles is much the same as at the Cascades.

Great numbers of salmon turn off and ascend the Snake river, to be captured at the Great Shoshonee Falls by the Snake and Bannock Indians. We follow on the vanguard of the swimming army, passing numberless tributaries, up which detachments make their way, right and left, into the heart of the country—supplies for tribes living near the different streams—to the great falls of the Columbia, the 'Kettle Falls;'* why so named is not very clear. These falls, except when the river is at its highest flood, form an impassable barrier to the salmon's progress; the distance from the sea is about 700 miles, and the first arrivals are usually about the middle of June.

The winter-quarters of the Boundary Commission were about two miles above the falls, and close to the falls is a trading-post of the Hudson's Bay Company, Fort Colville. The gravelly plateau on which the trading-post stands, together with one or two houses belonging to old employés, was clearly once a lake-bottom. The water at some remote period filling the lake ap-

* *Vide* Illustration.

pears to have broken its way out through the rocks at the falls, and left this flat dry land. Patches of wheat and barley are grown, but the soil is far too poor to repay the labour of cultivation.

About three weeks preceding the arrival of the salmon, Indians begin to assemble from all directions. Cavalcades may be seen, day after day, winding their way down the plain; and as the savage when he travels takes with him all his worldly wealth—wives, children, dogs, horses, lodges, weapons, and skins—the turn-out is rather novel. The smaller children are packed with the baggage on the backs of horses, which are driven by the squaws, who always ride astride like the men. The elder girls and boys, three or four on a horse, ride with their mothers, whilst the men and stouter youths drive the bands of horses that run loose ahead of the procession. A pack of prick-eared curs, simply tamed prairie-wolves, are always in attendance.

A level piece of ground overlooking the falls (the descent from which to the rocks is by a zig-zag path, down a nearly vertical cliff) is rapidly covered with lodges of all shapes and sizes. The squaws do the work appertaining to camping, and are literally 'hewers of wood and drawers of water.' The men, who are all, when at the fishery, under one chief, whom they designate the 'Salmon Chief,' at once commence work—some in repairing the drying-sheds, which are placed on the rocks (as are also numbers of lodges) at the foot of the zigzag; others are busy making or mending immense wicker hampers, about thirty feet in circumference, and twelve feet in depth. Little groups are dragging down huge trees lopped clear of their branches—rolling, twisting, and tumbling them over the rocks, to be fixed at last by massive boulders, the ends hanging over the foaming water not unlike so many gibbets. These trees being secure and in their right places, the next work is to hang the wicker baskets to them, which is a risky and most difficult job: but many willing hands and long experience work wonders; with strong ropes of twisted bark, the baskets are at last securely suspended. By this time the river begins to flood rapidly, and soon washes over the rocks where the trees are fastened, and into the basket, which is soon in the midst of the waterfall, being so contrived as to be easily accessible from the rocks not overwashed by the flood.

Whilst awaiting the coming salmon, the scene is one great revel: horse-racing, gambling, love-making, dancing, and diversions of all sorts, occupy the singular assembly; for at these annual gatherings, when all jointly labour in catching and curing the winter supply of salmon, feuds and dislikes are for the time laid by, or, as they figuratively express it, 'The hatchet is buried.'

The medicine-men (doctors and conjurors) of the different tribes busily work their charms and incantations to insure an abundant run of fish. One of the illustrations is drawn from a photograph of the falls. The Indians at first steadily refused to allow the photographer and his machine to come near the falls, declaring it a box of bad 'medicine' that would surely drive every salmon away; and not until an old Romish priest who was at the trading-post explained it to them, did they permit a photograph to be taken.

The watchers announce the welcome tidings of the salmon arrival, and the business begins. The baskets are hung in places where past experience has taught the Indians salmon generally leap, in their attempts to clear the falls. The first few that arrive are frequently speared from the rocks. They are in such vast numbers during the height of the 'run,' that one could not well throw a stone into the water at the base of the falls without hitting a fish: fifty and more may be seen in the air at a time, leaping over the wicker traps, but, failing to clear the 'salmon-leap,' fall back, and are caged. In each basket two naked Indians are stationed all day long; and as they are under a heavy fall of water, frequent relays are necessary. Salmon three or four at a time, in rapid succession, tumble into the basket. The Indians thrust their fingers under the gills, strike the fish on the head with a heavy club, and then fling them on the rocks. I have known three hundred salmon landed from one basket betwixt sunrise and sunset, varying in weight from twenty to seventy-five pounds.

From the heaps of fish piled on the rocks, boys and girls carry and drag them back to the squaws seated round the curing-houses; with sharp knives they rip the salmon open, twist off the head, and cleverly remove the backbone; then hanging them on poles, close under the roofs of sheds the sides of which are open, they dry them slowly, small fires being kept constantly smouldering on the floors. The smoke serves to keep away the flies, and perhaps also aids in the preservation of the fish. The only portions eaten by the Indians during the catching are the heads, backbones, roes, and livers, which are roasted, skewered on sticks.

When thoroughly dried the fish are packed in *bales* made of rush-mats, each bale weighing about fifty pounds, the bales being tightly lashed with bark-ropes. Packing in bales of equal weight facilitates an equitable division of the take. Horses are purposely brought to carry the fish back to winter-quarters, and two bales are easily packed on each horse. The fishing-season lasts for about two months: then the spoils are divided, and the place abandoned to its wonted quietude, until the following summer brings with it another harvest.

During the drying, silicious sand is blown over the fish, and of course adheres to it. Constantly chewing this 'sanded salmon' wears the teeth as if filed down, which I at first imagined them to be, until the true cause was discovered. I have an under-jaw in my possession whereon the teeth are quite level with the bony sockets of the jaw, worn away by the flinty sand.

I question if in the world there is another spot where salmon are in greater abundance, or taken with so little labour, as at the Kettle Falls, on the Columbia river. In all streams emptying into Puget's Sound, in the Fraser river, and rivers north of it to the Arctic Ocean, salmon ascend in prodigious abundance. In the Fraser there are no obstructions as far as Fort Hope to the salmon ascent; hence fishing is carried on by each village or family for themselves, and not by the combined labour of many, as on the Columbia. Near the mouth of the river large iron gaff-hooks are generally used; with these ugly weapons salmon are hooked into the canoes. Higher up, at the mouths of the Sumass, Chilukweyuk, and other tributary streams, they use a very ingenious kind of net worked between two canoes, with which large numbers of salmon are taken. Stages, too, are hung over the eddies from the rocks, and round nets used as at the Cascades.

On the Nanimo river the Indians have a very ingenious contrivance for taking salmon, by constructing a weir; but, instead of putting baskets, they *pave* a square place, about six feet wide and fourteen feet long, with white or light-coloured stones. This pavement is always on the lower side of the weir, leading to an opening. A stage is erected between two of these paved ways, where Indians, lying on their stomachs, can in an instant see if a salmon is traversing the white paved way. A long spear, barbed at the end, is held in readiness, and woe betide the adventurous fish that runs the gauntlet of this perilous passage!

But the most curious contrivance I saw was at Johnson's Narrows. I have said salmon readily take a bait when in saltwater. The Indians when fishing use two spears, one about seventy feet in length; the other shorter, having a barbed end, is about twenty feet long. In a canoe thus equipped, favourable fishing-grounds are sought, the Indian having the long spear being also provided with a small hollow cone of wood, trimmed round its greater circumference with small feathers, much like a shuttlecock; this he places on the end of the longer spear, and presses it under water, until down the full length of the handle; a skilful jerk detaches this conelike affair from the spear-haft, when it wriggles up through the water like a struggling fish. The savage with the short spear intently watches this deceiver; a salmon runs at it, and it is speared like magic.

Next in importance amongst the Salmonidæ is the Oregon Brook Trout, *Fario stellatus* (Grd. Proc. Acad., Phil. Nat. Soc., viii. 219).

Specific Characters.—Head rather large, contained four-and-a-half times in the total length; maxillary reaching a vertical line drawn behind the orbit. Colour of the back bright olive-green, sides pinkish-yellow, belly white, profusely speckled over with minute black spots.

This trout lives everywhere, and is to be met with in the lakes and rivers in Vancouver Island, in all streams flowing into Puget's Sound, and away up the western sides of the Cascades. Crossing to the eastern side, and descending into the valley of the Columbia, again he puts in an appearance. Climb the western slope of the Rocky Mountains up to the summit, 7,000 feet above the sea-level, there too he lives—always hungry and voracious. These trout are very delicious, varying from eight ounces up to three pounds in weight.

My first exploit in fishing for trout may be worth relating:—I was sitting on the bank of a stream that rippled gaily on its rocky course, down the western slope of the Rocky Mountains; and which, here and there lengthening out into a long stickle, and curling round a jutting rock, lazily idled by the grassy bank; anon leaping a sudden fall, and widening into a glassy pool. Butterflies gambolled and flitted recklessly; dragonflies clad in brilliant armour waged cruel war on the lesser forms of winged life, chasing them everywhere. The busy hum of insects, the air fragrant with the forest perfumes, the murmur of the water, and the songs of feathered choristers made one feel happy, though far away from civilisation. My reverie was broken by a sudden splash; a speckled tyrant, lurking under the bank on which I sat, had pounced upon a large grey fly that, unconscious of danger, had touched the water with its gauzy wings. Very well, Master Trout, you may perhaps be as easily duped as your more cautious *confrères*; so setting to work, I overhauled my 'possible sack,' found a few coarse hooks, a bit of gut, and some thread.

Among other materials wherewith to make a fly, feathers were indispensable. Shouldering my gun, I strode off to look for a 'white flesher,' alias ruffed grouse; soon stirred one up, bagged him, hauled out his glossy bottle-green frill; selected some feathers which I thought would turn a decent hackle, picked out a couple of brighter ones for wings, some red wool from my blanket for dubbing, and with these materials I tied a fly. Not the slightest resemblance, fancied or real, did it bear to anything ever created, but still it was a fly, and, as I flattered myself, a great achievement. A line was made from some ends of cord; then cutting a young larch, I made my tackle fast to the end, and thus equipped sallied to the stream.

My first attempt in the swift scour was a lamentable failure. Warily I threw my newly-created monster well across the stream, and, according to the most approved method, let it slowly wash towards me, conveying to the rod and line a delicate and tempting tremble; not a rise, not a nibble; my hopes wavered, and I began to think these trout wiser than I had given them credit for. I tried the pool as a last chance; so, leaning over the rock, I let my tempter drop into the water; it made a splash like throwing in a stone; but imagine my delight, ye lovers of the gentle art, when a tremendous jerk told me I had one hooked and struggling to get free! Depending on the strength of my tackle, I flung him out on the bank; and admitting all that may be said against me as being barbarous and cruel, I confess to standing over the dying fish, and admiring his brilliant colour, handsome shape, fair proportion—and, last thought not least, contemplated eating him! I pitied him not as, flapping and struggling on the grass, his life ebbed away, but thought only of the skill I had displayed in duping him, and the feast in store for me on returning to camp.

Having discovered a secret, I pressed eagerly on to turn it to the best advantage, and that day played havoc amongst the trouts. Some long willow-branches, cut with a crook at the end, served me in lieu of a basket. Passing the sticks under the gill-covers, and out at the mouth, I strung trout after trout until the sticks were filled; then tying the ends together, flung them across my shoulder and trudged along; a good plan when you have not a basket. I now turned my attention, and devoted all my ingenuity, to the manufacture of a more angler-like fly; and in this case the adage proved true, 'that a poor original was better than a good imitation.' My well-dressed fly was not one-half as much appreciated as the old one; there was a sham gentility about him that evidently led at once to suspicion, and it was only here and there I met with a fish weak enough to fall a victim to his polished exterior; I therefore abandoned the dandy, and returned again to the rough old red-shirted 'trapper' with which I first commenced.

There was a stream in which I had better sport than in any of the others, the Mooyee, on the western slope of the Rocky Mountains—a small stream, very rocky, clear as crystal, icy cold, and so densely wooded on each side that fishing in it, unless by wading, was impossible I remember one pool as being particularly productive—a rock-basin, with a little rivulet dancing into it through a pebbly reach; the water so beautifully clear, that everything in the pool was visible, as though one looked into an aquarium. I could not help standing and feasting my eyes on the trout playing about in it. To say the pool was full of fish is no exaggeration; all, with their heads toward the little stream, were gently sculling their tails to steady themselves. I gazed upon a mass of fish, big and little, from four ounces to three pounds in weight.

Having sufficiently indulged in admiring this host of trout (the like of which I had never seen before), I began the war. Dropping my 'sensation-fly' into the little stream, I let it sink and drift into the pool. Twenty open mouths rushed at it ravenously, and trout after trout was rapidly landed on the shingle. I continued this scheme until a heap of magnificent fish were piled at my side, and the pool was rapidly thinning. One crafty old fellow, however, that looked about three pounds in weight, defied all my efforts to tempt him. I let the fly drift over him, under his nose, above his nose; but he scorned it, and, if he could, I felt he would have winked his eye derisively at me.

To have him I was determined: so sitting down, I scooped out the eye of a fish, and put it on the point of the flyhook, then let it drift down the stream and into the pool; steadily it neared his nose, and in breathless expectation I awaited the result. He was evidently uneasy, and knew not what to do. It floated past him, and I thought my bait had failed; when round he turned, and dashing viciously at it, seized (pardon the joke) the hook and eye, and I had him fast. Being far too heavy to risk jerking, I let him get over his furious fit, then towed him ashore; hand over hand gathering up my line, I got close to him, and seizing him behind the gills, brought him upon the shingle; and a beauty he was!

I have tried various expedients—more as experiments than anything else—to find out what bait these trout really preferred. Grasshoppers they took readily, and I have often caught a trout when only one leg of the insect remained on the hook; the white meat from the tail of the river crayfish is also a very favourite diet. Earthworms I could not try, because they do not exist in British Columbia. But all my trials and experiments failed signally in discovering anything that could at all compare with my 'first fly.'

The trout spawn about October, or perhaps a little later, depositing their ova in gravel in the lesser streams.

SALMON TROUT.—*Salmo spectabilis* (Red-spotted Salmon Trout), Grd. Proc. Acad., Nat. Soc. Phild., viii. 218.—*Sp. Ch.*: Head a trifle more than a fourth of the total length; maxillary extending to a vertical line drawn posterior to the orbit. Colour of the back dark-greenish, inclining to grey, a lighter shade of the same colour on the sides—beneath silvery-white; thickly marked above the lateral line with yellowish spots, interspersed with others that are bright red.

In habits and distribution the salmon-trout differs in every respect from the preceding. There can be no doubt that this fish is anadromous, and comes up into the rivers to spawn at particular periods of the year, like the salmon, and then returns to sea. In October the great run begins. Into all the rivers emptying into Puget's Sound—the Dwamish, Nesqually, Puyallup, and several others, up the Fraser and its tributaries, into all the creeks and inlets about Vancouver Island, crowd in shoal after shoal. They vary in size; I have seldom seen them exceed three pounds in weight

The advent of these trout is the signal for a

general Indian fish-harvest. The banks of all the little streams are soon dotted with temporary lodges, and every one, from the naked little urchin to the stalwart chief, wages war upon these fish. All sorts of expedients are used to snare them. Boys, girls, and old squaws catch them with a hook and line, about eight or ten feet long, tied to the end of a short stick. The hook (made of bone or hard wood) is baited with salmon-roe. The Indians never use the roe fresh; dried in the sun it becomes extremely tough, and acquires a very rank oily smell. The fish take it greedily, and in this manner large numbers are captured.

Another bait equally fatal is made by cutting a small strip from the belly of a trout, and keeping the shiny part outermost—winding it tightly round the hook, from the barb, to about an inch up the line, securing it by twisting white horsehair closely round it. A small pebble is slung about a foot from the baited hook, and the line tied to the canoe-paddle close to the hand; paddling slowly along, this bait is trolled after the canoe. The intention is manifestly to imitate a small fish, as we troll with minnow or spoon-bait in our waters. All the larger fish are generally taken in this way. They rise readily to a gaudy fly, and afford admirable sport.

But the great haul of hauls is effected by a most ingeniously-contrived basket, in principle the same as our eel-baskets. It is made of split vine-maple, lashed together with strips of cedar-bark. These baskets vary in size; some of them are fifteen feet long, and six in circumference. The crafty savages place their wicker traps in the centre of the stream; a dam of latticework on each side reaches to the bank, so that no fish can get up-stream unless through the trap. Another plan, and a very good one where the water is shallow, is to build a little wall of boulders, rising about a foot above water, slanting the wall obliquely until the ends meet in the centre of the stream at an acute angle; at this point they place the basket. By this plan all the water is forced through the basket, increasing the depth and strength of the current. In happy ignorance of their danger, the fish ply steadily up-current, until they suddenly find themselves caged.

When a sufficient number of fish are in the basket, an empty one is carried out and set, the other brought ashore; its contents are turned out upon the grass. Squaws, old and young, knife in hand, squat round, looking eagerly on; and as the captives lie flapping on the sward, in the harpies rush, seize a trout, rip him up, remove the inside, and then skewer him open with two sticks. Poles, having a fork at the end, are placed firmly in the ground, about fifteen feet apart. Other sticks, barked and rubbed very smooth, are placed in these forked ends, on which the split trout are strung. Small fires are kept smouldering below the strung-up fish. When thoroughly dry, they are packed in small bales, and lashed with the bark of the cedar-tree.

CANDLE-FISH.—The Candle-fish or Eulachon, *Salmo* (*mallotus*) *Pacificus*, Rich. F. B. A., p. 227; *Thaleichthys Pacificus*, Grd.—*Sp. Ch.*: Head somewhat pointed and conical; mouth large, its fissure extending back to the anterior margin of the orbit; opercule terminated by a rounded angle, lower jaw projecting a little beyond the upper one; tongue rough, teeth on the pharyngeals; lower jaw, palatines, and vomer devoid of teeth; eye rather small; adipose fin, placed opposite the hind portion of the anal; scales subelliptical. Dorsal region greenish-olive colour, generally silvery-white, sparsely spotted with dirty yellow; a dark spot, nearly black, over each orbit.

A human body is a kind of locomotive furnace, that has to be kept up to a given temperature by fuel, its food. Under a tropical sun, not much fuel is needed, and that of a sort that will not keep up a large fire. Man, therefore, wears clothes made from a vegetable fibre, and eats fruit and rice, the lowest in the scale of heat-making materials. Far north among the polar ice, where you cannot touch metal without its taking the skin off your fingers, the human locomotive is protected by thick coverings of fur: the native takes the jackets from his furry-footed companions, and covers his own skin with them. But the grand oil-springs—the locomotive's necessary coal-mines in another form—are in the bodies of the great seals and whales. Oil and blubber burn rapidly, and give out a large amount of heat. With a fur-suit outside, and inside a feed of seal's flesh washed down with seal's oil, the steam of life is kept up very easily.

But all the fat of the sea is not in the bodies of those great blubbering whales and seals. There is a fish, small in size, not larger than a smelt, that is fat beyond all description, clad in glittering silver armour, and found on the coasts of British Columbia, Russian America, Queen Charlotte and Vancouver Islands, which is called by the natives *Eulachon* or Candle-fish. I have had both leisure and opportunity to make this fish's intimate acquaintance; played the spy upon its habits, its coming and going, and have noted how it is caught and cured.

Picture my home—an Indian village, on the north shore of British Columbia. The village is prettily situated on a rocky point of land, chosen, as all Indian villages are, with an eye to prevention of surprise from concealed foes. Rearward it is guarded by a steep hill, and it commands from the front the entrance to one of those long canals, which, as I have previously stated, resemble the fiords of Norway, often running thirty or forty miles inland.

The dwellings consist of ten or fifteen rude sheds, about twenty yards long and twelve wide, built of rough cedar-planks; the roof a single slant covered with poles and rushes. Six or eight families live in each shed. Every family has its own fire on the ground, and the smoke, that must find its way out as best it can through cracks and holes (chimneys being objected to), hangs in a dense upper cloud, so that a man can only keep his head out of it by squatting on the ground: to stand up is to run a risk of suffocation. The children of all ages, in droves, naked and filthy, live under the smoke; as well as squaws, who squat round the smouldering logs; innumerable dogs, like starving wolves, prick-eared, sore-eyed, snappish brutes, unceasingly engaged in faction-fights and sudden duels, in which the whole pack immediately takes sides. Felt, but not heard, are legions of bloodthirsty fleas, that would try their best to suck blood from a boot, and by combined exertions would soon flay alive any man with a clean and tender skin.

The moon, near its full, creeps upward from behind the hills; stars one by one are lighted in the sky—not a cloud flecks the clear blue. The Indians are busy launching their canoes, preparing war against the candle-fish, which they catch when they come to the surface to sport in the moonlight. As the rising moon now clears the shadow of the hills, her rays slant down on the green sea, just rippled by the land-breeze. And now, like a vast sheet of pearly nacre, we may see the glittering shoals of the fish—the water seems alive with them. Out glides the dusky Indian fleet, the paddles stealthily plied by hands far too experienced to let a splash be heard. There is not a whisper, not a sound, but the measured rhythm of many paddlers, as the canoes are sent flying towards the fish.

To catch them, the Indians use a monster comb or rake, a piece of pinewood from six to eight feet long, made round for about two feet of its length, at the place of the hand-grip; the rest is flat, thick at the back, but thinning to a sharp edge, into which are driven teeth about four inches long, and an inch apart. These teeth are usually made of bone, but, when the Indian fishers can get sharp-pointed iron nails, they prefer them. One Indian sits in the stern of each canoe to paddle it along, keeping close to the shoal of fish; another, having the rounded part of the rake firmly fixed in both hands, stands with his face to the bow of the canoe, the teeth pointing sternwards. He then sweeps it through the glittering mass of fish, using all his force, and brings it to the surface teeth upwards, usually with a fish impaled, sometimes with three or four upon one tooth. The rake being brought into the canoe, a sharp rap on the back of it knocks the fish off, and then another sweep yields a similar catch.

It is wonderful to see how rapidly an Indian will fill his canoe by this rude method of fishing. The dusky forms of the savages bend over the canoes, their brawny arms sweep their toothed sickles through the shoals, stroke follows stroke in swift succession, and steadily the canoes fill with their harvest of 'living silver.' When they have heaped as much as this frail craft will safely carry, they paddle ashore, drag the boats up on the shelving beach, overturn them as the quickest way of discharging cargo, relaunch, and go back to rake up another load. This labour goes on until the moon has set behind the mountain-peaks and the fish disappear, for it is their habit rarely to come to the surface except in the night. The sport over, we glide under the dark rocks, haul up the canoe, and lie before the log-fire to sleep long and soundly.

The next labour is that of the squaws, who have to do the curing, drying, and oil-making. Seated in a circle, they are busy stringing the fish. They do not gut or in any way clean them, but simply pass long smooth sticks through their eyes, skewering on each stick as many as it will hold, and then lashing a smaller piece transversely across the ends, to prevent the fish from slipping off the skewer. This done, next follows the drying, which is generally achieved in the thick smoke at the top of the sheds, the sticks of fish being there hung up side by side. They soon dry, and acquire a flavour of wood-smoke, which helps also to preserve them. No salt is used by Indians in any of their systems of curing fish.

When dry, the candle-fish are carefully packed in large frails made from cedar-bark or rushes, much like those one buys for a penny at Billingsgate; then they are stowed away on high stages made of poles, like a rough scaffolding. This precaution is essential, for the Indian children and dogs have an amiable weakness for eatables; and as lock-and-key are unknown to the redskins, they take this way of baffling the appetites of the incorrigible pilferers. The bales are kept until required for winter. However hungry or however short of food an Indian family may be during summer-time, it seldom will break in upon the winter 'cache.'

I have never seen any fish half as fat and as good for Arctic winter-food as these little candle-fish. It is next to impossible to broil or fry them, for they melt completely into oil. Some idea of their marvellous fatness may be gleaned from the fact, that the natives use them as lamps for lighting their lodges. The fish, when dried, has a piece of rush-pith, or a strip from the inner bark of the cypress-tree (*Thuja gigantea*), drawn through it, a long round needle made of hard wood being used for the purpose; it is then lighted, and burns steadily until consumed. I have read comfortably by its light;

the candlestick, literally a stick for the candle, consists of a bit of wood split at one end, with the fish inserted in the cleft.

These ready-made sea-candles — little dips wanting only a wick that can be added in a minute — are easily transformed by heat and pressure into liquid. When the Indian drinks instead of burning them, he gets a fuel in the shape of oil, that keeps up the combustion within him, and which is burnt and consumed in the lungs just as it was by the wick, but only gives heat. It is by no mere chance that myriads of small fish, in obedience to a wondrous instinct, annually visit the northern seas, containing within themselves all the elements necessary for supplying light, heat, and life to the poor savage, who, but for this, must perish in the bitter cold of the long dreary winter.

As soon as the Indians have stored away the full supply of food for the winter, all the fish subsequently taken are converted into oil. If we stroll down to the lodges near the beach, we shall see for ourselves how they manage it. The fish reserved for oil-making have been piled in heaps until partially decomposed; five or six fires are blazing away, and in each fire are a number of large round pebbles, to be made very hot.

By each fire are four large square boxes, made from the trunk of the pine-tree. A squaw carefully piles in each box a layer of fish about three-deep, and covers them with cold water. She then puts five or six of the hot stones upon the layers of fish, and when the steam has cleared away, carefully lays small pieces of wood over the stones; then more fish, more water, more stones, more layers of wood, and so on, until the box is filled. The oil-maker now takes all the liquid from this box, and uses it over again instead of water in filling another box, and skims the oil off as it floats on the surface.

A vast quantity of oil is thus obtained; often as much as seven hundredweight will be made by one small tribe. The refuse fish are not yet done with, more oil being extractible from them. Built against the pine-tree is a small stage, made of poles, very like a monster gridiron. The refuse of the boxes, having been sewn up in porous mats, is placed on the stage, to be rolled and pressed by the arms and chests of Indian women; and the oil thus squeezed out is collected in a box placed underneath.

Not only has Nature, ever bountiful, sent an abundance of oil to the redskin, but she actually provides ready-made bottles to store it away in.

The great seawrack, that grows to an immense size in these northern seas, and forms submarine forests, has a hollow stalk, expanded into a complete flask at the root-end. Cut into lengths of about three feet, these hollow stalks, with the bulb at the end, are collected and kept wet until required for use. As the oil is obtained, it is stored away in these natural quart-bottles, or rather larger bottles, for some of them hold three pints.

Some fifty years ago, vast shoals of eulachon used regularly to enter the Columbia; but the silent stroke of the Indian paddle has now given place to the splashing wheels of great steamers, and the Indian and the candle-fish have vanished together. From the same causes the eulachon has also disappeared from Puget's Sound, and is now seldom caught south of latitude 50° N.

CHAPTER IV.

THE ROUND-FISH, HERRINGS, AND VIVIPAROUS FISH.

THE ROUND-FISH (*Coregonus quadrilateralis*).—*Sp. Ch.*: Colour, yellowish-brown, paler on the sides and belly than on the back; scales bright and glittering, each edged with a narrow border of dark-grey; cheeks, fins, and tail, a deeper tint of the same colour as that on the back; head one-sixth of the length (without the caudal); mouth very small, under-jaw shorter than the upper—no teeth perceptible.

This fish has a very wide geographical range, being found as far north (according to Sir J. Richardson) as the Mackenzie and Coppermine rivers, east of the Rocky Mountains, and latitude 49° N. the western side; how much farther they range north of 49° I had no opportunity of judging.

This handsome and delicious fish, one of the *Salmonidæ*, is most valuable as an article of food to the Indians, west of the Rocky Mountains, the White-fish (*Coregonus albus*), or 'Attihawmeg' (which means 'reindeer of the sea'), being of like importance to those residing east of the mountains. There the Indians frequently have to subsist entirely on white-fish, and, at many of the fur-trading stations, the traders get very little else to eat during nine months of the twelve.

'In one small lake (Lake St. Ann's), near Fort Edmonton, forty thousand white-fish were taken, of an average weight of three to four pounds, in the course of three weeks.' (*Palliser's Exp.*)

Two modes are adopted for preserving them—one that of sun-drying, the other by freezing, in which state they may be kept perfectly sweet and free from taint for the whole winter.

The Round-fish is seldom taken over two pounds in weight, and prior to spawning they are loaded with fat, which on the shoulders almost amounts to a hump, but becomes thin, watery, and insipid, after the all-important duty of providing for their offspring is accomplished. I am not quite sure when they return to the sea, as nothing is seen of them after the ice sets in, towards the end of November, until their arrival on the following year. The ova are deposited in much the same way as that of other *Salmonidæ*:

a hollow made in the gravel contains the eggs and milt, which are covered over and abandoned—the young fish, on its emergence from the egg, taking care of itself as best it can.

One may journey a long way to witness a prettier or more picturesque sight than Round-fish harvesting on the Sumass prairie : the prairie bright and lovely ; the grass fresh, green, and waving lazily; various wild flowers, peeping coyly out from their cosy hiding-places, seem making the most of the summer; a fresh, joyous hilarity everywhere, pervading even the Indians, whose lodges in great numbers lie scattered about. From the edges of the pine-forest, where the little streams came out from the dark shadow into the sunshine, up to the lake, the prairie was like a fair. Indians, old and young; chiefs, braves, squaws, children, and slaves; were alike busy in capturing the round-fish, that were swarming up the streams in thousands: so thick were they that baits and traps were thrown aside, and hands, baskets, little nets, and wooden bowls did the work; it was only requisite to stand in the stream and bale out the fish. Thousands were drying, thousands had been eaten, and as many more were wasting and decomposing on the bank. Supposing every fish escaping the Indians, otters, and the various enemies that it meets with in ascending the rivers, succeeded in depositing its ova, where or how they find room to spawn, or what becomes of the offspring, is more than I know.

Round-fish are cured by splitting and sun-drying, precisely in the same manner as salmon. I have had very good sport angling for round-fish, by using a rough gaudy fly. They rise readily, and struggle obstinately, when hooked, but soon give up; turning on their side, they permit themselves to be dragged upon the bank without attempting a flap of resistance.

Some of these fish remain permanently, or at any rate for some time, in fresh-water. I have often taken them in the Na-hoil-a-pit-ka river, to get into which they must have leaped the Kettle Falls during a high flood, being quite 800 miles from the sea; and as they are caught in the spring, I think it fair to conclude they do not invariably return to the sea after spawning.

HERRINGS.—The Vancouver Island Herring (*Malletta cœrulia*, Grd.).—*Sp. Ch.*: Head, about one-fifth of the total length of the body, slender, its shape in profile somewhat fusiform; back, bright steel-blue colour, shading away on the sides to brilliant silvery-white: fins, yellow-white, but uniform in colour; posterior extremity of maxillary bone extending to a vertical line drawn through the middle of the orbit; eye, subcircular, large; colour, copper-red in the freshly-caught fish; anterior margin of the dorsal fin, nearer the extremity of the snout than the insertion of the caudal. The average length is somewhat about ten inches. Indian name along the coast, *Stole*; Skadget Indian, *Lo-see*.

There are three distinct herring arrivals, one beginning in February and March; these fish are small, and somewhat lean. About the beginning of April the run commences; these are finer, full of spawn, and in high condition: in June and July, and extending through the summer, small shoals occasionally make their appearance, but never as fine as the April fish.

Toward the middle of April herring legions commence arriving from seaward in real earnest; brigade follows brigade in rapid succession, until every bay, harbour, inlet, estuary, and lagoon is literally alive with them. Close in their rear, as camp-followers hang on the skirts of an army, come shoals of dogfish, salmon, and fish-eating sea-birds.

I have often seen a shoal of herrings, when hotly pursued by the dogfish, dash into a little rock-bound nook, the water lashed into white spray by a thousand tails and fins, plied with all the power and energy the poor struggling fish could exert to escape the dreaded foe. A wall of rocks, right and left, ahead the shelving shingle—on they go, and hundreds lie high-and-dry, panting on the pebbles. It is just as well perhaps to die there, as to be torn, bitten, and eaten by the piratical cannibals that are waging fearful havoc on the imprisoned shoal. The dogfish wound ten times as many as they eat, and, having satiated and gorged their greedy stomachs, swim lazily away, leaving the dead, dying, and disabled to the tender mercies of the sea-birds watching the battle, ever ready to pounce upon the unprotected, and end its miseries.

Garnering the herring-crop is the Coast Indian's best 'sea-harvest;' lodges spring up like mushrooms along the edges of the bays and harbours; large fleets of canoes dot the water in every direction, their swarthy crews continually loading them with glittering fish; paddling ashore, they hand the cargo to the female part of the community, and then start again for a similar freight.

Indians have various plans for catching herrings. Immense numbers are taken with small hand-nets, literally dipping them out of the water into the canoes; they also employ the 'rake,' already described as used for taking candle-fish. One savage, sitting in the stern of his canoe, paddles along, keeping in the herring shoal; another, having the rounded part of the rake firmly fixed in both hands, sweeps it through the crowded fish, from before aft, using all his force: generally speaking, every tooth has a herring impaled on it, sometimes three or four. It is astonishing how rapidly an Indian will fill his canoe with herrings, using this rude and primitive contrivance.

A wholesale system of capture is practised in Puget's Sound, Point Discovery, and Port Townsend, where large mud-flats run out for long distances into the sea, which are left quite dry at low-tide. Across these flats Indians make long dams of latticework, having here and there openings like our salmon-traps, allowing herrings to pass easily in, but preventing their return. Shoal after shoal pass through these 'gates,' but are destined never to get back to their briny home. It is not at all uncommon to take from two to three tons of fish at one tide, by this simple but ingenious method.

When the tide is well out, and the flats clear of water, the Indians bring down immense quantities of fir-branches, and stick them in the mud, lay them on the ground, and, in all sorts of ways, distribute them over the flats, within the weir-dam. On these branches the herring-spawn gets entangled; when covered with spawn the branches are carried to the lodges, and the fish-eggs dried in the sun. Thus dried, and brushed into baskets, it is in appearance very much like coarse brown sand; it is then stored away, and when eaten mixed with fish-oil is esteemed by the Indians as the very perfection of feeding. This spawn is to Indians what *caviare* is to Russians; but as I do not like either, it may be I am not an authority on its merits as a table dainty.

All herrings taken in the weirs are not eaten; the Indians dry or otherwise preserve them, but the great use to which they appropriate them is to extract the oil. This is a grand process, and carried on entirely by squaws. It would be a great blessing, and save much annoyance, if you could only leave your nose at home, or at some distance away, during your visit to an Indian village in herring-time, or whilst oil-making. The entire atmosphere appears saturated with the odour of decomposing fish, rancid oil, Indians, and dogs—a perfume the potency of which you only realise by having a thorough good sniff. Then, if you ever forget it, or wish to indulge your olfactory organ again, your tastes and mine, gentle reader, must widely differ. The oil is extracted and stored away (as described in a previous chapter) in native bottles.

I have no hesitation in stating my conviction that herring-fisheries established east and west of Vancouver Island, or at different points along the mainland coast, in the Straits of Juan de Feuca, oramidst the islands in the Gulf of Georgia, would turn out most remunerative speculations. It is true that herring-fishing has been tried, but only on the most limited scale. To make it pay; for that, after all, is the primary consideration; capital must be employed, and skilled hands to manage the drying, curing, and packing. Salt can be obtained in any quantities; wood in abundance, to make casks, build houses, boats, or ships; herrings within *millions*, requiring neither risk nor skill to catch. The rapidly-growing colonies of Vancouver Island and British Columbia offer ready markets for home consumption; China, Japan, the Sandwich Islands, and the entire coast southward from San Francisco to Mexico, afford facilities for disposing of almost any quantity of preserved fish. Those who undertake herring-fishing in North-western waters on a large scale, judiciously applying capital, skilled labour, and good management, will reap an ample harvest, and become the real 'Herring Kings' of the far North-west.

VIVIPAROUS FISH.—We are so accustomed to associate the production of young fishes with eggs and milt, familiar to all as hard and soft roe in the cured herring, that it is difficult to believe in the existence of a fish bringing forth live young, just as do dogs, cats, rats, and mice—only with this difference, that, in the case of the fish, the young are perfect in every detail, when launched into the water, as the parent, and swim away self-dependent, to feed or be fed on, as good or ill-luck befals the little wanderer. The woodcut represents the female fish with the young *in situ*, together with others scattered round her, having fallen out when the walls of the abdomen were dissected open: the drawing was made from a female fish I brought from Vancouver Island, and now exhibiting in the Fish Room of the British Museum.

At San Francisco, as early as April, I saw large numbers of viviparous fish in the market for sale; but then, it is an open question whether these fish really arrive at an earlier period of

the year in the Bay of San Francisco than at Vancouver Island. I think not. That they are taken earlier in the year is simply due to the fact, that the fishermen at San Francisco have better nets and fish in deeper water, than the Indians, and consequently take the fish earlier. The habit of the fish is clearly to come into shallow water when the period arrives for producing its live young; and from the fact that some of these fish are occasionally taken at all periods of the year, I am induced to believe that they do not in reality migrate, but only retire into deeper water along the coast, there to remain during the winter months, reappearing in the shallow bays and estuaries in June and July, or perhaps earlier, for reproductive purposes; here they remain until September, and then entirely disappear.

They swim close to the surface in immense shoals, and numbers are very craftily taken by the Indians, who literally frighten the fish into their canoes. At low-tide, when a shoal of fish is in the bay, or up one of those large inlets that intersect the coast-line, the savages get the fish between the bank (or the rocks, as it may be) and the canoe, and then paddle with all their might and main among the terror-stricken fish, lashing the sea with their paddles, and uttering the most fiendish yells. Out leap the fish from the water, in their panic to escape this (to their affrighted senses) terrible monster; and if not 'out of the fryingpan into the fire,' it is out of the sea into the canoes—which in the long run I take to be pretty much the same thing.

It appears to be a singular trait in the character of viviparous fish, that of leaping high out of the water on the slightest alarm. I have often seen them jump into my boat when rowing through a shoal, which is certainly most accommodating. The Indians also spear them: they use a long slender haft with four barbed points, arranged in a circle, but bent so as to make them stand at a considerable distance from each other. With this spear they strike into a shoal of fish, and generally impale three or four; many are caught with hooks, but they bite shily, the only baits I have seen taken being salmon-roe nearly putrid, or bits of crab.

Just prior to my leaving Vancouver Island, numbers were netted by some Italian fishermen who had a seine. They found a ready sale for them in the market, but as a table-dainty they are scarcely worth eating; the flesh is insipid, watery, and flabby, and I am convinced that no system of cooking or culinary skill would ever convert it into a palatable fish.

The geographical range of viviparous fish, as far as I have any opportunity of judging, is from the Bay of San Francisco to Sitka. It may perhaps (and I have but little doubt that it does) extend much farther south along the Mexican coast; but this I can only surmise, never having seen them beyond the limits above stated. It frequents all the bays and harbours on the east and west sides of Vancouver Island, and is equally abundant in the Gulf of Georgia and the Straits of Juan de Feuca; making its appearance about the same period, or perhaps somewhat earlier, in the various inlets on the Oregon coast, from Cape Flattery to the Bay of San Francisco. It will be just as well perhaps, before I go into the subject of its specific characters and singular reproductive organs, I should mention how I first stumbled upon the fact of its being viviparous.

Soon after I arrived at Vancouver Island, I at once set to work to investigate, as far as it lay in my power, the habits and periods of migration of the different species of fish periodically visiting the North-west coast. The sole means then at my disposal to obtain fish for examination, or as specimens to send home, was to employ Indians or catch them myself; so it happened, some of these fish were first brought me by Indians. Cutting one down the side (the plan I usually adopt to skin a fish, keeping the opposite side untouched), to my intense surprise, out tumbled a lot of little fish! My wildest dreams had never led me to suppose a fish I then thought was a bream, or one of the perch family, could be viviparous. I at once most hastily arrived at the conclusion that the greedy gourmand had eaten them. Dropping my knife, I sat in a most bewildered state looking at the fish.

The first ray of light that shone in to illumine my mystification seemed to spring from the fact, that each little fish was the model, counterpart, and facsimile of the larger, and in shape, size, and colour were exactly alike: from the position too they occupied in the abdomen of the larger fish, I was led at once to see the error of my first assumption, that they had been swallowed. Carefully dissecting back the walls of the abdomen, I discovered a delicate membranous bag or sac having an attachment to the upper or dorsal region, and doubled upon itself into numerous folds or plaits, and between each of these folds was neatly packed away a little fish; the bag was of a bluish-white colour, and contained fourteen fish. I had no longer any doubt that the fish was viviparous, and that it was a true and normal case of ovarian gestation. So much for my first discovery; the details of my subsequent examinations I shall again have occasion to refer to.

It happened most curiously that a Mr. Jackson (I believe a government officer of the United States) was, about this same period, amusing himself by fishing at Salsalita, and caught two viviparous fish, a male and a female. On cutting open the female, to obtain a piece of the belly for bait, he, like myself, was astonished at seeing a whole bevy of tiny fish come scrambling out, and at first imagined, as I did, that they had been swallowed. He immediately wrote a letter to Professor Agassiz, sending the mutilated fish, having previously satisfied himself that they had not been devoured, and stating at length his singular discovery. The professor was astonished, and disbelieved the possibility of the fish being viviparous, imagining some error had crept into the statement sent him by Mr. Jackson; but other fish in a similar state were subsequently obtained by Mr. Carey, and forwarded to the learned professor. The fact was then most undeniably established, that this and many other species were strictly viviparous.

I have spoken of this at some length, because it is a curious coincidence that the same fact should have been discovered by two men a long distance apart, about the same date, and by both in the same way,—by sheer accident.

Now we come to a ticklish question: how are the young fish vitalised in the abdomen of the mother? In this case I shall adopt what I conceive to be the most straightforward course, which is candidly to give my own thoughts, and solicit from abler, older, and better physiologists their opinions or theories—for I sincerely think this is a question well worth careful investigation. I believe the ova, after impregnation, at first goes through the same transformations in the ovarium as it would do, supposing it to have been spawned and fecundated in the ordinary spawning-bed, but only up to a certain point; then, I think, the membrane enfolding the ova, that have by this time assumed a fishlike type, takes on the character and functions of a placental membrane, and the young fish are supplied by an umbilical cord, just as in the case of a fœtal mammal. But a third change takes place. There can be no doubt that the young fish I cut out, and that swam away, had breathed before they were freed from the mother; hence I am led to think that, a short time prior to the birth of the young, sea-water has access to this marsupial sac, washes over the infant fish, the gills assume their normal action, and the regular systemic circle is established. Maturity attained, the umbilical attachment snaps, and the little fish, perfect in every detail of its organisation, is launched into the deep, to brave its many perils, and shift for itself. The strong transverse muscles attached to the powerful sphincter (constituting the genital opening acting from the abdominal walls), I imagine, are in some way concerned in admitting the sea-water, and it appears to me a contrivance admirably adapted to effect such a purpose; but how impregnation takes place, I may at once honestly confess—I do not know.

The male is much like the female, but more slim, and the milt just like that of other fish. I can only conjecture that fecundation is accomplished through the medium of the sea-water, admitted by the curiously-contrived floodgate of the female, carrying in the milt-germs, and washing them over the ova.

The actual period of utero-gestation I am by no means sure about, but I am inclined to think they breed twice in the year. It is worthy of remark that the young mature fish are very large, when compared with the size of the mother. In a female fish eleven inches in length, the young were three inches long--the adult fish four-and-a-half inches high, the young an inch.

The only instance I can find recorded of a viviparous fish bearing any analogy to the *Embiotocidæ* is the viviparous blenny (*Zoarces viviparus*, Cuv.). Of course I exclude the sharks and rays. Of the viviparous blenny little or nothing appears to me to be known. On reference to Pennant's 'British Zoology,' all he says is, that it was discovered by Schonevelde, and that Sir Robert Sibbald afterwards found it on the Scotch coast, and it was mentioned by Linnæus in his account of the Swedish Museum.

I quote the following paragraph verbatim from Pennant's 'British Zoology.' Speaking of the blenny, he goes on to say: 'It is viviparous, *bringing forth two or three hundred young at a time.* Its season of parturition is a little after the depth of winter; before midsummer it quits the bays and shores, and retires into the deep, where it is commonly taken. It comes into the mouth of the River Esk at Whitby, Yorkshire, where it is frequently taken from off the bridge.'

In Cuvier's 'Animal Kingdom' (vol. i. 'Fish'), all I can glean is that the blenny is viviparous. Yarrel, in his 'British Fishes,' speaks of a Mr. Low, who put a number of the small fishes (the young of the blenny) in a tumbler of sea-water, in which they increased in size, but eventually died from the want of fresh-water. Again, he quotes a Mr. Neil, who saw in the Edinburgh market, in 1807, several dozens of young fish escape alive from the female. 'The arrangement of the perfectly-formed young in the fœtal sac of the gravid female is very remarkable.'

It is quite clear from the above quotations that there is an analogy, if not a close one, between the reproductive organs of the blenny and those of the viviparous fish from the North-west seas; for 'the fœtal sac of the gravid female' evidently means that there is a kind of placental sac, in which the young are contained; but it leaves us quite as much in the dark as ever as to how fœtal life is supported. As the ova deposited in the usual way (when fecundated) contains all that is requisite for the development of the embryo, it is just possible that the same process goes on in the womb of the female viviparous fish, and that the fœtal sac is only a wrapper, formed by the widened end of the ovary. But still I maintain that it fulfils a far more important duty.

I fear I have been rather prolix in the foregoing descriptions, but I must plead the novelty and importance of the subject as my excuse. The most beautiful of all the species of these fish is the sapphire perch (so called by the traders), very plentiful in Puget's Sound. Eighteen exquisitely beautiful mazarine-blue lines or stripes mark its entire length from head to tail; and above and below this line are a number of spots of most dazzling blue, arranged in a crescent shape, about the eyes and gill-covers. Between these spots the colour changes, as it does in the dolphin, throwing off a kind of phosphorescent light of varying shades of gold, purple, and green—the back bright-blue, but darker than the stripes; the belly white, marked by golden-yellow streaks.

But now for the most important feature in the history of these fish—that of bringing into the world their young alive, self-dependent, and self-supporting, as perfect in their minutest organisation as the parent-fish that gives them birth. The generative apparatus of the female fish when in a gravid state may be defined as a large bag or sac. Ramifying over its surface may be seen a most complicated and strangely beautiful vascular arrangement—a network of vessels, the use of which is clearly to convey the lifegiving fluid to the infant fish, and carry it back again, after having served its destined purpose, to be revivified for future use. The way this sac is, as it were, folded, and the different compartments made for the accommodation of the embryonic fish, is most singular, and very difficult to describe clearly.

The best illustration I can think of is an orange. You must imagine the orange divided into its regular number of little wedge-shaped pieces, and each piece to represent a fish; that the rind of the orange is a delicate membrane, having a globular shape, and easily compressed or folded. You now desire to fit the pieces together again in the original orange-shape, but you must begin on the *outside* of the globular membrane, pressing in with each section a fold of membrane (remember that each represents a fish); when each piece is in its place, you will still have the sac in its rounded form, but the rind or membrane has been folded in with the different pieces. If I have made myself understood, it will be seen that there must be a double fold of membrane between each portion of orange. This is exactly the way the fish are packed in this novel placental sac. If it were practicable to remove each fish from its space, and the sac retain its normal shape, there would be twelve or fourteen openings (depending upon the number of young fish), the wall of each division being a double fold of membrane — the double-edges wrapping or, as it were, folding over the fish. Now make a hole in the end of this folded bag, and *blow* it full of air, and you get at once the globe-shaped membranous sac I have likened to an orange.

The fish are always arranged to economise space: when the head of a young fish points to the head of its mother, the next to it is reversed, and looks towards the tail. I am quite convinced that the young fish are packed away by doubling or folding the sac in the way I have endeavoured to describe. I have again and again dissected out this ovarian bag, filled with fish in various stages of development, and floating it in salt-water, have, with a fine-pointed needle, opened the edges of the double membranous divisions that enwrap the fish—(the amount of overlapping is of course greater when the fish is in its earlier stages of development). On separating the edges of the sac, out the little fishes pop. I have obtained them in all stages of their growth,

—but sometimes (and this not once or twice, but often) have set free the young fish from its dead mother. Thus prematurely cut loose from its membranous prison, the infant captive, revelling in its newly-acquired liberty, swam about in the saltwater, active, brisk, and jolly, in every particular, as well able to take care and provide for itself as its parent. The female external genital opening is situated a little posterior to the anal opening; the orifice is at the apex, and in the centre of a fleshy conical protuberance, which is in fact, a powerful sphincter muscle, *moored*, as it were, in its place by two strong muscular ropes, acting from and attached to the walls of the abdomen.

Dr. Günther, in the British Museum Catalogue of Fishes, uses the generic title of *Ditrema*, which I have adopted. The first glance at the fish, as it lies on the table or on the beach, would lead you to pronounce it a *Pomotis* (belonging to the family *Percidæ*): the northern *Pomotis* (*P. vulgaris*) is a good example, and very common along the shores of Lake Huron, where I have often caught them. Or, on the other hand, you would be perhaps tempted to call it a *Sparus*; the gilthead (*S. auratus*) may be taken as a type suggesting the resemblance. This fish is taken in large numbers in the

Mediterranean, and occasionally on the French and Spanish coasts. But a close investigation into the more marked generic and specific characters, apart from their reproducing organs, at once clearly shows they belong neither to the one family nor the other; they differ much more from the percoids than from the sparoids, but the cycloid scales remove them at once from the sparoids, in which the scales present a very uniform ctenoid type.

The illustration represents a female *Ditrema argenteum*, Brit. Mus. Cat., 'Fishes.'

Amphistichus argenteus, Agass., Am. Journ., 1854; Soc. Nat. Hist., 1861, p. 131; Pacif. R. R. Exp., 'Fishes,' p. 201.

Mytilophagus fasciatus (Gibbons).

Amphistichus similes (Grd.).

The middle dorsal spines are either nearly as long as, or somewhat longer, than the posterior; scales on the cheek, in five series, somewhat irregularly disposed. The height of the body is rather more than a fourth of the total length (without caudal); jaws equal anteriorly; the maxillary extends to below the centre of the orbit; lips thin, the fold of the lower interrupted in the middle. For description of species, *vide* Appendix, vol. ii.

CHAPTER V.

STICKLEBACKS AND THEIR NESTS—THE BULLHEAD—THE ROCK-COD—THE CHIRUS—FLATFISH.

The genus *Cottoidæ* (fish having mailed cheeks) has a great many representatives, common on Vancouver Island and the British Columbian coasts. The least of the family, the stickleback, is so singularly different from most other fishes in its habits, as to merit the first consideration.

In the months of July and August it would be difficult to find a stream, large or small, swift or slow, lake, pool, or muddy estuary, east and west of the Cascade Mountains, that has not in it immense shoals of that most irritable and pugnacious little fish the stickleback, ever ready on the slightest provocation to engage in a battle. Let friend or foe but rub against his royal person, or come nearer his private subaqueous garden than he deems consistent with safety or good behaviour, in a moment the spines are erected like spear-points, the tiny eyes glow with fury, the colours decking his scaly armour intensify, and flash with a kind of phosphorescent brightness, until the diminutive gladiator looks the impersonation of rage and fury; but as we cultivate his acquaintance, and gain a better knowledge of his real character, we shall discover that his quarrelsome disposition is not so much attributable to a morose temper, and a love of fighting for fighting's sake, as to a higher and more praiseworthy principle.

No amount of thinking would lead one to imagine that his pugnacity arises from intense parental affection: a love of offspring, scarcely having a parallel in the living world, prompting him to risk his life, and spend a great deal of his time in constantly-recurring paroxysms of fury and sanguinary conflicts, in which it often happens that one or more of the combatants gets ripped open or mortally stabbed with the formidable spines arming the back. Skill in stickleback battles appears to consist in rapidly diving under an adversary, then as suddenly rising, and driving the spines into his sides and stomach. The little furies swim round and round, their noses tightly jammed together; but the moment one gets his nose the least bit under that of his foe, then he plies his fins with all his might, and forcing himself beneath, does his best to drive in his spear, if the other be not quick enough to dart upwards and escape the thrust; thus squaring they fight round after round until the death or flight of one ends the combat.

I have often, when tired, lain down on the bank of a stream, beneath the friendly shade of some leafy tree, and gazing into its depths watched the sticklebacks either guarding their nests already built, or busy in their construction. The site is generally amongst the stems of aquatic plants, where the water always flows, but not too swiftly. He first begins by carrying small bits of green material, which he nips off the stalks, and tugs from out the bottom and sides of the banks; these he attaches by some glutinous material, that he clearly has the power of secreting, to the different stems destined as pillars for his building. During this operation he swims against the work already done, splashes about, and seems to test its durability and strength; rubs himself against the tiny kind of platform, scrapes the slimy mucus from his sides, to mix with and act as mortar for his vegetable bricks. Then he thrusts his nose into the sand at the bottom, and bringing a mouthful scatters it over the foundation; this is repeated until enough has been thrown on to weight the slender fabric down, and give it substance and stability. Then more twists, turns, and splashings, to test the firm adherence of all the materials that are intended to constitute the foundation of the house, that has yet to be erected on it. The nest or nursery, when completed, is a hollow, somewhat rounded, barrel-shaped structure, worked together much in the same way as the platform fastened to the water-plants; the whole firmly glued together by the viscous secretion scraped from off the body. The inside is made as smooth as possible, by a kind of plastering system; the little architect continually goes in, then turning round and round, works the mucus from his body on to the inner sides of the nest, where it hardens like a tough varnish. There are two apertures, smooth and symmetrical as the hole leading into a wren's nest, and not unlike it.

All this laborious work is done entirely by the male fish, and when completed he goes a-wooing. Watch him as he swims towards a group of the fair sex, enjoying themselves amidst the water-plants, arrayed in his best and brightest livery, all smiles and amiability: steadily, and in the most approved style of stickleback love-making, this young and wealthy bachelor approaches the object of his affections, most likely tells her all about his house and its comforts, hints delicately at his readiness and ability to defend her children against every enemy, vows unfailing fidelity, and, in lover-fashion, promises as much in a few minutes as would take a life-time to fulfil. Of course she listens to his suit: personal beauty, indomitable courage, backed by the substantial recommendations of a house ready-built, and fitted for immediate occupation, are gifts not to be lightly regarded.

Throwing herself on her side, the captive lady shows her appreciation, and by sundry queer contortions declares herself his true and devoted spouse. Then the twain return to the nest, into which the female at once betakes herself, and therein deposits her eggs, emerging when the operation is completed by the opposite hole. During the time she is in the nest (about six minutes) the male swims round and round, butts and rubs his nose against it, and altogether appears to be in a state of defiant excitement. On the female leaving he immediately enters, deposits the milt on the eggs, taking his departure through the backdoor. So far, his conduct is strictly proper, but, I am afraid, morality in stickleback society is of rather a lax order. No sooner has this lady, his first love, taken her departure, than he at once seeks another, introduces her as he did the first, and so on wife after wife, until the nest is filled with eggs, layer upon layer—milt being carefully deposited betwixt each stratum of ova. As it is necessary there should be two holes, by which ingress and egress can be readily accomplished, so it is equally essential in another point of view. To fertilise fish-eggs, running water is the first necessity ; and as the holes are invariably placed in the direction of the current, a steady stream of water is thus directed over them.

For six weeks (and sometimes a few days more) the papa keeps untiring sentry over his treasure, and a hard time he has of it too: enemies of all sorts, even the females of his own species, having a weakness for new-laid eggs, hover round his brimming nest, and battles are of hourly occurrence; for he defies them all, even to predatory water-beetles, that, despite their horny armour, often get a fatal lance-wound from the furious fish. Then he has to turn the eggs, and expose the under ones to the running water: and even when the progeny make their appearence, his domestic duties are far from ended, for it is said (although I have never seen him do it), 'When one of the young fish shows any disposition to wander from the nest, he darts after it, seizes it in his mouth, and brings it back again.'

There are three species that come into the fresh-waters of British Columbia, to nest and to hatch their young:—

Gasterosteus serratus, the Saw-finned Stickle-back (Ayres, Proc. Cal. Acad. Nat. Sc. 1855 p. 47).—*Sp. Ch.*: Body entirely plated; peduncle of tail keeled; the three dorsal spines conspicuously serrated on their edges; anterior fin a little in advance of the base of the pectoral; insertion of ventrals in advance of the second dorsal spine—their own spines serrated on both edges; posterior margin of caudal somewhat hollowed. The colour of the freshly-caught fish is greyish-olive along the dorsal line; but on the sides, particularly in the male, it shades away into an iridescence, like that seen on mother-o'pearl, again changing to pure silvery-white on the abdomen.

Gasterosteus Pugettii, the Puget Sound Stickle-back (Grd., Proc. Acad., Nat. Sc. Phil., viii. 1856).—*Sp. Ch.*: Body only in part plated, peduncle of tail not keeled; the three dorsal spines without serrations; the anterior one inserted immediately behind the base of the pectorals; ventrals inserted anterior to the second dorsal spine. The colour is very much like that of *G. serratus*, but more decidedly purplish on the sides; the eyes bright red in both species, when fresh from the water.

Gasterosteus concinnus, the Tiny Stickleback (Rich., F. B. A., p. 57, vol. iii.).—*Sp. Ch.*: Head one-fourth of the total length, mouth small, and teeth but feebly developed; dorsal spines nine, seventh and eighth smaller than the preceding ones, the ninth longer than any of the others. The abdomen is protected by a bony cuirass, and the ventrals represented by two spines. All the spines are moveable, and destitute of serrations. Colour of the back a bright sea-green, sides purplish-pink, shading away to a silvery-white on the belly; the entire body speckled with minute black spots.

This handsome little stickleback, though smaller in size than his brethren, is vastly more abundant. Sir J. Richardson speaks of it 'as being common in the Saskatchawan, ranging as far north as the 65th parallel.' So abundant are they in the lakes and pools about Cumberland House, east of the Rocky Mountains, that sledge-loads are dipped out with wooden bowls, and used for feeding the dogs. I have seen cartloads of these tiny fish in a single pool, left by the receding waters after the summer floods, on the Sumass prairie and banks of the Chilukweyuk river. As the water rapidly evaporated, the miserable captives huddled closer and closer together, starving with hunger and panting for air, but without the remotest chance of escape. The sticklebacks die and decompose, or yield banquets to the bears, weasels, birds, and beetles; the pool dries, and in a few weeks not a trace or record remains of the dead host of fishes. In the smaller streams, a bowl dipped into the water where the sticklebacks were thickest, could be readily filled with fish.

Sticklebacks are the most voracious little gourmands imaginable, devourers of everything, and cannibals into the bargain; tearing their wounded comrades into fragments, they greedily swallow them. I have often taken this species (*G. concinnus*) in Esquimalt Harbour, where they are very plentiful during the winter months. The natives of Kamtschatka make use of a stickleback (*G. obolarius*), which they obtain in great quantities, not only as food for the sledge-dogs, but for themselves also, by making them into a kind of soup. West of the Rocky

Mountains I have never seen the Indians use them as an article of diet, not from any dislike to the fish, but simply because there are larger and better fishes quite as abundant, and as easily procurable. Whether there are any species in the North-west, strictly marine, building their nests in the sea and never entering fresh-water, I am unable to say.

The Fifteen-spine Stickleback (*Gasterosteus spinachia*) is along our own coasts strictly a tenant of the ocean, and makes a nest of seaweeds glued together with an adhesive mucus, in the same way as the nests of our little friends are cemented, that seek as their nursery the clear cold streams of British Columbia, Oregon, and Vancouver Island.

THE BULLHEAD.—The stickleback has a near relative, with a name nearly as ugly as the owner, '*Bullhead*' being certainly not suggestive of beauty! With such a name, we are the less disappointed to find the entire family of our friends ill-favoured, prickly, hard-skinned, and as uncomfortable to handle as to look at. Plates of scaly armour cover the head, from which sprout sharp spines, like a crop of horns; between these are tubercles that have the appearance of being rivets. The body looks like an appendage, tapering away to a mere nothing at the tail. There are many species frequenting the lakes and rivers of British Columbia, during the summer months, for the purpose of spawning. On their return to the sea, swarms of young bullheads, of various species, regularly follow the ebb and flow of the tide; and in rough weather every breaker, as it rushes up the shelving shingle, carries a freight of tiny fish, that are left struggling amid the pebbles in thousands, to be dragged back and floated out again by the succeeding wave, or to find a last home in the stomachs of the sea-birds.

The bullhead does not actually build a nest, like the stickleback, but makes an egg-house, on the bottom of some slowly-running stream. The male usually selects a hollow under a boulder, or a space betwixt two stones, and shoves out the lesser pebbles and gravel, to form a pit. This accomplished, several females are in turn induced to deposit their roe, having done which they are driven off by the male, who supplies the milt, then shovels the sand and pebbles, with his huge horny head, over the treasure, until it is completely covered: more females, more eggs and milt, more shovelling, until the affair is completed to the bullhead papa's satisfaction. Now stand clear all thievish prowlers! Let anything of reasonable size venture near—then head down, and plying all his propellers to their utmost power, he charges at them, driving his horns in to the very hilt; free again, seizes hold with his mouth — thus biting and stabbing, until he kills or routs his foe. I am not able to say exactly how long the eggs are incubating, but, as nearly as I could observe them (in the Sumass and Chilukweyuk streams), in about eight weeks the young escape from the egg-house. The females were invariably driven away, with the same ferocity as other unwelcome guests, from the depositing the spawn to the exit of the infant fish: then old and young disappear into deeper water, and are seldom seen again.

During the winter, I constantly obtained the bullheads from out the seine-nets used in Esquimalt Harbour to procure fish for the supply of Victoria market. Rejected by the fishermen, the Indians greedily gathered up the despised fishes, broiled them over the lodge-fire empaled on a slender twig, then feasted right-royally on the grilled remains of the spiny martyrs.

The genus *Centridermichthys* is characterised as follows:—Head more or less depressed, rounded anteriorly; head and body covered with soft and scaleless skin, more or less studded with prickles or granulations; teeth in the jaws, on the vomer and palatine bones.

Centridermichthys asper (*Coltus asper*, Rich. F. B. A. 'Fishes,' p. 295), the Prickly-skinned Bullhead.—*Sp. Ch.*: Gill-openings separated beneath, by an isthmus; three opercular spines; crown with very small warts, back of the body with very minute spines; colour light yellowish brown, thickly dotted with spots nearly black. The length of the adult fish is seldom over three-and-a-half inches.

These tiny bullheads are common in all the streams east and west of the Cascades. They are not fond of going very far from the sea, but leave the larger rivers soon after entering them, seeking the clear rivulets and shallow lakes. In the streams flowing through the Sumass and Chilukweyuk prairies, in those flowing into Puget's Sound, and north of it on the mainland to Fort Simpson, and in all the streams draining Vancouver Island, the prickly-skinned bullhead can be easily found in July and August. Similar in habits, and frequenting the same localities as the preceding, are several species described in the Appendix.

The Rock Cod.—Belonging to the same family

is the rock cod, as it is usually styled by the fishermen who provide the Victoria and San Francisco markets; one of the best and daintiest table-fish caught in the seas round Vancouver Island. It often attains a considerable size, and being in tolerable abundance, constitutes an article of some commercial value.

As numbers are taken all through the year, and as I never saw them in fresh-water, it is fair to assume they are strictly marine. Their appearance is not prepossessing, giving one the idea of being all head, fins, and bones, as they lie gasping on the shingle; an error of the eye only, as you discover when testing the substance and quality of a large one, smoking hot from the fish-kettle. Three species are commonly offered for sale in the markets, one of which is also taken in Japanese seas. They vary in size; I have often seen a rock cod thirty inches in length. Biting greedily at any bait, they are constantly caught by the Indians when trolling for salmon.

The one usually seen in the Victoria markets is *Sebastes inermis* (Cuv. and Val., p. 346; Faun. Japon., 'Poiss.,' p. 47, pl. 21, figs. 3, 4), the Weak-spined Rock Cod.—*Sp. Ch.*: The height of the body equals the length of the head; the upper surface of the head flat, with some depressed spines behind the orbit. The fourth and fifth dorsal spines are the largest, longer than those of the anal, and nearly half the length of the head. Colour, uniform brownish.

THE CHIRUS.—On the fish-stalls in Victoria and San Francisco markets the visitor may generally see, lying by the side of the dingy, spiny rock cod, a handsome, shapely fish, about eighteen inches in length. Its sides, though somewhat rough, rival in beauty many a tropical flower: clad in scales, adorned with colours not only conspicuous for their brilliancy, but grouped and blended in a manner one sees only represented in the plumage of a bird, the wing of a butterfly, or the petals of an orchid, this 'ocean swell' is known to the ichthyologist as the Chirus—the *Terpugh* (a file) of the Russians—the *Idyajuk* of the Aleutian Islanders—the *Tath-le-gest* of the Vancouver Islanders.

Quite as delicious to the palate as pleasant to the eye, the chirus is altogether a most estimable fish. Its habit is to frequent rocky places, particularly where long ledges of rocks are left bare at low-water, and sheltered at the same time from the surge of the sea in rough weather. Here the chirus loves to disport his gaily-dressed person, amidst the gardens of sea plants: for in these gardens dwell jellyfish, tender little crustaceans, soft-bodied chitons, crisp shrimps, and juicy annalides—all dainty viands, on which this gay lounger delights to regale himself.

At low-tide, when strolling over the slippery rocks that everywhere gird the eastern side of Vancouver Island, in the larger rock-pools I was certain to see lots of these fish imprisoned, having lingered imprudently at their feasts. This indulgence constantly costs the idler his life: gulls, herons, shags also prowl over the rocks, well knowing what admirable preserves these aquariums are. Once spied out, it is of no avail to hide amidst the seaweeds, or cower under the shelving ledges draped with coralines. The large pincer-like beak follows, nips him across the back; a skilful jerk gets the head first—then down a lane he goes from which no chirus ever returns.

We might as reasonably attempt to describe, the flushing changing colours of the Aurora Borealis as seen in high latitudes, or the phosphorescence of a tropical sea, or the wing of the diamond-beetle, as to hope by word-painting to give the faintest conception of the colourings that adorn the chirus: red, blue, orange, and green are so mingled, that the only thing I can think of as a comparison is a floating flower-bed, and even then the gardener's art, in grouping, is but a bungle contrasted with Nature's painting!

There are three species of chirus common along the island and mainland coasts. The one usually sold is *Chirus hexagrammus* (Cuv., Regne An., 'Poiss.,' pl. 83), the Six-lined Chirus.—*Sp. Ch.*: A skinny tentacle over each orbit; palatine teeth none; two muciferous channels, between the lateral line and dorsal fin; scales ciliated.

FLATFISH.—In all the muddy estuaries and on the sandy flats about Puget's Sound, at the mouths of the Columbia and Fraser rivers, several species of flatfish are found in great abundance. These fish have always formed an important article of food to all the sea-fishing Indians, and, since the influx of white settlers, are caught for the supply of the Victoria and San Francisco markets.

Only the larger species are taken with hook and line, the smaller flounders being usually speared by the Indians. And a pleasant sight it is, too, to watch a little fleet of canoes, each one slowly paddled by a dusky squaw gliding along the sandy shallows, the spearman in the bow 'prodding' for the fish hidden in the mud and sand. The flounder, thus disturbed, scuds along the bottom, and stirs up the sand like a trail, marking its line of progress. The sharp-eyed savage notes the spot where the dirt-line ends, paddles up to it, dashes in the spear, and, quick as thought, transfers the '*flat*' fish from its fancied hiding-place to the bottom of the canoe. Immense numbers are taken in this manner at every tide. The following are the species usually sold in the markets:—

Pleuronectes bilineates (*Platessa bilineata*, Ayres, in Proc. Calif. Acad., 1855, p. 40), the Two-lined Flatfish.—*Sp. Ch.*: The height of the body is a little less than one-half of the entire length, the length of the head nearly one-fourth; snout somewhat projecting, not continuous in direction with the descending profile of the nape; eyes on the right side large, their diameter being two-sevenths of the length of the head, separated by a strong prominent ridge, which is partly covered with scales; lower jaw prominent; a single even row of strong blunt teeth in each jaw, less developed on the coloured side than on the blind; scales very conspicuous, those on the head and on the tail ciliated; lateral line with a strong curve above the pectoral: a second series of pores commences above the eye, and follows the dorsal profile to the vertical, from the opercular angle, where it terminates—it communicates with the true lateral line by a branch; the dorsal fin rises over about the anterior third of the orbit, and terminates at a distance from the caudal equal to the breadth of the eye; anal spine prominent; pectoral fin half as long as the head. Colour, light greyish-brown, with lighter blotches. More abundant at San Francisco than at Vancouver Island and north of the Fraser.

Pleuronectes digrammus (Günther, Brit. Mus. Catalogue, 'Fishes,'), the Two-lined Flounder (Nov. Spec.).—*Sp. Ch.*: The height of the body rather less than one-third of the entire length, the length of the head two-ninths, and that of the caudal two-thirteenths; snout with the lower jaw prominent, equal in length to the diameter of the eye, which is nearly one-fifth of that of the head; maxillary as long as the eye; the upper jaw with a series of twenty-eight small truncated teeth on the blind side, those of the other side being few in number and very small; eyes separated by a very narrow, naked, bony ridge; scales small but conspicuous; lateral line, with a very slight curve above the pectoral; a second series of pores commences above the eye, and follows the dorsal profile to the twenty-sixth dorsal ray, where it terminates; dorsal and anal rays quite smooth—the dorsal commences above the anterior third of the orbit, and terminates at a distance from the caudal nearly equal to the depth of the free portion of the tail; anal spine prominent—the longest dorsal rays are somewhat behind the middle of the fin, rather shorter than the pectoral, and half as long as the head; uniform brownish; length, eight inches. I obtained this new species of flounder in Mackenzie's Arm, a tidal inlet continuous with Victoria Harbour.

Pleuronichthys guttulatus (Gerard, in Proc. Acad., Nat. Sc. Philadel., 1856, p. 137, and U. S. Pacif. R. R. Expd., 'Fishes,' p. 152).—*Sp. Ch.*: The height of the body is somewhat more than one-half of the total length (with the caudal), the length of the head one-fourth, and that of the caudal one-fifth. The interorbital space is exceedingly narrow, and raised ridgelike ; snout very blunt and short; mouth small, with the jaws even. The dorsal commences above the anterior part of the orbit, and terminates at a short distance from the caudal; its longest rays are on and behind the middle of the fin. Scales, very small, cycloid. The lateral line is slightly arched above the pectoral; a similar series of pores runs from the upper eye, along the base of the dorsal fin, to about the middle of the length. There is a connecting branch between both lines, across the occipital region. Colour greyish, densely dotted with black and white spots. Common at Vancouver Island and San Francisco. For further description of species, *vide* Appendix, vol. ii.

CHAPTER VI.

HALIBUT FISHING — DOGFISH — A TRIP TO FORT RUPERT — RANSOMING A SLAVE — A PROMENADE WITH A REDSKIN — BAGGING A CHIEF'S HEAD — QUEEN CHARLOTTE'S ISLANDERS AT NANAIMO.

HALIBUT.—The Halibut, a giant amongst flat-fishes, is taken by the Indians on the western side of Vancouver Island; a veritable ground-feeder, frequenting deep-sea sandbanks, and devouring anything and everything that comes within reach of his terrible mouth. The halibut, at Vancouver Island, attains to an immense size, 300 lbs. being no unfrequent weight.

The Indians are most skilful in securing this leviathan of the deep, as I had an opportunity of seeing, when visiting the northern end of the island. Picture to yourselves an Indian village, built on a plateau overlooking an open roadstead; a crowd of Indians on the shingly beach, watching the departure of a large canoe, manned by four savages, awaiting my arrival. This being a special occasion, they were more elaborately painted than usual. A brief description of one will serve to portray the other three. Tailors are entirely unknown in the land of the red-skin; a small piece of blanket or fur, tied round the waist, constitutes the court, evening, and morning costume of both chief and subject.

My crew were *kilted* with pieces of scarlet blanket. Imagine, if you can, a dark swarthy copper-coloured figure leaning on a canoe-paddle, his jet-black hair hanging down nearly to the middle of his back, the front hair being clipped close in a straight line across the forehead. Neither beard, whisker, nor moustache ever adorns the face of the redskin, the hair being tweezered out by squaws in early life, and thus destroyed. A line of vermilion extends from the centre of the forehead to the tip of the nose, and from this 'trunk line' others radiate over and under the eyes and across the cheeks. Between these red lines white and blue streaks alternately fill the interstices. A similar pattern ornaments chest, arms, and back, the frescoing being artistically arranged to give apparent width to the chest; the legs and feet are naked. A 'fire-bag,' made from the skin of the medicine-otter, elaborately decorated with beads, scarlet cloth, bells, and brass buttons, slung round the neck by a broad belt of wampum, completed the costume of my coxswain.

The canoe was what is commonly called a 'dug-out,' that is, made from a solid log of wood. Coiled round the sharp bow of the canoe, like a huge snake, was a strong line about sixty fathoms in length, made from the inner bark of the cypress, neatly twisted. Lying along each side, extending far beyond both bow and stern, were two light spear-hafts, about sixty feet long; whilst stowed away in the bow were a dozen shorter spears, one end being barbed, the other constructed to fit on the longer spear, but so contrived that the spearman can readily detach it by a skilful jerk. Tied lightly to the centre of each of the smaller spears was a bladder made from sealskin, blown full of air, the line attaching it being about three fathoms in length.

I had hardly completed my investigation of the canoe, its crew, and contents, when, to my intense astonishment, the four Indians lifted me, as they would a bale of fur, or a barrel of pork, and without a word deposited me in the bottom of the canoe, where I was enjoined to sit, much in the same position enforced on a culprit in the parish stocks. I may mention, incidentally, that a canoe is not half as enjoyable as poets and novelists, who are prone to draw imaginary sketches, would lead the uninitiated to believe. It would be impossible to trust oneself in a more uncomfortable, dangerous, damp, disagreeable kind of boat—generally designated a 'fairy barque,' that 'rides, dances, glides, threads its silvery course over seas and lakes, or, arrow-like, shoots foaming rapids.' All a miserable delusion and a myth! Getting in (unless lifted, as I was, bodily, like baggage) is to any but an Indian a dangerous and difficult process; the least preponderance of weight to either side, and out you tumble into the water to a certainty. Again, lowering oneself into the bottom is quite as bad, if not worse, requiring extreme care to keep an even balance, and a flexibility of back and limb seldom possessed by any save tumblers and tightrope-dancers. Down safely, then, as I have said, you are compelled to sit in a most painful position, and the least attempt to alter it generally results in a sudden heeling-over of the canoe, when you find yourself sitting in a foot of cold water.

We are off, and, swiftly crossing the harbour, the beach grows indistinct in the distance; but we still see the dusky forms of the Indians, the rough gaudily painted huts, the gleam of many lodge-fires, and wreaths of white smoke slowly ascending through the still air; the square substantial pickets shutting in the trade-fort, its roof and chimneys just peeping above, backed by the sombre green of the pine-trees, altogether presented a picture novel and pretty in all its details.

A few minutes and we rounded the jutting head-land, keeping close along the rocky shore of the island, gliding past snug bays and cozy little land-locked harbours, the homes and haunts of countless wildfowl; soon we leave the shore, and stand away to sea. The breeze is fresher here, and a ripple, that would be nothing in a boat, makes the flat-bottomed canoe unpleasantly lively. Save a wetting from the spray, and occasional surge of water over the gunwale, all goes pleasantly. The far-away land is barely distinguishable in the grey haze. No canoes are to be seen in the dark-blue water; the only sign of living things—a flock of sea-gulls waging war on a shoal of fish, the distant spouting of a whale, and the glossy backs of the black fish as they roll lazily through the ripple. The line at the bow is uncoiled, a heavy stone enclosed in a net attached as a sinker, a large hook made of bone and hardwood, baited with a piece of the octopus, (a species of cuttle-fish), is made fast to the long line by a piece of hemp-cord; then comes a heavy plunge of the sinker, the rattle of the line as it runs over the side of the canoe, and—we wait in silence for the expected bite.

A tug, that came unpleasantly near to upsetting all hands, lets us know that a halibut was bolting the tempting morsel, hook and all. A few minutes gave him time fairly to swallow it, and now a sudden twick buries the hook deeply in the fleshy throat; the huge flatfish finds, to his cost, that his dinner is likely seriously to disagree with him, whilst in the canoe all hands are in full employ. The bowman, kneeling, holds on tightly with both hands to the line; the savage next him takes one of the long spears, and quickly places on the end of it a shorter one, baited and bladdered; the other two paddle warily.

At first the hooked fish was sulky, and remained obstinately at the bottom, until continued jerks at the line ruffled his temper, and excited his curiosity sufficiently to induce a sudden ascent to the surface; perhaps to have a peep at his persecutors. Awaiting his appearance stood the spearman, and when the canoe was sufficiently near, in he sent the spear, plucking the long haft or handle from the shorter barbed spear, which remained in the fish, the bladder, floating like a life-buoy, marking the fish's whereabouts. The halibut, finding his reception anything but agreeable, tries to descend again into the lower regions, a performance now difficult to accomplish, as the bladder is a serious obstacle. Soon reappearing on the surface, another spear was sent into him, and so on, until he was compelled to remain floating. During all this time the paddlers, aided by the line-man, followed all the twistings and windings of the fish, as a greyhound courses a doubling hare.

For some time the contest was a very equal one, after the huge fish was buoyed and prevented from diving. On the one side the halibut made desperate efforts to escape by swimming, and on the other the Indians, keeping a tight line, made him tow the canoe. Evident signs of weariness at last began to exhibit themselves, his swimming became slower, and the attempts to escape more feeble and less frequent. Several times the canoe came close up to him, but a desperate struggle enabled him once more to get away. Again and again we were all but over; the fish, literally flying through the water, sometimes towed the canoe nearly under, and at others spun it suddenly round, like a whipped top; nothing but the wonderful dexterity of the paddlers saved us from instant shipwreck and the certainty of drowning. I would have given much to have stood up; but no; if I only moved on one side to peep over, a sudden yell from the steersman, accompanied by a flourish of the braining-club—mildly admonitory, no doubt, but vastly significant—ensured instant obedience. I forgot cold, wet, and fright, and indeed everything but the all-absorbing excitement attendant on this ocean-chase. The skill and tact of uneducated men, pitted against a huge sea-monster of tenfold strength, was a sight a lover of sport would travel any distance to witness.

Slowly and steadily the sturdy paddlers worked towards the shore, towing the fish, but keeping the canoe stern-first, so as to be enabled to pay out line and follow him, should he suddenly grow restive: in this way the Indians gradually coaxed the flat monster towards the beach; a weak, powerless, exhausted giant, outwitted, captured, and subdued, prevented from diving into his deep-sea realms by, what were to him, anything but life-buoys. We beached him at last, and he yielded his life to the knife and club of the redskin.

I believe the species to be the *Pleuronectes hippoglossus* of Linnæus, but of this I am by no means perfectly clear, as I had only an opportunity of examining this single specimen, that I estimated as weighing over 300 lbs.; and it was quite impossible to investigate its specific character, inasmuch as the Indians immediately set to work to cut the body in pieces, some to be there and then devoured, after a very brief roasting on a temporary fire; the remainder, packed into the canoe,was taken to the village.

Halibut are said to spawn in the middle of February; the roe, which is bright red, being esteemed a great dainty by all the Coast Indians.

Cod.—The true Cod, although I never saw it offered for sale in the Victoria market, is taken both at the northern extremity of Vancouver Island, and near Cape Flattery, at its southern end. The Indians fish for them with hooks and lines, and adopt very much the same system for landing heavy obstinate fish as I have already described as used to subdue the halibut. No regular system of deep sea fishing had, when I left the island, been tried by white men; neither had the trawl ever dragged up the treasures hidden at the bottom; so that deep-sea fish are still comparatively unknown. But of this I am quite sure—whenever fisheries are established along the island coasts, the trawl and deep-sea line, used by experienced hands, will bring up treasures from mines of wealth as yet unworked, to which gold and fur are nothing.

Dogfish.—The Western Dogfish (*Acanthius Suckleyi*), Grd., Proc. Acad., Nat. Sc. Phil., vii. 1854.—*Sp. Ch.*: Head contained in a sixth of the entire length; snout blunt, nostrils near to its apex. Eye large and bright, sea-green in the newly-taken fish. Anterior margin of the first dorsal, midway betwixt the pupil and anterior margin of the second dorsal. Colour reddish brown, above thickly spotted with white, overspread with bronze reflections.

This most predaceous race of sharks, although they never grow to a size dangerous to man, are nevertheless most bloodthirsty and implacable enemies to all the finny tribes inhabiting the waters of the North-west. They appear to live everywhere, in every harbour, up the long inland canals, in the lagoons, and nearly as far as the tide flows; the dogfish is ever to be found up the tidal rivers. Hunting in packs like wolves, they often chase a shoal of fish upon the shingle, then bite and maim six times as many as they can possibly eat. I have often seen them seize dead and even wounded birds, drag them below the surface, and tear them into shreds.

Angling where there are dogfish, and it is hard to discover a spot where they are not plentiful, is simply to waste time, and lose one's temper; your bait hardly touches the water ere it is gorged, and an ugly dogfish dangles at the end of the line. To unhook the thief is a service of danger, unless knocked senseless, and his fearfully-armed jaws are propped open with a piece of stick. But, with all his faults, the dogfish is most useful and valuable to the Indians, who spear incredible numbers, split them, and take out their livers. From these fatty livers a quantity of clear oil is extracted, by heat and pressure, applied in such a clumsy manner, that at least one-third is wasted. I was credibly informed that one small tribe of Indians, living on the west coast of Vancouver Island, by their bungling process of oil-making, managed to obtain seven cwt. of oil in one season: surely oil making alone would pay a company a handsome return for a judicious outlay of skill and capital. Several naval surgeons have assured me they had fairly tested its curative powers—in diseases where oil is said to be efficacious—and found it in every respect quite equal to the finest cod-liver oil.

Whilst occupied in collecting the fishes previously described, the Honourable Hudson's Bay Company's steamer 'Otter' was about to make her usual trip to Fort Rupert, in order to carry up the necessary supplies to the chief trader in charge of the fort, and bring back to Victoria the furs traded during the year. Being a good opportunity to visit so remote a part of Vancouver Island (not accessible, at that time, in any other way), leave was obtained from His Excellency the Governor, and a passage provided for me.

On a bright but cold morning in October the 'Otter' twisted, puffed, and worked her way through the somewhat intricate passage leading out of Victoria Harbour. Leaving the harbour, the scenery opens out like a magnificent panorama, indescribably wild and beautiful. In front, the sharp jagged mountains of the coast range, wooded to the sea-line, tower in the far distance to the regions of eternal snow; to the left, the rounder hills of the island slope easily to the water's edge, in grassy glades and lawnlike openings, belted with scrub-oaks; higher up, the hill-sides are overshadowed by the Douglas pines and cedars; whilst just visible in our course, like a green speck, is the famed island of St. Juan; and bending away to the right, as far as eye could reach, dense forests look like one vast unbroken sea of green.

We had a delightful run along the coast and amidst islands, and anchored in the evening near the narrows. These same narrows are only used by the initiated as a short cut, being too risky for large vessels navigated by unskilled hands. There is a channel, a quarter of a mile long and seventy yards wide, between a small island and the Island of Vancouver. Through this rocky canal the tide rushes with fearful velocity. We ran it safely in the morning, although it struck me as being the most ticklish bit of navigation I ever experienced. Through these narrows, we were soon in Nainimo, where we called for a supply of coals; the town, at this early stage of its history, consisting of about a dozen log-shanties, inhabited by the coal-miners and employés of the fur-trading establishment.

Whilst 'coaling,' a deputation of Indian braves, headed by a young chief, waited on the captain of the steamer. Squatted in a circle on the deck, and the all-essential pipe smoked, the object of their visit was disclosed. The Fort Rupert Indians, residing at the Indian village and trading-post we were *en route* to visit, had very recently made a raid on the Nainimo savages. In the foray, the old chief had been killed, several braves seriously injured, and, what was worse than all, the favourite wife of the deceased dignitary had been seized, and carried off a slave. The young chief, it seems, had loved the wife of his predecessor, and was willing to pay any ransom for his lost darling. After a long 'wa-wa' (talk), the captain consented to effect a purchase, if possible, and bring back, on our return, the lost one to the arms of her sable lover.

We had a pleasant run across the Gulf of Georgia, and anchored at 10 P.M. in Billings' Harbour (much like a small duck-pond), in Faveda Island. The next morning, again under weigh at 6 A.M., raining, as the captain said, 'marlinespikes,' we steamed past a group of islands, behind which is Malospina Strait. From this strait, Jarvis's Inlet runs like an immense canal for a distance (I believe) of fifty miles inland.

Here the gulf widens out like the open sea, and little can be seen of the land until the extreme south-east point of Valdes Island is reached, known as Point Mudge, betwixt which and Vancouver Island is a narrow channel, not more than a mile in width, called Discovery Passage.

About a mile from its entrance, we passed a large Indian village, the home of the Tah-cul-tas, a powerful band, of most predatory habits, and generally at war with the different tribes north and south of them; they own a large fleet of canoes, a great many slaves, and scalp and plunder all they can lay hands on.

For a distance of fourteen miles Discovery Passage is much the same width, until reaching Menzies Bay, where the rapids commence. At the base of these rapids, the channel, barely a quarter of a mile wide, suddenly opens out into a large pond-like space. The tide rushes down the narrow passage at the rate of ten knots an hour, and to get up through it was as much as our little steamer could accomplish. Panting and struggling, and sometimes hardly moving, at others she was carried violently against the shore, until by slow degrees she breasted the current and got safely through. I could not help wondering how Captain Vancouver ever managed to get his ship up this terrible place, so difficult even when aided by the power of steam.

Above the rapids the passage again widens to Point Chatham, the north-west termination of Discovery Passsge. We puff by Thurlow Island, divided from Valdes Island by the Nodales Canal, and anchor in a snug harbour named Blenkinsop's Anchorage. We start again at sun-up, the fifth morning since leaving Victoria. As we steamed steadily along through Johnston's Straits, I could recall to my remembrance no scenery that was comparable, in wild grandeur and picturesque grouping, to the scenery on my left. The coast-line of Vancouver Island presented a series of small projecting headlands; the bays and creeks between, seldom rippled by the breeze, are very Edens for wildfowl. In the background, the hills rise sharp and conical, at this time crowned with snow, but all alike densely timbered. In the distance, Hardwicke Island, like a floating emerald, hid the water beyond it. To the right, islands of all sizes and shapes, so thick that one might suppose it had rained islands at some time or other: on the least of them grew pine-trees, any of which would have made a mainmast for the largest ship ever built. I have again and again threaded the intricate passages through the 'Lake of a Thousand Islands,' in the Great St. Lawrence; but I say, without fear of contradiction, that the scenery from Chatham Point to the mouth of the Nimkish river is wilder, bolder, and in every respect more beautiful, lovely as I admit the Canadian scenery to be.

The ship-channel hugs the shore of Vancouver Island, passing close to Cormorant, Haddington, and Malcolm Islands, and the mouth of the Nimkish river, navigable for canoes some considerable distance. This stream is used by the Hudson's Bay traders to reach the western side of Vancouver Island. Ascending it in canoes as far as practicable, about two days' walking brings them to Nootka Sound.

At the mouth of the river, I saw the village of the Nimkish Indians, situated on a table-land overhanging the sea, and inaccessible save by ascending a vertical cliff of smooth rock—a feat nothing but a fly could manage, unaided; but the redskins have a ladder, made of cedar-bark rope, which they can haul up and lower at will. The ladder up, the place is impregnable. Safe themselves, they can quietly bowl over their enemies, and sink their canoes.

These Nimkish Indians speak of another tribe that they call Sau-kau-lutuck, who have never seen or traded with white people. Their story, as interpreted for me by Mr. Moffat, the chief trader at Fort Rupert—who told me he quite believed it to be true—was as follows:—

'In crossing over to the west side of the island, on a war-path, the Nimkis discovered these Indians by accident, took several of them prisoners, whom they subsequently used as slaves, taking also skins, and what other property they had worth plundering. They are said to live on the edge of a lake, and subsist principally on deer and bear, and such fish as they can take in the lake. They own no canoes, neither do they know the use of firearms, their only weapons being the bow, arrow, and spear.'

The wind came on to blow as we left this interesting spot, and soon increased to a gale from the south-east, making the Otter rock most unpleasantly in the cradle of the deep. About 10 A.M. we ran into Beaver Harbour, our destination. This so-called harbour, being nothing more than an open roadstead, is disagreeably rough; a heavy sea rolls angrily in, dashing in foamy breakers on the rocky coast.

We anchor about a mile from shore, the captain deeming it unsafe to venture nearer. To announce our arrival, a gun is to be fired: this, I observed, was rather a service of danger to the sailor who had to touch it off, as it was just an equal chance whether the bulk of the charge came through the barrel or the touch-hole; the latter having become so capacious from rust and long usage, as to necessitate the employment of an enormously long wand, with a piece of lighted slow-match tied to the end of it. All hands having cleared away, and carefully concealed themselves, the wand slowly appears from a secure hiding-place, and the wheezy bang proclaims 'all 's safe.'

The report was still echoing through the distant hills, when countless tiny specks were discernible, dancing over the waves like birds. On they came, a perfect shoal of them, nearer and nearer, all evidently bound for the ship. I could make out clearly now, that these specks were canoes filled with Indians. By this time our boat was lowered; how I got into it, I never clearly remember: I have a dim recollection of descending a rope with great rapidity, and finding myself sprawling in the bottom, and being dragged up by the captain, much after the fashion adopted by clowns in a pantomime to reinstate the prostrate pantaloon upon his legs. At any rate I was safe, and the boat, propelled by four sturdy rowers, neared the shore.

On looking round, I observed the canoes had all turned towards us, and we were soon surrounded by the most extraordinary fleet I had ever beheld. The canoes were of all sizes, varying from those used for war purposes, holding thirty men, to the cockleshell paddled by a squaw. With the exception of a bit of skin, or an old blanket tied round the waist, the savages were all perfectly nude; their long black hair hung in tangled elf-locks down their backs, their faces and bodies painted in most fantastic patterns, with red and white. Keeping steadily along with us, they continually relieved their feelings by giving utterance to the most wild and fiendish yells that ever came from human throats.

As we neared the landing, I could see the chief trader of the Hudson's Bay Company, conspicuously white amidst a group of redskins, waiting to receive us. The boat grated on the shingle some distance from the beach, white with spray. 'Surely you don't expect me to go ashore like a seal?' I appealingly enquired of the captain. Before he had time to reply, four powerful savages, up to their waists in water, fisted me out of the boat; and two taking my heels, and two my shoulders, they bore me safely to the shore.

Having handed my letters of introduction from his Excellency the Governor to the chief trader, I was presented to the chiefs as a *Hyas tyee* (great chief), one of 'King George's' men. So we shook hands, and I attempted to move towards the fort; it was not to be done. To use the mildest term, I was 'mobbed;' old savages and young savages, old squaws and young squaws, even to boy and girl savage, rushed and scrambled to shake hands with me. Had I been a 'pump' on a desert, surrounded by thirst-famished Indians, and each arm a handle, they could not have been more vigorously plied. Being rescued at last by the combined efforts of trader and captain, I was marched into the fort, the gates shut with a heavy clang, and most thankful was I to be safe from any further demonstrations of friendship. The evening passed rapidly and pleasantly; mine host was a thorough sportsman, full of anecdote, and hospitable to a fault.

Awaking early, I wandered out, and up into the bastion of the fort. The sun was creeping from behind the ragged peaks of the Cascade Mountains, tinting with rosy light their snow-clad summits; the wind had lulled, or gone off to sea on some boisterous errand; the harbour, quite smooth, looked like burnished silver. There was a wild grandeur about the scene, that awoke feelings of awe rather than admiration; everywhere vast piles of craggy mountains, clad from the snow-line to the sea with dense pine-forests; not an open grassy spot, or even a naked mass of rock, peeped out to break the fearful monotony of these interminable hills.

The trading-post is a square, enclosed by immense trees, one end sunk in the ground; the trees are lashed together. A platform, about the height of an ordinary man from the top of these pickets, is carried along the sides of this square, so as to enable anyone to peep over without being in danger from an arrow or bullet. The entrance is closed by two massive gates, an inner and outer; all the houses—the chief trader's, employés', trading-house, fur-room, and stores—are within the square. The trade-room is cleverly contrived so as to prevent a sudden rush of Indians; the approach, from outside the pickets, is by a long narrow passage, bent at an acute angle near the window of the trade-room, and only of a sufficient width to admit one savage at a time. (This precaution is necessary, inasmuch as, were the passage straight, they would inevitably shoot the trader.)

At the angles nearest the Indian village are two bastions, octagonal in shape, and of a very doubtful style of architecture. Four embrasures in each bastion would lead the uninitiated to believe in the existence of as many formidable cannon, with rammers, sponges, neat piles of round-shot and grape, magazines of powder, and ready hands to load and fire—and, at the slightest symptom of hostility, to work havoc and destruction, on any red-skinned rebels daring to dispute the supremacy of the Hudson's Bay

Company. Imagine my surprise, on entering this fortress, to discover all this a pleasant fiction; two small rusty carronades, buried in the accumulated dust and rubbish of years, that no human power could load, were the sole occupants of the mouldy old turrets.

The bell for breakfast recalling me, I jokingly inquired of the trader if he had ever been obliged to use this cannon for defensive purposes. He laughed as he replied, 'There is a tradition that, at some remote period, the guns were actually fired, not at the rebellious natives, but over their heads; instead of being terror-stricken at the white man's thunder, away they all scampered in pursuit of the ball, found it, and, marching in triumph back to the fort-gate, offered to trade it, that it might be fired again!'

Breakfast finished, the trader, captain, and myself started for the village. Clear of the gates, we scrambled down a rocky path, crossed a mountain-burn, dividing the Indians from the fort, and entered 'the city of the redskins;' which consists of a long row of huts, each hut nearly square, the exterior fantastically frescoed in hieroglyphic patterns, in white, red, and blue; having however a symbolical meaning or heraldic value, like the *totum* of the Indians east of the

Rocky Mountains; four immense trees, barked and worked smooth, support each corner; the tops are carved to resemble some horrible monster: the hut is constructed of cedar-plank, chipped from the solid tree with chisels and hatchets made of stone: many hands combine to accomplish this; hence a hut becomes the joint property of several families. Five tribes live in this village:—

Qua-kars,	numbering	about	800	warriors.
Qual-quilths	,,	,,	100	,,
Kum-cutes	,,	,,	70	,,
Wan-lish	,,	,,	50	,,
Lock-qua-lillas	,,	,,	80	,,

The entire population, even to the dogs, turned out on our advent; it was puzzling to imagine where they all came from. We soon formed the centre of the vilest assemblage man ever beheld. The object of our visit made known, a ring was immediately formed by chiefs and braves, the squaws and children being outside. Had any charming princess, captive in an enchanted castle, been guarded by such a collection of painted ragamuffins as now surrounded us, he would have been a valorous knight that dared venture to release her.

The first question discussed being the price, a

much larger sum was asked than we felt disposed to pay. Although the slave belonged solely to one Indian, the power to sell resting with him only, still every one had their say. Men gurgled and spluttered strange unintelligible noises, women chattered and screamed like furies, whilst children engaged in small battles outside the ring.

Thirty blankets and two trade-guns—equal to about 50*l*. sterling—were the terms at last agreed on. We then adjourned to the shed where the slave was a prisoner. I was in a great state of expectation, picturing to myself an Indian Hebe, limbs exquisitely moulded, native grace and elegance in every movement, gorgeous in 'wampum,' paint, and waving feathers, such as I had read of as 'Laughing Water,' or 'Prairie Flower.'

Being carried, so to speak, into the shed—a waif in the stream of savages rushing like a human torrent to get in—with all the breath squeezed out of me, I was deposited somewhere; but as my head was enveloped in a dense cloud of pungent smoke, it was some time ere I discovered I was close to the captain. 'Sit down,' he roared; 'you will die of suffocation if you keep your head in the smoke.' At once I seated myself on the floor, and now quite understand what being suffocated in a chimney is like.

Once more enabled to see, it was easy to discover the secret: there being no place for the smoke to escape, it accumulates at the top of the shed, and one literally, not figuratively, 'lives under a cloud.' There was a hum and a burr, as in a nest of angry hornets; a din increased by the dogs, that fought and rolled in where I sat; and being by no means particular whether they bit my legs or any other man's, it required unwonted agility to keep clear.

During an interval of peace, it was easy to make out that the slave was coming. Alas! how fleeting are imaginary pictures—poetic dreams—castles in the air! Half crouching, and waddling rather than walking, came my ideal; her only covering, a ragged, filthy old blanket, her face begrimed with the dirt and paint of a lifetime; short, fat, repulsive, the incarnation of ugliness, a very Hecate! All my romance vanished like a dissolving-view. For this had I been squeezed nearly to death, suffocated, poisoned with a noxious stench, my legs imperilled by infuriated curs, my ears deafened, half devoured by insatiable blood-suckers?—to aid in paying 50*l.* for the ugliest old savage eyes ever beheld!

All the chiefs assembled at the fort in the evening to receive payment, and hand over the slave. Squatting on their heels, nose and knees together, their backs against the wall, they formed a circle. The pipe produced (nothing can be done without it); I say pipe, for *one* only is used; filled and lighted, it passes from mouth to mouth; each, taking a good pull, puffs the smoke slowly from his nostrils. The thirty blankets and two guns being piled in the centre of this strange assemblage, the slave was led in. Each blanket underwent a most careful inspection; the guns, snapped and pointed, were finally approved of. A husky grunt, from each of the council, denoting general approval, the guns and blankets were carried off in triumph, and we became the fortunate possessors of this strange purchase.

Whilst in the fort I was tolerably exempt from the insatiable and most annoying curiosity, that induces Indians to watch everything a stranger does. One oily old chief, however, always contrived to get into my room in time to see me dress. He used to stalk in, squat down rolled in a dirty blanket, and testify his pleasure by a series of grunts slightly varied in tone. He was certainly the most blubbery-looking man I ever beheld. Everything about him was suggestive of oil, from his head to his heels, blanket included; like a compound of salmon and seal's flesh, he smelt quite as oily as he looked. Outside, however, there was no help for it: go where I would, a bodyguard of savages (real untamed savages too, not semi-civilised articles) was always in attendance.

Once I managed to escape through the pickets at the back of the fort, and stealthily reaching the beach, under cover of the trees, imagined myself safe. A light misty rain fell thickly, and a flock of sanderlings, running along in the ripple, completely absorbed my attention. I was suddenly startled by hearing the 'crunch, crunch' of a foot in the shingle behind me. I had looked right and left on reaching the beach, but not a trace of Indian was visible. Turning suddenly round, you can picture my surprise at finding myself face to face with a savage, unclad from head to heel, carrying—what should you imagine?—not a scalping-knife, or a war-club, or bow or spear or gory scalp: it was an immense green gingham umbrella, a thoroughbred 'Gamp,' with horn crook, battered brass ferule, furled with a ring such as curtains are hung on. He politely offered me a part, and scarcely deeming it safe to refuse, I paraded the beach, linked arm-in-arm with the ugliest specimen of humanity eyes ever beheld. I wonder if, before or since, a naked savage and civilised man ever walked together on the sea-beach, listening to 'what the wild waves were saying,' sheltered from the rain by a green gingham umbrella! I trow not. I should have been no more astonished at seeing a seal, or old Neptune himself, with an umbrella, than I was at a naked Indian so protected on the beach at Fort Rupert.

This was not my only adventure whilst staying at the fort. The beach runs out very flat for a long distance seaward; the rocks appear a slaty kind of shingle, with seams of coal cropping out in every direction. The pines (*Abies Douglassii*) grow down to highwater-mark, attaining a height of 250 feet and over, straight as a flagstaff. On the branches are placed quaint-looking affairs, that you discover, on inquiry, to be coffins; but how the friends of the departed get the boxes up into the trees, or how they keep them there when they are up, is more than I can tell. The coffin is usually an old canoe, lashed round and round, like an Egyptian mummy-case, with the inner bark of the cedar-tree; but of this, and other singular customs, I shall have to speak more at length in a future chapter.

Near one of these arboreal cemeteries, I observed a high pole, and dangling from it a head, fresh, bloody, and ghastly; the scalp had been removed, and a rope, passing through the under-jaw, served to suspend it. Horribly revolting as the face appeared, still I could not help going close to it. Never had I seen so singular a head; it looked in shape like a sugarloaf, the apex of the skull terminating in a sharp point. On returning to the fort, I inquired if they could tell me anything about this mysterious head. It appeared that, a day or so before our arrival, a war-party of the Qua-kars had returned from a raid on the mainland coast, and brought with them a number of slaves. (Prisoners taken in war, or in any other manner, are invariably used as slaves, bought and sold, whipped or killed, as best befits the whim or caprice of their owner.) Amongst the wretched captives, was a chief. Soon after landing, he was made fast to a temporary cross erected on the beach, shot, scalped, and beheaded, and it was his head I had seen in my rambles. On hearing further that the tribe to which he belonged was one that elongate instead of flatten the head, I determined at any risk to have the skull.* Extreme caution was needed, or a like fate would probably be mine; a white chief's hairless head might possibly adorn the same pole as that of the painted savage. I made several attempts, but each time signally failed to accomplish my purpose.

The night preceding our departure, all hopes of obtaining the coveted head were nearly abandoned. Fortune at last smiled upon me; unobserved, I upset the pole, and *bagged* the head; and pushing it into my game-bag, got safely into the fort. Still in terror of being seen, I hid it in the bastion, and eventually headed it into a pork barrel, with stones and sand; then had it rolled boldly out, and put on board the steamer.

On our departure the following morning, I was rejoiced to find the head had not been missed, but somewhat frightened, on learning I was to be paddled to the steamer, in the state-canoe of the chief to whom the trophy belonged. In grand procession, we marched from the fort to the canoe, marshalled by the dingy dignitary, who, in happy ignorance of the wrong I had done him, was all smiles and grins; the final hand-shaking being accom-

* *Vide* Illustration.

plished, I was lifted into the canoe in the same fashion as I had been previously lifted out, and rapidly reached the steamer.

The chief came on board the steamer whilst the anchor was being weighed. Imagine what I felt when he seated himself deliberately upon the cask wherein I had hid his property. The wished-for moment came, the wheels splashed slowly round, my plundered friend was bowed over the side, and not until the smoke of the lodge-fires, and the fading outline of the village, grew dim in the distance, did I feel my scalp safe. The head is now in the Osteological Room of the British Museum, and well worth investigation by any who may be curious to compare the effect of circular pressure with that of the flat-head.* Skulls similarly flattened were also brought by me from Vancouver Island.

We again called at Nanaimo on our return, and, whilst 'coaling,' delivered the ransomed lady safely into the hands of her owner. At the same time three hundred Indians from Queen Charlotte's Island landed, *en route* to Victoria, arriving in large canoes, each holding about twenty Indians and their baggage. These canoes were not at all similar to any I had seen

* *Vide* Illustration.

at Fort Rupert, or to those used by the Coast and Fraser river Indians. The shape was similar to the boats one sees in very old pictures, filled with sailors in armour, the bow and stern carved to represent a neck, bearing on it some hideous grinning monster's head.

Their chief, named Edin-saw, once saved the crew of a small schooner, the 'Susan Sturges,' from being killed by the islanders under his control. The vessel was wrecked on Queen Charlotte's Island, and the crew subsequently ransomed. This little army of savages reached Victoria safely, having taken four months to make the voyage; threading all the difficult and dangerous straits, with the risk of capture from other tribes, exposed to all the vicissitudes of weather, in open canoes as easily upset as a child's cradle.

Reaching Victoria in safety, I proceeded up the Fraser, and for the first time witnessed sturgeon-spearing.

CHAPTER VII.

STURGEON-SPEARING—MANSUCKER—CLAMS.

THE Sturgeon found in North-western waters differs only in some unimportant specific distinctions from the one living in the pond of the Zoological Society's Gardens, in the Regent's Park. *Accipenser transmontanus* is the name given by Sir J. Richardson to sturgeon that frequent rivers that flow into the St. Lawrence, on the east side of the Rocky Mountains, but unknown in streams that fall into the Arctic Ocean. On the western side sturgeon abound in the Columbia, Fraser, and most other rivers as far north as lat. 53° N. It is certainly not a handsome fish to look at, reminding one of a shark in armour; yet, clad as he is from head to tail in bony mail, every movement is easy and graceful.

Sp. Ch.—Five rows of plates encase the body: the row along the back is most prominent, and contains fifteen shields. The cheeks are flat, the snout terminating in an acute point, remarkably flexible and trunklike in its movements. Four barbels dangle from beneath the snout, situated about mid-distance between its point and the orbit. The mouth is underneath, resembling a huge flabby sucker in the freshly-caught fish. Nevertheless, as his habit is to prowl about the mud and gravel at the bottom, it is in reality the very best kind of mouth that could have been given. The barbels that hang before are clearly delicate feelers, intended to give warning, that game suitable for food—disturbed probably by the flexible nose—is near; the nose is employed to stir up the mud, turn over stones, or in exploring the hiding-places of prey amidst the rocks and heavy boulders. The eyes are small and golden-yellow in the newly-caught fish, but change immediately after death.

The great extent and strength of the pectorals, which are nearly horizontal, show us that, in addition to their acting as oars and rudder, they are also powerful assistants in bringing the great fleshy mouth to bear upon anything discovered by the barbels. Female fish are taken full of roe in the Fraser during the month of June, and sometimes later; but where they deposit the ova or what becomes of the young after leaving the eggs, are mysteries. I never saw a small sturgeon, but have no doubt most of the young fish descend to the sea, although it is equally certain numbers remain entirely in the fresh-water. Madame Sturgeon's family is by no means a small one: a bushel of eggs is not an unusual quantity for a female fish to yield; a great many thousands, although I do not know how many eggs a bushel contains. The Indians dry these eggs in the sun and devour them with oil, as we eat currants and cream. It would surely pay to prepare cauiare on the Russian plan, even to send it to the English market. A rough kind of isinglass was at one time prepared by the Fraser river Indians and traded by the Hudson's Bay Company, but even that branch of industry has ceased to flourish since the 'Golden Age.' Indians are exceedingly fond of sturgeon-flesh, and usually demand a high price for it.

Few fish have a wider geographical range than sturgeon. On our own coasts, we find them frequenting the mouths of rivers and muddy estuaries. When caught in the Thames, within the jurisdiction of the lord mayor of London, it is considered a royal fish; implying, that the fish ought to be sent to the king, though how far the sovereign's rights in the matter are actually considered, seems to be somewhat doubtful. It is said, however, that the sturgeon was exclusively reserved for the table of the king in the time of Henry I.

In the Fraser and Columbia rivers, and in all the streams of any magnitude from latitude 46°19′ N. to Sitka, latitude 53° N., the sturgeon is found abundantly; as also in Northern Asia, where it forms an article of vast commercial value, the well-known and much-prized caviare being made from its roe, and that almost indispensable household necessary, isinglass, from its air-bladder. The long ligamentous cord, traversing the entire length of the spine, constitutes another delicacy, called *vesiga*, much relished by the Russians. The flesh also is eaten, cooked in various ways, and held in no mean estimation. Turkey, Italy, Germany, and Greece (especially the two latter) are great markets for caviare.

Pliny speaks of the sturgeon as being in great repute among the Greeks and Romans: 'the cooked fish was decked with garlands, as were the slaves who carried it to table;' and altogether it was an affair of great pomp and ceremony, when a sturgeon was to be demolished.

Sturgeon arrive in the Columbia early in February, and a little later in the Fraser, although a great number above the Kettle Falls, at Fort Colville, must remain permanently in the fresh-water. They ascend the rivers to incredible distances, in the Fraser as high as Fraser Lake, quite up in the Rocky Mountains. In the Columbia sturgeon have been taken eight hundred miles above the Kettle Falls, which are, speaking roughly, eighteen hundred miles from the sea, and, in accomplishing this, several very serious obstacles have to be overcome. Up the Snake river, at the great Shoshonee Falls (a salmon-station of the Snake Indians), sturgeon are often taken. The Snake river, tributary to the Columbia, is about fourteen hundred miles from the sea.

One would never imagine a fish clad in stiff unyielding armour could ascend rapid torrents and leap falls that puzzle even the lissom salmon; but the strength of the sturgeon is immense, and the power it can exert with the tail would be almost incredible to those, who have never seen the rapid twists, plunges, and other performances this fish goes through, when it has a barbed hook in the jaws, or a spear between the joints of its mail.

The first glance at a sturgeon would lead any one accustomed to fish, to decide at once that it must be a ground-feeder: the form and position of the mouth, the lengthened snout, the barbels, the ventral fins so far back, the large size of the pectorals — as I have already stated—all clearly evidence a habit of grubbing-up food of various kinds near the bottom, and browsing off shelled molluscs adhering to sticks or stones. They also indulge in small fish: eulachon are oily dainties they seem particularly to appreciate; and the Indians say sturgeon are never so fat and good as in 'eulachon time.' Small blame to the sturgeon for appreciating such delicious fish.

During the time the Fraser and Columbia rivers are rising,—and the rise is very rapid, about thirty feet above the winter level, owing to the melting snow,—sturgeon are continually leaping. As you are paddling quietly along in a canoe, suddenly one of these monsters flings itself into the air many feet above the surface of the water, falling back again with a splash, as though a huge rock had been pitched into the river by some Titan hand. It appears to be only play, as they never leap for insect-food; neither have I ever observed them do it during low-water; perhaps the intense cold of the snow-water begets a desire for exercise.

The systems of catching sturgeon in use amongst the Indians of the Fraser and Columbia rivers are widely different, as indeed are all their modes of taking fish. This mainly arises from the fact of the Columbia river having numerous deep falls, that impede the ascent of all fish going up to spawn. These falls, as I have said, are quite impassable for even the salmon until the snow-water floods the river. The Fraser, on the other hand, offers no hindrance at all until after Fort Hope is passed, and the principal Indian fishing-stations are all below this point: hence it is that on the Columbia, the fish, both salmon and sturgeon, are speared, trapped in baskets or weirs, and the sturgeon also taken with hook and line; whereas, on the Fraser, salmon are principally taken in nets, and sturgeon speared.

I shall first describe the mode adopted by the Indians of the Columbia to catch sturgeon with hook and line. The best months for fishing are February and March, and the time of day either early in the morning, or late in the evening. The Dalles is a favourite fishing-station.

The first thing is to prepare the bait. The old

wooden fish-hook is now amongst the things that *were*, its place having been supplied by its civilised Birmingham brother, bartered by the Indians from the Hudson's Bay Company. The fishing line is either made of native hemp, or the inside bark of the cypress-tree spun into cord. The bait is a long strip cut from the under-side of a trout, at one end of which the point of the hook is inserted; the strip being then wound tightly and evenly round the hook, and up the line about three inches, the silvery side outer-most. It is then firmly whipped over with white horsehair, a pebble slung on as a sinker, and the deception is complete. Five or six long barbed spears are stowed away in the canoe, the line coiled carefully in the bow, and the baited hook laid on it. Two wily redskins man this frail bark, the paddler squatting on his heels in the stern, the line-man standing in the bow.

A few skilful turns of the paddle sends the canoe to the mudbank on which King Stur-geon is dozing, and awaiting his matin or ves-per meal. The dainty-looking morsel, bearing all the external semblance to a fish (but, like the Trojan horse, pregnant with mischief), sinks noiselessly and slowly to the bottom; the canoe drifts with the current, and in this manner the bait is towed along; it nears the sturgeon's nose, and, being far too tempting to be refused, the great pendulous lips close upon it; but ere it reaches the gullet, a sharp twitch of the line buries the hook in the tenacious gristle. At once discovering he has been miserably done, anger and obstinate resistance are in the ascendant; so he comes to the surface with a rush and a splash.

The paddler now exerts all his skill to keep a slack line, for the hooked fish would otherwise inevitably upset the canoe; the bowman, with the line in one hand and a spear poised in the other, quietly bides his time; then he hurls the spear into the sturgeon's armour-clad back; down darts the fish, but soon returns to the surface, when in goes another spear, and so on again and again, until, towed ashore, it is dragged out of the water with a powerful gaffhook. Large numbers besides such as are thus speared are netted in passing through the narrow rock-channels.

On the Fraser river sturgeon-spearing is the most exciting sport imaginable. Hooking, playing, and landing a noble salmon is an achievement every fisherman is truly proud of; but I unhesitatingly assert that to spear and land a sturgeon five or six hundred pounds in weight, with only a frail canoe, which the slightest inequality of balance will upset in an instant, requires a degree of skill, courage, and dexterity that only a lifetime's practice can bestow.

I have already said the Fraser has no falls below Fort Hope, but a great many stiff rapids; below these rapids it widens out into long slowly-running shallows, generally speaking having large sand and gravel-banks—*bars*, as the miners call them, and on these bars the Indians live during the fishing-season. The time for fishing being generally soon after sunrise, four canoes, each manned by two Indians, usually start for sturgeon-capture; the paddler, who squats in the stern, looks in the direction in which the canoe is to go, not, as we sit in rowing, with our backs to the bow, but facing it; he is always chosen for his greater strength, tact, and dexterity with the paddle, for on his skill depends in a great degree the safety and success of the spearman.

The spearman stands in the bow, armed with a most formidable spear—the handle,* from seventy to eighty feet long, is made of white pine wood; fitted on the spear-haft is a barbed point, in shape very much like a shuttlecock, supposing

* *Vide* Illustration.

STURGEON-SPEARING ON THE FRASER

each feather represented by a piece of bone, thickly barbed, and very sharp at the end. This is so contrived that it can be easily detached from the long handle by a sharp dexterous jerk. To this barbed contrivance a long line is made fast, which is carefully coiled away close to the spearman, like a harpoon-line in a whale-boat.

The four canoes, alike equipped, are paddled into the centre of the stream, and side by side drift slowly down with the current, each spearman carefully feeling along the bottom with his spear, constant practice having taught the crafty savages to know a sturgeon's back when the spear comes in contact with it. The spear-head touches the drowsy fish—a sharp plunge, and the redskin sends the notched points, through armour and cartilage, deep into the leather-like muscles. A skilful jerk frees the long handle from the barbed end, which remains inextricably fixed in the fish; the handle is thrown aside, the line seized, and the struggle begins.

The first impulse is to resist this objectionable intrusion, so the angry sturgeon comes up to see what it all means : this curiosity is generally repaid by having a second spear sent crashing into him. He then takes a header, seeking safety in flight, and the real excitement commences. With might and main the bowman plies the paddles, and the spearman pays out line, the canoe flying through the water. The slightest tangle, the least hitch, and over it goes; it becomes, in fact, a sheer trial of paddle *versus* fin. Twist and turn as the sturgeon may, all the canoes are with him: he flings himself out of the water, dashes through it, under it, and skims along the surface; but all is vain—the canoes and their dusky oarsmen follow all his efforts to escape as a cat follows a mouse.

Gradually the sturgeon grows sulky and tired, obstinately floating on the surface. The savage knows he is not vanquished, but only biding a chance for revenge; so he shortens up the line, and gathers quietly on upon him, to get another spear in. It is done—and down viciously dives the sturgeon; but pain and weariness begin to tell, the struggles grow weaker and weaker, as life ebbs slowly away, until the mighty armour-plated monarch of the river yields himself a captive to the dusky native in his frail canoe.

The Clam.—Amongst the edible shellfish found on the coasts of Vancouver Island and British Columbia, the Great Clam, as it is there styled (*Lutraria maxima*), or the Otter-shell of conchologists, is by far the most valuable. Clams are one of the staple articles of winter food on which all Indian tribes in a great measure depend who inhabit the north-west coast of America. The clam to the Indians is a sort of molluscous cereal, that they gather and garner during the summer months; and an outline sketch of this giant bivalve's habits and style of living, how captured, and what becomes of it after being made a prisoner, may be interesting; its habits, and the uses to which, if not designed, it is at least appropriated, being generally less known than its minute anatomy. Clams attain an immense size; I have measured shells eight inches from the hinge to the edge of the valve. We used them as soap-dishes at our head-quarters on Vancouver Island.

The clam has a very wide range, and is thickly distributed along the mainland and Vancouver Island coasts; his favourite haunts are the great sandbanks, that run out sometimes over a mile from the shore. The rise and fall of the tide is from thirty to forty feet, so that at low-water immense flats or beaches, consisting of mud and sand, are laid bare.

There is nothing poetical about the clam, and its habits are anything but clean; grovelling in the mud, and feeding on the veriest filth it can find, appears to constitute the great pleasure of its life; the stomach is a kind of dusthole, into which anything and everything finds ready admission. Its powers of digestion must be something wonderful; I believe clams could sup on copper tacks, and not suffer from nightmare. Spending the greater part of its time buried about two feet deep, the long syphon, reaching to the surface, discovers its whereabouts, as the ebbing tide leaves the mud, by continually squirting up small jets of water, about six or eight inches high. The sand flats dry, out marches an army of squaws (Indian women), as it is derogatory to the dignity of a man to dig clams. With only a small bit of skin or cedar-mat tied round the waist, the women tramp through the mud, a basket made from cedar-root in one hand, and in the other a bent stick about four feet long.

Thus armed, they begin to dig up the mud-homes of the unsuspecting clam: guided by the jets of water, they push down the bent stick, and experience has taught them to make sure of getting it well under the shell: placing a stone behind the stick, against which the squaw fixes her foot firmly, she lifts away: the clam comes from darkness into daylight ere he knows it, and thence into the Indian's basket. The basket filled, the clam-pickers trudge back again to the lodge—and next to open him. He is not a *native* to be astonished with an oyster-knife; once having shut his mouth, no force, saving that of dashing his shell into atoms, will induce him to open it. But the wily redskin, if she does not know the old fable of the wind and the sun trying their respective powers on the traveller, at least adopts the same principle on the luckless clam; what knife and lever fail to do a genial warmth accomplishes. The same plan the sun adopted to make the traveller take off his coat (more persuasive, perhaps, than pleasant) the Indian squaw has recourse to in order to make the clam open his shell.

Hollowing out a ring in the ground, about eight inches deep, they fill the circle with large pebbles, made red-hot in the camp-fire near by, and on these heated stones put the bivalve martyr. The heat soon finds its way through the shelly armour, the powerful ropes that hold the doors together slacken, and, as his mansion gradually grows 'too hot to hold him,' the door opens a little for a taste of fresh air. Biding her chance, armed with a long, smooth, sharp-pointed stick, sits the squaw—dusky, grim, and dirty—anxiously watching the clam's movements.

The stronghold opens, and the clam drinks draught after draught of the cool life-giving air; then down upon him the savage pounces, and astonishes his heated and fevered imagination by thrusting, with all her force, the long sharp stick into the unguarded house: crash it goes through the quivering tissues; his chance is over! Jerked off the heated stones, pitilessly his house is forced open; ropes, hinges, fastenings crack like packthread, and the mollusc is ruthlessly dragged from his shelly home, naked and lifeless.

Having got the clam out, the next thing is to preserve it for winter: this is effectually accomplished by stringing-up and smoking. A long wooden needle, with an eye at the end, is threaded with cord made from native hemp; and on this the clams are strung like dried apples, and thoroughly smoked, in the interior of the lodge. A more effectual smoking-house could hardly be found. I can imagine nothing in the 'wide, wide world' half as filthy, loathsome, and disgusting as the interior of an Indian house. Every group has some eatable—fish, mollusc, bird, or animal—and what the men and squaws do not consume, is pitched to the dusky little savages, that, naked and dirty, are thick as ants in a hill; from these the residue descends to the dogs, and what they leave some lower form of animal life manages to consume. Nothing eatable that is once brought in is ever by any chance swept, or carried, out again, and either becomes some other form of life, or, decomposing, assumes its elemental condition.

An old settler once told me a story, as we were hunting together, and I think I can vouch for the truth of what he related, of having seen a duck trapped by a clam:—'You see, sir, as I was a-cruising down these flats about sun-up, the tide jist at the nip, as it is now, I see a whole pile of shoveller ducks snabbling in the mud, and busy as dogfish in herring-time; so I creeps down, and slap I lets 'em have it: six on 'em turned over, and off went the pack gallows-scared, and quacking like mad. Down I runs to pick up the dead uns, when I see an old mallard a-playing up all kinds o' antics, jumping, backing, flapping, but fast by the head, as if he had his nose in a steel trap; and when I comes up to him, blest if a large clam hadn't hold of him, hard and fast, by the beak. The old mallard might a' tried his darndest, but may I never bait a martin-trap again if that clam wouldn't a' held him agin any odds 'til the tide run in, and then he'd a' been a gone shoveller sure as shooting; so I cracked up the clam with the butt of my old gun, and bagged the mallard.'

Any one who has travelled in America must have eaten clam-chowder, or, more probably perhaps, tried to eat it. It is a sort of intermediate affair between stew-proper and soup. How it is made I do not know, but I do know that to my palate it is the vilest concoction I ever tasted; and I always look upon a man who can eat clam-chowder with a kind of admiration almost akin to envy; for I feel and know that if he can eat chowder, short of cannibalism he can eat anything. I have tried smoked clam, but that I cannot say I enjoy; it is remarkably like chewing good old tarry ropeyarn, and, save the slight difference in nutritive power, about an equally agreeable repast.

If any of my readers should be curious to see the shells of these monster clams, they will find many I have recently brought home in the Shell Room of the British Museum.

MANSUCKERS.—The three kinds of cuttlefish best known in British seas are, first, the sepia, the creature whose backbone is the 'cuttlefish' of the apothecaries' shops; second, the 'loligo,' or 'calamary,' that has a beautiful penlike bone, and, from the presence of a bag containing a black fluid, is sometimes called the 'pen-and-ink' fish; and third, the 'octopus.'

The octopus as seen on our coasts, although even here called a 'mansucker' by the fishermen, is a mere Tom Thumb, a tiny dwarf, as compared to the Brobdignagian proportions he attains in the snug bays and long inland canals along the east side of Vancouver Island, as well as on the mainland. These places afford lurking-dens, strongholds, and natural sea-nurseries, where the octopus grows to an enormous size, fattens, and wages war, with insatiable voracity, on all and everything it can catch. Safe from heavy breakers, it lives as in an aquarium of smooth lake-like water, that, save in the ebbing and flowing of the tide, knows no change or disturbance.

The ordinary resting-place of this hideous 'sea-beast' is under a large stone, or in the wide cleft of a rock, where an octopus can creep and squeeze itself with the flatness of a sand-dab, or the slipperiness of an eel. Its modes of locomotion are curious and varied: using the eight arms as paddles, and working them alternately, the central disc representing a boat, octopi row themselves along with an ease and celerity comparable to the many-oared caïque that glides over the tranquil waters of the Bosporus; they can ramble at will over the sandy roadways intersecting their submarine parks, and, converting arms into legs, march on like a huge spider. *Gymnasts* of the highest order, they climb the slippery ledges, as flies walk up a window-pane; attaching the countless suckers that arm the terrible limbs to the face of the rocks, or to the wrack and seaweed, they go about, back downward, like marine sloths, or, clinging with one arm to the waving algæ, perform series of *trapèze* movements that Leôtard might view with envy.

The size, of course, varies. I have seen and *measured* the arm five feet long, and as large at the base where it joins the central disc as my wrist; and were an octopus by any chance to wind its sucker-dotted cable-arms round a luckless bather, fatal would be the embrace, and horrible to imagine, being dragged down and drowned by this eight-armed monster; a worse death than being crushed by coiling serpents like ill-fated Laocoon.

I have often when on the rocks, in Esquimalt Harbour, watched my friend's proceedings; the water being clear and still, it is just like peering into an aquarium of huge proportions, crowded with endless varieties of curious sea-monsters; although grotesque and ugly to look at, yet all alike displaying the wondrous works of Creative wisdom. In all the cosy little nooks and corners of the harbour the great seawrack (*Macrocystis*) grows wildly, having a straight round stem that comes up from the bottom, often with a stalk three hundred feet long; reaching the surface, it spreads out two long tapering leaves that float upon the water: this sea-forest is the favourite hunting-ground of octopi.

I do not think, in its native element, an octopus often catches prey on the ground or on the rocks, but waits for them just as the spider does, only the octopus converts itself into a web, and a fearful web too. Fastening one arm to a stout stalk, stiffening out the other seven, one would hardly know it from the wrack amongst which it is concealed. Patiently he bides his time, until presently a shoal of fish come gaily on, threading their way through the sea-trees, joyously happy, and little dreaming that this lurking monster, so artfully concealed, is close at hand. Two or three of them rub against the arms: fatal touch! As though a powerful electric shock had passed through the fish, and suddenly knocked it senseless, so does the arm of the octopus paralyse its victim; then, winding a great sucker-clad cable round the palsied fish—as an elephant winds its trunk round anything to be conveyed to the mouth—draws the dainty morsel to the centre of the disc, where the beaked mouth seizes, and soon sucks it in.

I am perfectly sure, from frequent observation, the octopus has the power of numbing its prey; and the sucking-discs along each ray are more for the purposes of climbing and holding-on whilst fishing, than for capturing and detaining slippery prisoners. The suckers are very large, and arranged in triple rows along the under-surface of the ray, decreasing in size towards the point, and possessing wonderful powers of adhesion.

As illustrating the size of these suckers, I may as well confess to a blunder I once made. It was an extremely low tide, and I was far out on the rocks at Esquimalt Harbour, hunting the pools, when I saw what I fancied a huge actinia, as big as an eggcup, its tentacles hauled in, and, having detached its disc from the rocks, was waiting for the tide: placing the fancied prize safely in my collecting-box, to my disgust, on examining my new species, it turned out to be only the sucking-disc of an octopus.

Tyrants though they be, an enemy hunts them with untiring pertinacity. The Indian looks upon the octopus as an alderman does on turtle, and devours it with equal gusto and relish, only the savage roasts the glutinous carcase instead of boiling it. His mode of catching octopi is crafty in the extreme, for redskin well knows, from past experience, that were the octopus once to get some of its huge arms over the side of the canoe, and at the same time a holdfast on the wrack, it could as easily haul it over as a child could upset a basket; but he takes care not to give a chance, and thus the Indian secures his prize.

Paddling the canoe close to the rocks, and quietly pushing aside the wrack, the savage peers through the crystal water, until his practised eye detects an octopus, with its great ropelike arms stiffened out, waiting patiently for food. His spear is twelve feet long, armed at the end with four pieces of hard wood, made harder by being baked and charred in the fire: these project about fourteen inches beyond the spear-haft, each piece having a barb on one side, and are arranged in a circle round the spear-end, and lashed firmly on with cedar-bark. Having spied out the octopus, the hunter passes the spear carefully through the water until within an inch or so of the centre disc, and then sends it in as deep as he can plunge it. Writhing with pain and passion, the octopus coils its terrible arms round the haft; redskin, making the side of the canoe a fulcrum for his spear, keeps the struggling monster well off, and raises it to the surface of the water. He is dangerous now; if he could get a hold-fast on either savage or canoe, nothing short of chopping off the arms piecemeal would be of any avail.

But the wily redskin knows all this, and has taken care to have ready another spear unbarbed, long, straight, smooth, and very sharp, and with this he stabs the octopus where the arms join the central disc. I suppose the spear must break down the nervous ganglions supplying motive power, as the stabbed arms lose at once strength and tenacity; the suckers, that a moment before held on with a force ten men could not have overcome, relax, and the entire ray hangs like a dead snake, a limp, lifeless mass. And thus the Indian stabs and stabs, until the octopus, deprived of all power to do harm, is dragged into the canoe, a great, inert, quivering lump of brown-looking jelly.

CHAPTER VIII.

MULE-HUNTING EXPEDITION FROM VANCOUVER ISLAND TO SAN FRANCISCO—THE ALMADEN QUICKSILVER MINES—POISON-OAK AND ITS ANTIDOTE.

THE Commission, in 1860, were to commence the work of marking the boundary-line on the eastern side of the Cascades. A large addition to our staff of pack-mules being indispensable, I was despatched to San Francisco to purchase them; and instructed to rejoin the Commission, as soon as practicable, at the Dalles, already mentioned as a small town on the upper part of the Columbia river.

I introduce the journal of my mule-hunting adventures at this part of the volume, as it enables me to explain the systems of transport and travelling resorted to in wild countries, where roads and railways are unknown. I transcribe my journal, the events of each day as hastily recorded:—

Feb. 29th, 1860.—Left Esquimalt Harbour in

the steamer 'Panama,'—my destination San Francisco,—my mission to purchase mules. The island is still in its winter garb; not a bud has burst into leaf, and very few migratory birds have made their appearance. At 10.30 a.m. we are steaming out of the harbour; no wind, water smooth as a lake; run pleasantly down the Straits of Juan de Fuca, and pass Cape Flattery about 4 p.m. Wind blowing unpleasantly fresh, and a heavy tumbling swell makes the 'Panama' disagreeably lively. Passengers rapidly disappear; various gulping sounds, heavy sighs, and impatient calls for the steward, tell clearly enough that the most terrible leveller next to death, sea-sickness, has begun its work below.

March 1st.—A bleak misty morning, a heavy sea, wind dead ahead, and cold driving hail-showers. The ship, rolling from side to side, renders it difficult for even practised hands to guide anything spillable to the mouth; and walking, save to a sailor or a housefly, is an impossible performance.

March 2nd.—Managed to scramble on deck about 7 a.m., by going through a series of acrobatic performances, that came near to dislocating all my joints; wind moderated, but a heavy sea still rocked us very rudely. We are close inshore, passing Cape Blanco, 350 miles below Cape Flattery. Port Orford, a place celebrated for its cedar, is just visible through the haze; the rounded hills behind it are quite white with snow. Kept close inshore all day, but the weather is too cold, and sea too rough, for one to enjoy the scenery.

March 3rd.—Scrambled on deck again about 7 a.m.; wind still ahead, but altogether a better morning than yesterday. Had a good look at Cape Mendozena, a bold rocky headland, to the south of which is Mendozena city, consisting of a few houses and a groggery. The coast-line is exceedingly picturesque and pretty: between this headland and Point Arena a series of undulating hills, capped with massive pine-trees; their sides and grassy slopes, reaching down to the sea-line, remind me of English hayfields; it seems almost like enchantment, the change in the vegetation three days only from Vancouver Island.

March 4th.—At sunrise I am on deck, called by the captain, to get a peep at the 'Golden Gate.' There is just enough light to reveal a stupendous mass of bold mountain scenery, rising apparently from the sea, and towering up 3,000 feet and over, until lost in the haze of the morning.

Under the shadow of these hills we are puffing towards an opening, as if cut purposely through a solid wall of rock. On the right stands an immense fortress, built of red brick. Alcatraz Island, right ahead, is dimly visible, like a grey spot in the line of water. The ripple, touched by the sunbeams that are slanting into the bay, seems converted into revolving cylinders of brilliants. As we steam through this magnificent portal, the finest harbour in the world opens out to the southward and westward. On the curving shore of the bay, I can see the city of San Francisco, built on the slopes of three hills; to the left the island of Yerba Buena; farther to the right a forest of masts, from which flags representing every nation flutter in the breeze; ahead a long stretch of water, as far as eye could follow it—the continuation of the harbour.

We ran alongside an immense pier at 6 a.m. I am mobbed by touters from every hotel in San Francisco, and have hard work to keep my luggage from being equally divided amongst them. Passengers appear, for the first time since leaving Vancouver Island, blanched like celery or seakale. By dint of strong arms and stronger language, I get my luggage fastened to a grating that lets down by machinery, at the end of an omnibus marked 'Oriental Hotel.' I am hustled into the 'bus with three pale passengers, and we are rapidly whirled off to the 'Oriental.' The mail-packet from Panama has also just arrived; all the beds are taken at the hotel, so I bide my chance of some one leaving before night.

Called on the Consul, and through his kindness am located in the Union Club House, a grand improvement on the 'Oriental.'

March 5th.—Occupied in giving my letters of introduction, and arranging money-matters. The club-house in which I am staying is a massive granite building. The granite, beautifully faced and fitted, was all hewn in China; the house was put together there, to see everything was properly finished, then taken to pieces, packed, and shipped for San Francisco. Chinese builders came with it, brought their own scaffolding (made entirely from bamboo), put it together, built up the granite edifice in which I transcribe this, as handsome a structure as any San Francisco can boast of.

March 6th.—Having nothing particular to do, determine to visit the New Almaden quicksilver mines. There are two routes to these mines—one per stage the whole distance (56 miles), the other per steamer to the head of the Bay of San

Francisco, and thence by stage to San José. Past experience had taught me, whenever possible, scrupulously to avoid stage travelling. Being tossed in a blanket, or rolled down a steep hill in a cask, produce much the same bruised and general state of sprain and dislocation as a day's ride in a stage. Choosing the steamer lessened the chance of jolting by quite one-half, at the same time affording a good opportunity of seeing the famed Bay of San Francisco.

I embark at seven from a wooden pier—early as it is, alive with the hum, buzz, and bustle of the awakening city—and steam away over the unrippled waters of the bay. The temperature is delicious; a few fleecy clouds are swept rapidly over the clear blue sky by a light breeze blowing softly from the land, laden with the perfume of wild flowers and forest trees. A run of a few hours brought us to the embarcadero, or landing, at the head of the bay, from whence a stage bumped me over the road about four miles, to the old town of San José.

Pueblo San José stands at the entrance of a lovely valley. The town consists of a collection of adobe houses; a few in the main street are built of wood, painted white, with brilliant green jalousies outside the windows. The older houses are scattered round an open space, the plaza: trees of greenest foliage, in double rows, shade one from the burning sun, and everywhere spacious orchards and flower-gardens testify to the fertility of the soil.

Having a note from a friend in San Francisco to the host of '—— House,' more than ordinary civility was accorded me, and by some superhuman means a buggy would be ready in about two hours to take me to the mines. Crossing the Alameda, a grove of willows and oaks, planted by the padres, leads to the old crumbling walls of what was once a very spacious mission, now rapidly falling to decay. The interior of the old church is decorated with rude carvings, paintings of the Crucifixion, and frescoed figures of saints and martyrs, clad in garments of dazzling colours. One old shaven priest, with a particularly dirty cassock, and a face so begrimed with layers of filth as to be mosquito-proof, was the only ecclesiastic visible. Thousands of cliff swallows (*Hirundo lunifrons*) were busy building their bottle-shaped mud nests under the dilapidated roof

Discovered little worth looking at in the town. Found the buggy waiting: my coachman, a regular Yankee, puffing vigorously at an immense cigar, was seated in readiness, his legs resting on the splash-board. Without removing the cigar from his mouth, he drawled out, 'Say, Cap'en, guess you'd better hurry up if you mean making the ranch before sundown. Bet your pants this child ain't agwine that road in the dark nohow.' 'What's to happen?' I mildly enquired. 'Happen! Wal, maybe upset; maybe chawed up by a grisly; maybe cleaned slick out by the greasers. You'd better believe a man has to keep his eye skinned in the daytime; so hurry up, Cap.' Without further parley I scrambled in, and away we went.

Our road lay over broad plains and through occasional belts of timber; deep, gravelly arroyos, in and out of which we dashed with a plunging scramble, marked the course of the floods. Everything was steaming hot; the baked ground reflected back the scorching sun-rays, until the atmosphere quivered as one sees it over a limekiln; the mustangs in a fog of perspiration; the Jehu, denuded of coat and vest, continually yelled 'A git along,' with a rein in each hand, steering rather than driving, was red-hot in body and temper. But this was nothing to my state of broil. Exposed to a temperature that would have made one perspire sitting in the shade; to be kept in a state of bodily fear of instant upset; to undergo a continuous exercise that would have been good training for an athlete, to avoid being shot out of the buggy like a shell from a mortar, would have set an Icelander in a glow. The rapidity with which we whirled along, and the eccentric performances of the vehicle, destroyed, in a measure, the enjoyment of a scene quite new to me.

We rattled through the splendid valley of Santa Clara, passing here and there a fertile ranch; on either side, the wooded slopes looked like lawns of Nature's own contriving; far on my left, the bay glimmered like a line of silver light, the ground carpeted with flowers, brilliant escholtzia and blue nemophila were most conspicuous amidst a natural harvest of wild oats and grass; and on all sides, from amongst the clumps of buck-eye and oak, the cheery whistle and chirp of birds rang pleasantly on the ear.

Reaching the 'Halfway House' (as a small wooden building is named, midway betwixt San José and the mine), we stopped to water the mustangs and refresh the inward man — a respite most acceptable. A 'tall drink' worked wonders on my hitherto taciturn coachman, who, as we jogged along the remaining half the journey, related such wonderful stories, that it seemed to me we had hardly left the 'Halfway House' ere we rattled under a grove of trees completely shutting out the fading light, and pulled up with a sudden jerk, that well-nigh pitched me over the mustangs. 'Guess we've made it, Cap'en; this here's the manager's.'

Giving my letters of introduction to Mr. Young, a hospitable invitation to be his guest was readily accepted. I cannot help devoting a line to the praise of a house most enjoyable in its minutest details, with a host and hostess it refreshes one's heart to recall to memory.

The lower village of Almaden consists of a long row of very pretty cottages, the residences of the workmen employed in smelting the ore; each cottage was completely buried with honeysuckle and creeping roses; the gardens in front filled with flowers, and at the back with vegetables and fruit. A small stream of water, clear and cold, ripples past the frontage, brought from a mountain-burn that runs swiftly at the back, a barrier dividing the gardens from the surrounding hills. An avenue of trees leads from the cottages to the spacious brick buildings used for smelting.

The discovery of these fabulously rich mines of

quicksilver is briefly told. Long ere gold was discovered in California, the padres and early settlers knew of a cavern in the hillside, about a mile and a half from the present village. Deeming it merely a natural fissure or cleft in the rock, explorations only were made by the more adventurous as to its extent, which proved to be in length one hundred feet, running into the mountain horizontally. No one ever thought it was an artificial excavation of great antiquity. When the vaqueros and old dons of the neighbourhood were questioned by a new-comer about the cave, a shrug of the shoulders, and the usual reply, 'Quien sabe? son cosas muy antiguas,' was the sole information obtained.

A gold-seeker, assaying some of the rock, salivated himself, and thus discovered it was rich in quicksilver. A grant, with the land adjoining, was procured, and the original opening widened; in clearing away the rubble and dirt at the end of the cave, several skeletons were discovered, together with rude mining-tools and other curious relics, clearly proving it an old excavation made by the natives for the purpose of procuring vermilion, so much used by all savages to paint themselves. The position of the skeletons in the rubbish covering them left no doubt that, having followed the vein of cinnabar without exercising due precaution to prop the loose ground overhead, they had been literally buried alive in a grave of their own digging. Further research soon revealed the immense value of the deposit. Many years rolled away, and very little was done until it passed from the hands of an English company into that of an American firm.

The mine is about a mile and a half from the smelting-works, on the side of a mountain; an admirable road leads to it by a gentle ascent, down which waggons drawn by mules bring the ore to be smelted. On reaching the summit I rested on a level plateau, on which the upper works are built; I am to descend presently into the depths of the mine to see how the ore is deposited, and trace, step by step, the various processes it has to go through before it is marketable.

The main entrance is a tunnel ten feet high, and about an equal width throughout, in which runs a tramway leading to the shaft. At the end of this tunnel a small steam-engine does the work of the poor 'tanateros,' or carriers, who, until very recently, brought the ore and rubbish from the bottom of the mine on their backs, a system still adopted in Spain and Peru, each man having to bring up a load of two hundred pounds, in a bag made of hide, fastened by two straps passing round the shoulders, and a broader one across the forehead, which mainly sustains the load. It was fatal work to the poor Mexicans who had to do it, the terrible muscular strain soon producing disease and death!

On reaching the engine I am undressed and rigged as a miner, a costume far more loose and easy than becoming. Three dip-candles dangled from a button on my jacket by the wicks, and one enveloped in a knob of clay for my hand, completed my toilet. The next process is to be lowered down into the mine. Squeezing myself into a huge kind of bucket, and assuming as near as practicable the shape and position of a frog, my candle lighted, 'All right!' says somebody, and I find myself rapidly descending a damp dismal hole, dripping with water like a shower. Of course I shudder, and have horrible ideas of an abyss, ending no one knows where; the candle hissed, sputtered, and went out; the bucket swang as the chain lengthened, and bumped unpleasantly against the rocks; now a sudden stop, and a lively consciousness of being dragged bodily out like a bundle of clothes, discloses the fact of my safe arrival at the bottom.

The swarthy Mexican miner deputed as guide leads the way along a narrow gulley, and down an incline to the mouth of another hole, the descent to which has to be effected on a slanting pole, with notches cut in it, very like a bear-pole, called by the miner an *escalera*, requiring a saltatory performance that would not have been so bad if I had only known where I should have landed in case of falling. After this we scramble down a flight of steps cut in the rock, and reach the lowest excavation, about one thousand feet from the surface.

The cinnabar is found in large pockets, or in veins, permeating a kind of trap-rock; and as the miners dig it out, large columns or pillars are left to support the roof, and prevent the chance of its falling in. A small charcoal-fire burned slowly at the base of one of these massive columns, and as its flickering light fell dimly, illuminating with a ruddy glow the bronzed faces and nearly nude figures of the miners, the vermilion hue of the rugged walls and arched roof, sparkling with glittering crystals, forcibly reminded me of a brigand's cave, such as Salvator Rosa loved to paint.

All the work is done by contract: each gang taking a piece of ground on speculation, is paid according to the amount of ore produced; the ore averaging about thirty-six per cent. for quicksilver, although some pieces that I dug myself produced seventy-five per cent. Many mines in Europe have been profitably worked when the cinnabar has yielded only one per cent.

A shrill whistle rings through the mine; the miners from all directions rush towards the pillars. Thinking, at least, the entire concern was tumbling in, I was about to scamper off, when the guide, seizing my arm, drags me behind a projecting mass of rock, simply saying, 'A blast!' For a while there was a deathlike silence—not a sound save the hiss of the fusee, and the heavy breathing of the men; then the cave lighted up with a lurid flash, shedding a blinding glare over every object like tropical lightning. The dark galleries appeared and disappeared in the twinkling of an eye, whilst the report, like countless cannon, was echoed and reechoed through the cavernous chamber. Showers of fragments came rattling down in every direction, hurled up by the force of the powder. On the smoke clearing, the miners set to work to collect the scattered fragments of cinnabar. If a blast has been successful, often many tons of rock are loosened and torn out, to be broken into small pieces and conveyed to the bucket, and hauled by the engine to the surface. The mining operations are continued night and day, seventy-four pounds of candles being consumed every twenty-four hours.

I finish the survey of this singular mine perfectly free from foul air or fire-damp; ascend as I came down; and, by vigorous rubbing with soap-and-water, am slowly restored from bright vermilion to my normal colour.

The ore, on reaching the surface, is conveyed by the tram-cart to the sorting-shed, where it is broken and carefully picked over by skilful hands, great caution being needed in selection, as much valuable ore might be thrown away, or a large quantity of useless rock taken to the smelting-furnaces. The picked ore is placed in large bags made of sheepskin, weighed; and then hauled by the mules to the lower works.

Near the mine is a primitive kind of village, the abode of the miners, sorters, and ore-carriers, who are principally Mexicans; dirty señoras in ragged finery, dirtier children devoid of garments, together with dogs, pigs, poultry, and idle miners playing monte on the doorsteps, contrast sadly with the exquisite little village at the works.

Descending from the mine to the level ground by a short track down the hillside, through scenery indescribably picturesque, I reach the smelting furnaces; these, occupying about four acres of land, are built of brick, admirably neat, and well contrived. As quicksilver is found in several forms—namely, native quicksilver, occurring in small drops, in the pores or on the ledges of other rocks, argental mercury, a native silver amalgam, and sulphide of mercury or cinnabar, different processes are requisite for its reduction. Here it is found solely in form of cinnabar, and to reduce it a kind of reverberatory furnace is used, three feet by five, placed at the end of a series of chambers, each chamber seven feet long, four wide, and five high. About ten of these chambers are arranged in a line, built of brick, plastered inside, and secured by transverse rods of iron, fitted at the ends with screws and nuts, to allow for expansion. The top is of boiler iron, securely luted.

The first chamber is the furnace for fire, the second for ore, separated from the first by a grated partition, allowing the flame to pass through and play over the cinnabar. This ore-chamber, when filled, contains ten thousand pounds of cinnabar. The remaining chambers are for condensing the metal, communicating by square holes at the opposite corners; for instance, the right upper corner and lower left, and *vice versâ*, so that the vapour has to perform a spiral course in its transit through the condensers. Leaving the chambers, the vapour is conducted through a large wooden cistern, into which a shower of water continually falls, and thence through a long flue and tall chimney carried far away up the hillside.

The mercury is collected, as condensed, in gutters running into a long conduit outside the building, from which it drops into an iron pot sunk in the earth. As the pot fills, the mercury is conveyed to a store-tank that holds twenty tons. So great is its density, that a man sitting on a flat board floats about in the tank on a lake of mercury without its flowing over the edges of his raft. From this tank the metal is ladled out, and poured into iron flasks containing each seventy pounds (these flasks are made in England, and sent to New Almaden): in this state it is shipped for the various markets.

Although every possible care has been taken to prevent the mercurial fumes from injuring the smelters, still a great deal of it is necessarily inhaled, most injurious to health. Clearing out the furnace is the most hurtful process, the men employed working short spells, and resting a day or two between. A furnace charged with ore, I am told, takes about eight days to sublime and cool.

It is difficult to obtain a correct statement of the absolute yield of this mine; proprietors, for many reasons, deeming it inexpedient to let the world know the extent of their riches. The export of quicksilver from San Francisco, a few years back, may, I think, be averaged at 1,350,000 pounds of mercury per annum, valued at 683,189 dollars; and this, together with the large amount consumed in California, was the sole produce of the New Almaden mines.

There are fourteen furnaces, arranged with passages ten feet wide between them, the whole covered with a roof sufficiently high to allow a current of air to circulate freely. Between the furnaces and on all the open spaces are innumerable bricks, just as we see them in a brickyard to harden before baking. On inquiring what these were made for, I discover that all the fragments and dust-cinnabar are pounded together, mixed with water, and made into bricks: in this form the ore can be conveniently built into the furnace, securing intervening spaces for the flame and heat to act on; thus more perfect sublimation is secured, and a great saving of metal effected. There are blacksmiths' and carpenters' shops and a sawmill adjoining the furnaces.

Until recently all the ore was brought down from the mine packed on the backs of mules, a most costly system of transport as compared to the one now in use. The vegetation only suffers immediately round the chimney, and even there not to any alarming degree. The flue, being of great length, carried at a moderate slope up the hill, and terminating in a very tall chimney, completely condenses all mercurial and arsenical fumes. Before this flue and stack were constructed, even the mules and cattle grazing in the pastures died from the poisonous effects of the mercurial vapour; and its deadly action on vegetation was like that of the fabled upas-tree. The workmen now, as a rule, enjoy very good health, and are admirably cared for; the village boasts a capital hotel, and stages run daily to San José and San Francisco.

A spring of native soda-water, bubbling up in the centre of the village, protected and fitted like a drinking-fountain, is said to work wonders as a curative agent in all maladies arising from the effects of mercury. This spring is supposed to be under the especial care of a 'Saint Somebody,' a lady whose image, attired in very dirty finery, figures in niches cut in the rocks at the mine. No miner ever leaves or enters the mine without prostrating himself before this dirty effigy.

March 9th.—Return to San Francisco by road; dine at San Mateo, as lovely a spot as I ever gazed on. The grass is kneedeep, and the clumps of buck-eye (*Esculus flava*) and handsome oaks besprinkling the rounded hills and banks of the clear stream winding its way past the village to the Bay of San Francisco, like a lake glistening in the distance, reminded me of a park in fertile Devonshire. Completely shut in, and sheltered from the wind that blows nearly all the summer, withering up the vegetation exposed to its influence, everything round about this favoured spot grows in wild luxuriance. In the garden belonging to the roadside house, the summer flowers are in full bloom, and vegetables of all kinds in rare abundance, such as for size and quality equal anything Covent Garden Market can show.

The bay runs inland about forty miles, and the land on its shores is particularly fertile, and employed in great measure for dairy-farms and stock-ranches.

For the first time I gather the poison-oak (*Rhus toxicodendron*), a pretty plant, that climbs by rootlets, like the ivy, and trails gracefully over both rocks and trees. Some persons are most seriously affected by it, especially such as are of fair complexion, if they only venture near where it grows. It produces swelling about the eyes, dizziness, and fever; the poisonous effects are most virulent when the plant is bursting into leaf. I picked, examined, and walked amidst the trees over which it twined thickly, but experienced not the slightest symptoms of inconvenience. Still, I know others that suffer whenever they come near it. Where the poison-oak thrives, there too grows a tuber known to the settlers as Bouncing Bet, to the botanist as *Saponaria officinalis*, the common soapwort. The tuber is filled with a mucilaginous juice which, having the property of entangling air when whisked up, makes a lather like soap. This lather is said to be an unfailing specific against the effects of the poison-oak—the poison and its antidote growing side by side!

CHAPTER IX.

SACRAMENTO — STOCKTON — CALIFORNIAN GROUND-SQUIRRELS — GRASS VALLEY—STAGE TRAVELLING—HYDRAULIC WASHINGS—NEVADA—MARYSVILLE—UP THE SACRAMENTO RIVER TO RED BLUFFS—A DANGEROUS BATH.

March 10th.—At San Francisco this morning a friend took me to see the 'What Cheer House,' a very large hotel, supported by gold-miners, where they make up six hundred beds, every lodger having a small room to himself, with marble wash-stand, looking-glass, and dressing-table. Each story shuts off from the next by fireproof doors, and the water is forced to the top of the house, where there are hoses, fire-buckets, and axes enough to fit out a fire-brigade. A large steam-engine is the cook's assistant, doing everything that hands usually do; it kneads the bread, rolls the dough, drives the roasting gear, grinds coffee, peals apples and potatoes, beats the eggs (twelve hundred dozen a week), washes, irons, dries, and mangles the clothes; heats the water for the bathing-houses, which are perfect in every detail; does all the pumping, and cleans the knives.

Adjoining the dining-room is a well-selected library, general reading-room, and museum, containing a capital collection of stuffed birds, and other useful objects of Natural History. The rate each miner pays is five dollars, equal to 1*l.* per week: this includes eating and drinking. The house is strictly a temperance one, no fermented liquor being allowed within it.

Wandering about San Francisco would be much more enjoyable, if the hills were less steep, and the wind, which is everlastingly blowing, freighted with fine sand, that finds its way into your very watchcase, could be stilled.

March 11*th.*—Steaming across the bay in a white steamer called the 'Eclipse,' propelled by the largest paddlewheels I ever saw. We are en route to Sacramento, which we reach late at night.

March 12*th.*—Strolled about. Hardly believe so vast a place can have grown up in ten years. I think I like it better than San Francisco. The streets running east and west are marked by numbers—1*st* street, 2*nd* street, and so on; those having a north and south bearing by letter, as—*A* street, *B* street, &c. Received a telegram from the Commissioner, who had just reached

San Francisco on his return from England, to join him.

Nothing material occurs in my journal until

March 23rd.—I am at the Webber House in Stockton, a very pretty city, built on what the Americans call a *slew*, or, in other words, a muddy arm of the San Joaquin river. The country round is perfectly flat, but fertile beyond description. To obtain water the inhabitants have only to bore an augur-hole about nine feet in depth, when it bubbles up like a fountain. In nearly every garden is a tiny windmill, employed to irrigate the peach-orchards and general crops. Hear of 700 mules that have just arrived from Salt Lake city.

March 24th.—Drive out in a buggy to the mule ranch. The country very bare of timber, but thickly covered with grass. Every hillock, I observe, is burrowed like a rabbit-warren by the Californian ground-squirrel (*Spermophilus Beechyii*). I am told that it is next to impossible to drive out or exterminate these most destructive pests; entire fields of young wheat are cleared off by them, as if mowed down; gardens are invaded, and a year's labour and gain destroyed in a single day. Trapping, shooting, and strychnine have failed to accomplish the work of extinction. Farmers often flood entire districts, 'to drown out the darned cusses!' Their habits are strictly diurnal; and pretty lively little fellows they are, scampering off to their holes on the approach of danger, where they sit up on their hind-legs, peering curiously at the intruder. You may come very near now: there is a safe retreat behind, and he knows it. When too close, however, for safety's sake, the squirrel gives a shrill defiant whistle, like the laugh of a sprite, and dashes into its burrow.

Purchased twenty-one mules, at 150 dollars per head; the others were team-mules, and too large for pack animals. My mules are to remain on the ranch until I have completed my other purchases.

March 25th.—Cross in the stage from Stockton to Sacramento, a distance of about forty miles, through a country fertile in the extreme. Wild flowers, in endless variety of colour, decked the grass-land. The hawthorn, white with blossom, perfumes the air; and the waving green cornfields contrast pleasantly with the foliage of the oaks and chestnuts scattered about in graceful clumps. We change horses at Woodbridge, Fugit Ranch, and Elk Grove, and at four o'clock pull up at the St. George's Hotel, Sacramento.

March 26th.—I am again on the road, this time bound to Grass Valley. A clumsy railway with *cars*, or carriages, like the yellow caravans giants, dwarfs, and wise pigs travel in, bumps me out to Fulsome, about thirty miles off. Here I am hustled into a stage, without a chance of seeing anything but mud, in which the horses are standing knee-deep.

This stage is different from any I have seen; loops, straps, and other contrivances, clearly meant to hold on by, evidence an inequality of motion and tendency to upset that give rise to disagreeable forebodings. Constructed to hold nine inside, the centre seat swings like a *bale* dividing horses in a stable, and being somewhat rounded and padded, looks very like it. Five passengers seat themselves. I have hardly time to look at them, when a loud cracking of whips, several voices yelling 'Hi! git up!' 'Hi! git along!' and a sudden jerk sends me upon the *bale* —a general splash and scramble—and we are off!

We do the first ten miles with a bearable amount of jolting, and stop to change horses. The five insiders get out, and we take a nip at the roadside house, or what would be such if there were any roads. I observe four most perverse, obstinate, wild-looking horses being cautiously fastened to the stage; they are clearly uneducated—'wild mustangs' one of the insiders called them. They are held tightly. 'All aboard, boys?' says the driver (they call him *Mose*)—in we scramble—bang slams the door—and with an awful lurch away we go! Now I can understand the suspicious-looking machinery, designed, on the principle of life-buoys, for stage-tossed travellers to cling to. Holding on to these we swing along as hard as the beasts can gallop.

I am told by a fellow-passenger that unless the 'mustangs start at a gallop, they either upset the stage, or kick themselves clear of the harness.' On this journey they were agreeable enough to gallop off, so we escaped the two contingencies. Several times *Mose* shouted, 'Get out, boys, and hang on awhile.' I discover that this means that we are to cling to the side of the stage, that our united weight may prevent its capsizing, when going along the side of a slope like the slant of a housetop.

Near dark we are requested by 'Mose' to walk up the last hill. A tall sallow man, with a face hollow and sunken, closely shaven, except a tuft at the chin, steps along with me, and we reach the top of the hill a good time before the stage. We are standing amidst some scrubby timber.

The long shadows of the trees are swallowed up in the gathering gloom, the music of the forest has died away, and, save the wind sighing through the leafy foliage, everything is still. My companion draws nearer. 'Stranger,' he began, in a voice that appeared to come from his boots, and get out at his nose, 'jist war we are standin', three weeks agone, a tarnation big grizzly come slick upon two men, jist waitin' for the stage, as we are; chawed up one, and would a gone in for t'other, but he made tall travellin' for the stage. When they came up Ephraim had skedaddled, and they never see him or old Buck-eye arter.'

This is refreshing! I hope if 'old Ephraim' does come, he may eat my tough companion. The stage came, but the bear did not. We reach our destination at 8 p.m.: how sore I am!

March 27th.—A good sleep has worked wonders. I find Grass Valley a romantic little mountain town, about 2,200 feet above the sea-level, on the western slope of the Sierra Nevada, owing its existence entirely to gold-mining. Visited Mr. A.'s mill—a magnificent quartz-crusher. Nine stamp-heads, each 900 lbs. in weight, are worked by one of Watts' engines. The fine-dust gold is collected on blankets, or bullocks' hides with the hair on, over which the water washes it, as it comes from the stamp-heads. Some of the most productive gold deposits in California were discovered in and about this quaint little place. I descend a shaft 240 feet deep. The gold is distributed through the mud and silt of what was clearly an ancient river-bed.

March 28th.—Ride on horseback to Nevada and Hunt's Hill. Nevada is a clean pretty *city*, with gay shops, brightly-painted houses, and planked streets. Near it are the famed hydraulic washings. The gold is disseminated through terraces of shingle conglomerates, often three hundred feet in thickness. These terraces are actually washed entirely off the face of the country, by propelling jets of water against them, forced under great pressure through a nozzle. To accomplish this, the water is brought in canals, tunnels, and wooden aqueducts, often forty miles away from the drift. This supply of water the miners rent.

As we near the washing-spot, in every direction immense hose, made of galvanized iron, and canvas tubes six feet round, coil in all directions over the ground, like gigantic serpents, converging towards a gap, where they disappear. On reaching this gap, I look down into a basin, or dry lake, 300 feet below me. The hose hangs down this cliff of shingle, and following its course by a zigzag path, I reach a plateau of rock, from which the shingle has already been washed. A man stands at the end of each hose, that has for its head a brass nozzle. With the force of cannon-shot water issues, in a large jet, from this tube ; and propelled against the shingle, guided by the men, washes it away, as easily as we could broom a molehill from off the grass.

The stream of water, bearing with it the materials washed from out the cliff, runs through wooden troughs called 'flumes,' floored with granite; these flumes extend six miles. Men are stationed at regular distances to fork out the heavy stones. Throughout its entire length transverse strips of wood dam back a tiny pond of mercury; these are called *riffles*—gold-traps, in other words—that seize on the fine-dust gold distributed throughout the shingle. The 'flumes' are cleaned about once a month, and the gold extracted from the mercury. Masses of wood occur, in every stage of change, from that of pure silica to soft asbestiform material, and pure carbon.

I am strongly disposed to think this immense hollow must have been the rocky shore of an inlet or a lagoon; the rocks underlying the shingle have all the appearance, when denuded by the washing, of sea-wear. I try with a powerful lens to detect gold amidst the material they are washing, but not a trace is discoverable, and yet it pays an immense profit to the gold-washers.

Hunt's Hill is a timbered mountain, about 3,500 feet in altitude. Washing its base is the Greenhorn river, on the banks of which some very rich gold-washings are carried on, as well as at Bear Creek, on the opposite slope of the ridge. Clothing the hill, towering high above the shanties of the miners, the sugar and nut-pines wave lazily; the immense cones of the latter, plentifully besprinkling the ground, afford a feast to the Indians and lesser rodent mammals.

March 29th.—Return to Marysville. Visited another hydraulic washing at Timbuctoo, on the Yuba river, much the same as that seen at Nevada. Marysville is about the third best city in California, situated on the bank of the Feather river, which is rapidly filling up, from the immense quantity of material brought down from the hydraulic washings. A single peach-orchard I visited was 200 acres, all fenced, and the trees in beautiful health; from it, I am told,

80,000 dollars were returned in a single year by the sale of the peaches.

I commence my journal again on

April 24th.—I am in the 'Victor' steamboat, a small crank flat-bottomed affair, pushed against the current by a huge stern-wheel—an ugly appendage, but very effective in navigating swift shallow streams. I am bound for Red Bluffs, 275 miles above Sacramento. Pass the exits of the Yuba and Feather rivers, and change the yellow muddy water for the pure sparkling stream fresh from the mountain.

April 25th. — Starting again—the 'Victor' having been fastened up all night, tethered to a tree, as one would tie up his horse—the scenery, as we wend along the sinuous course of the stream, rapidly changes its character. The banks get steep, and sharp hills take the place of the flat lands behind us. Wild grape-vines hang in clustering tangles of green luxuriance from the branches of the ilex, oak, and arbutus, forming a continuous arcade over the water.

The Bluffs are reached. A straggling town, built on a high bank beetling over the Sacramento river, peeps out, from amidst some tall trees. Men, women, children, and dogs are crowding down, marching like ants from a hill towards a recent discovery of eatables. The banks are red, the soil is red, and the houses are built of red brick —Red Bluffs, a proper and appropriate name.

Land, and put up at —— House, not remarkable for anything but dirt and discomfort.

April 26th.—Purchase 59 mules, with a complete pack and equipment. My mules and men, that I had sent by land from Stockton, arrive. Hire two additional hands, and order the provisioning for my intended trip.

April 27th.—Mules and men need rest; breakfast over.

'Now, Cap'en,' says mine host, as I was debating whether it would be wiser to remain quietly at home, and enjoy a thoroughly idle day, or join the hunters, 'I calkilate we've got to worry out this day somehow. S'pose we take a ride over to the Tuscan Springs. It's a mighty strange place, you bet your life; they say it's right over the devil's kitchen, and when he's tarnation hot, he comes up and pops out his head to get a taste of fresh air. The very water comes risin' up a-bilin', and the pools flash into flame like powder, if you put fire near 'um.'

'Why, Major,' I replied, 'it is the place of all others I should enjoy seeing. How far is it?'

'Waal, it ain't over ten mile, but a mighty bad road at that.—Here, Joe, saddle up, and bring round two mustangs.'

The mustangs are small compact horses, seldom exceeding fourteen-and-a-half hands in height, descended from Spanish stock, originally brought into Mexico on its conquest by the Spaniards. They run wild in large herds on the grassy prairies in California and Texas, and are just lassoed when needed. I may perhaps mention, *en passant*, that a lasso is from thirty to forty feet long, and made of strips of raw hide plaited together. When a mustang is to be caught, an experienced hand always keeps the herd to windward of him; sufficiently near he circles the lasso round his head, and with unerring certainty flings it over the neck of the horse he has selected.

The end of a lasso being made fast to a ring in the saddle, as soon as the horse is captured, the rider turns his steed sharp round, and gallops off, dragging the terrified and choking animal after him. The terrible noose becomes tighter and tighter, pressing on the windpipe, until, unable to offer further resistance, the panic-stricken beast rolls in agony, half suffocated, on the prairie. Never after this does the horse forget the lasso—the sight of it makes him tremble in every limb.

I have seen the most wild and vicious horses rendered gentle and docile in a minute, by simply laying the lasso on the neck behind the ears.

The breaking-in is a very simple affair: while the animal is down the eyes are bandaged, and a powerful Spanish bit placed in the mouth. This accomplished, he is allowed to get up, and the saddle is firmly 'synched.' The saddles commonly used in California differs very little from those used in Mexico. The stirrups are cut out from a block of wood, allowing only the point of the toe to be inserted; they are set far back, and oblige the rider to stand rather than sit in the saddle. One girth only is used, styled a 'synch,' made of horsehair, and extremly wide; no buckles or stitching is used, but all is fastened with strips of raw hide. Everything being complete, the rider fixes himself firmly in the saddle, and leaning forward jerks off the blind; it is now an open question who is to have the best of it. If the man succeeds in sitting on the mustang until he can spur him into a gallop, his wildness is soon taken out of him, and one or two more lessons complete the breaking.

Joe by this time had made his appearance with the mustangs. Mounting, away we went at a raking gallop!

I know no exercise half as exhilarating and exciting as the 'lope,' a kind of long canter, the travelling pace of a mustang; there is no jarring or jolting. All one has to do is to sit firmly in the saddle; the horse, obeying the slightest turn of the wrist or check of the rein, swings along for hours at a stretch, without any show of weariness.

Having crossed the Sacramento in a 'scow,' a kind of rough ferry-boat, our road lay over broad plains and through scattered belts of timber. The grass was completely burnt up, and the series of gravelly arroyos, in and out of which we continually plunged and scrambled, marked clearly the course of the winter streams.

The air felt hot and sultry, but fragrant with the perfume of the mountain cudweed. Not a cloud was visible in the lurid sky, and the distant mountains, thinly dotted with timber, seemed softened and subdued as seen through the blue haze. We entered a valley leading through a pile of volcanic hills that one could easily have imagined had been once the habitat of civilised man. The wooded glades had all the appearance of lawns and parks planted with exquisite taste; the trees, in nothing resembling the wild growth of the forest, were grouped in every variety of graceful outline.

On either side the hills were covered with wild oat as thick as it could grow; its golden-yellow tints, contrasting with the dark glossy-green of the cypress, the oak, and the manzanata, had an indescribably charming effect. As we advanced the valley gradually narrowed, until it became a mere *cañon* (the Spanish for funnel), shut in by vast masses of rock that looked like heaps of slag and cinder—bare, black, and treeless. A small stream of bitter, dark, intensely salt water trickled slowly through the gorge.

Following a rough kind of road, that led up the base of the hills for about two miles, we entered what I imagine was the crater of an extinct volcano; nearly circular, about a mile in diameter, and shut in on every side by columnar walls of basalt. There was a weird desolation about the place that forcibly reminded me of the Wolf's Glen in Der Freischütz—a fit haunt for Zamiel! Scarce a trace of forest-life was to be seen, not a tree or flower; everything looked scorched and cinderous, like the *débris* of a terrible fire, and smelt like a limekiln on a summer-night. A long narrow house, resembling a cattle-shed, stood in the centre of this circle.

'Waal, Cap'en, I guess we've made the ranch anyhow,' said the Major, as we drew up at the door of this most uninviting-looking establishment. 'A mighty tall smell of brimstone,' he further added, 'seems coming up from "Old Hoof's" stove-pipe. Calkilate he's doing a tallish kind of dinner below.'

I had no time to reply, ere the host, owner, and general manager of the Tuscan Springs made his appearance. 'How's your health, Doctor?' inquired the Major. 'I've brought up Cap'en —— to have a peep at your location; he's mighty curious about these kind of diggins.'

'Waal, Cap'en,' said the Doctor, in a long drawling voice, 'I am glad to see you. I raither guess you don't see such nat'ral ready-made places, for curin' jist every sickness, in the old country as we have in California.—Here, boy, put up the mustangs: and now step in, and I'll tell old aunty to scramble up some eggs and bacon, and then we can take a look round the springs.'

Aunty was a quaint specimen of the feminine gender, not at all suggestive of the gentler sex. Her features were small, but sharply cut. She was bent naturally, but not from age, and reminded me of a witch. One would not have felt at all astonished at seeing her mount a broomstick, and start on an aërial trip over the burnt-up rocks. But all honour to her skill as a cook,—she did her fixings admirably!

During dinner I had ample time to take stock of Doctor Ephraim Meadows. His face would have been a fortune as a study to a painter; his forehead high but narrow, his eyebrows thick, bushy, and overhanging; his hair would have joined his eyebrows, had not a narrow line of yellow skin formed a kind of boundary between them. Peering out from beneath his shaggy hair were two little twinkling, restless grey eyes, more roguish than good-natured. His nose, crooked and sharp, was like the beak of a buzzard; with thin dry lips that shut in a straight line, which told in pretty plain language he could be resolute and rusty if need be. The tip of his chin, bent up in an easy curve, was covered with a yellowish beard, that had been guiltless of comb or shears for many a day. His nether limbs were clad in leather never-mention-ums, kept up by a wide belt, from which dangled a six-shooter. A red shirt, with an immense collar that reached the point of the shoulders, and a dirty jean jacket completed his costume.

Our meal over, we started out to see the wonders of the doctor's establishment. The house or hospital, as he designated it, was a long frame-building, divided into numerous small rooms, all opening on a kind of platform that extended the entire length of the building; and sheltered overhead by a rough kind of verandah. A camp-bed, wash-basin, and stool constituted the furniture of each apartment. Four sickly-looking men were walking feebly up and down the platform. These, the Doctor assured me, were giants now as compared to what they had been ere they stumbled on the Tuscan Springs and his water-cure.

The springs are about ten in number, but not all alike. In some of them, the water rises at a temperature near to boiling, and densely impregnated with sulphuretted hydrogen-gas, perfectly poisoning the air with a most insufferable stench. In others, again, the waters bubble up tepid, but bitter and saline. From two of them, that widen into pools, gas (I imagine some compound of hydrogen) rises constantly to the surface; and when I applied a match to the water, a sudden flash lighted up the pool for a second or two, and this could be repeated at intervals of three or four minutes. This gas, by a simple contrivance, is collected and conveyed into a small shanty, dignified with the name of 'Steam Bath,' the gas being used to heat the water from one of the springs so as to fill a small room with steam.

It is one of the most singular and interesting places I have ever visited. There can be no doubt that the springs rise from the crater of an extinct volcano, and that there is some active volcanic action still going on in the depths below. Incrustations of various salts and sulphur covered the edges of the pools and rocks over which the water runs. The water they drink has to be brought from a spring the other side of the encircling hills.

Although at this place I observed more direct evidence of some great internal fire or subterranean laboratory, in which Nature is ever transforming the elemental forms of crude matter into available materials for the supply of organic life; still throughout Oregon and California I have constantly come across similar sulphurous and saline eruptions, particularly soda-water springs, where the water rises through the earth, thoroughly impregnated with carbonic-acid gas. At Nappa, not far from San Francisco, native soda-water is collected and bottled at the springs for the supply of the San Francisco market. Olympian nectar was never more grateful to the thirsty gods, than is this soda-water to the hot, parched, and thirsty hunter!

The Doctor had many strange and wild theories about these springs, and evidently entertained a lively belief in their close proximity to his Satanic Majesty's kitchen.

'Cap'en,' said the doctor, 'I calkilate you ain't a-goin' home without just tryin' a bath?'

I at first declined. I did not feel at all ill, and as I bathed every day grudged the trouble of undressing. It was of no use—the Major joined the Doctor; persuasion failing, mild force was hinted at if I did not comply. I was led, or rather hustled, into the bathing-house. In one corner of this dismal-looking shed was an immense square tray, and over it was a most suspicious-looking contrivance, like the rose of a giant's watering-pot. I shuddered, for I knew I should be held in that tray, and deluged from the terrible nozzle.

My miseries commenced by my being seized on by two brawny attendants (the bathers), and literally peeled like an onion, rather than undressed. This completed, a small door that I had not noticed before was opened, and disclosed a kind of cupboard, about six feet square. A flap of board was raised by an attendant, and supported by a bracket; a contrivance one frequently sees in small kitchens to economise room. On this I was laid; my janitors withdrew, the door slammed, and I was alone in the dark.

A sudden noise, between a hiss and a whistle, enlightened me as to the fact, that sundry jets of steam were turned on. The room rapidly filled, and the perspiration soon streamed from my skin. At first I fancied it rather pleasant; a sort of lazy sleepy feeling came over me, but as this passed away I felt faint and thirsty, and yelled to be let out. No reply. I began to think it anything but a joke, and again shouted: not a sound but the hissing steam.

My thirst grew insupportable; it seemed as if a live crab was gnawing and rending my stomach with his claws and nippers. I made several attempts to get off the table, but wherever I put my leg the burning-hot steam came like a flame against it, and there was not sufficient room to stand betwixt the table and the partition of my steam-prison. I called louder and louder; my reasoning powers were growing feeble, my presence of mind was rapidly abandoning me, and a thousand wild fancies passed through my brain; I had given up all hope, when

I saw a gleam of light. I have a vague remembrance of being dragged out, plunged into cold water, and savagely rubbed with a kind of hempen rasp.

As I became quite conscious of what was going on, I was partly dressed, and lying on the grass, the Doctor and the Major standing close by, the bathers rubbing my hands and feet; whilst Aunty, squatted on a log, was holding a cup containing some steaming mixture.

'O Doctor!' I said, as well as I could articulate, 'a little more, and you would have had to bury me; I was nearly gone!'

'Waal, Cap'en, I kind of guess you must have had a near shave for life, but it warn't meant nohow. You see the Major and me just strolled up to take a peep at the mustangs, and the darned brutes stampeded, breaking clean out of the "corral," and went past the bath-house like mad. The boys see 'em, and hearin' us a-hollerin', made tracks right after 'em, and never thought about your bein' a-steamin'. Old Aunty, by sheer luck, heard you a-screamin' and a-snortin', and it mighty nigh skeert the old woman to death, for she thought "Old Hoof" was a-bilin' himself. Up she came a-tearin' and a-shriekin' that somethin' unearthly was in the steam-room. "Thunder and grizzlys," says the Major, "the boys have forgot the Cap'en, and gone right after the mustangs!" You'd better believe we soon had you out, and you ain't none the worse for it, thank Providence!'

The combined powers of Aunty's mixture and the Major's whisky-flask rapidly restored me. The villanous mustangs—the cause of my mishap—were caught and saddled. Danger past is lightly thought of, and we enjoyed a hearty laugh as the Major quaintly told the story at the Bluffs of the Cap'en's bath at the Tuscan Springs.

CHAPTER X.

THE START FROM RED BLUFFS—MISHAPS BY THE WAY—DEVIL'S POCKET—ADVENTURE AT YREKA—FIELD-CRICKETS—THE CALIFORNIAN QUAIL—SINGULAR NESTING OF BULLOCK'S ORIOLE.

April 28th.—My pack-train is completed, my provisions arranged for packing on the mules. I have eighty-one mules and a bell-horse. To manage mules without a horse carrying a bell round its neck is perfectly impossible. The bell-horse is always ridden ahead, and wherever it goes the mules follow in single file. (But of this and packing I shall have more to say further on.)

April 29th.—Sunday.

April 30th.—I have determined to find my way through Oregon by an unknown route; doing this, I shall reach the Commission at least two months earlier than by taking the ordinary mail-route to Portland.

Again and again I am warned of the risk not only of losing my mules and men, but my own scalp into the bargain. The country swarms with hostile Indians, many large streams have to be crossed, the trail is bad, if any; and altogether the prospect is anything but cheering. I have, however, made up my mind to go.

The annoyances of a start got over—wild mules reduced to a state of discipline, packs adjusted, and men as sober as could reasonably be expected—all went pleasant as a marriage-bell until the second day, when my first misfortune happened.

May 1*st.*—I camp on a beautiful bit of ground, with grass in abundance, and a stream, clear as crystal and cold as ice, rippling past close to my fire. I place a guard over my mules, fearing accidents; and choosing as level a spot as I can see, roll myself in my blanket, and with my head in my saddle soon slept.

I awoke at sun-up, lit my pipe, and wandered off to see what had become of my mules. I found the trusty guard sound asleep, coiled up under a tree, but not a mule. A sharp admonition, administered through the medium of my foot, soon dispelled his dreams, and awoke him to a lively sense of reality. He rapidly uncoiled, started up, stared vacantly around, and thus relieved his feelings:—

'I guess they're gone, Cap'en, every tarnation coon of 'em, right slick back to the Bluffs.'

I could have pistolled the rascal there and then, but the mules had to be recovered; so I bottled up my wrath, roused all my sleeping camp, and we started in pursuit of the missing culprits.

May 4th.—Three days have elapsed. I have got the mules together, but three are still absent. Again we started. I made a long march, crossing Cottonwood Creek, through Major Raddon's ranch — one of the finest in California for grazing — struck the Upper Sacramento, and camped about sundown on a creek called Stillwater.

May 5th.—In the night it came on a deluge of rain, that regularly soaked through everything; but it cleared towards morning, and we dried ourselves in the sun as we rode along.

The next three days we travelled through a beautiful parklike country, very lightly timbered, covered with grass, and thickly dotted with magnificent ranches (farms); we struck Pitt river on the fourth day, crossed it safely, swam the mules, and ferried over the packs.

May 9th.—Our journey for the first twelve miles lay through a narrow rocky gorge—the trail; simply a ledge of rock, barely wide enough for a mule to stand upon. Three hundred feet below rolled the river. The least mistake—a single false step, and over goes mule or man, as it may be, and you see the last of him.

Here I passed a most curious place called the Devil's Pocket; the trail winds along the very edge, and you peer down into an immense hollow kind of basin, that looks as if it had once been a lake, and suddenly dried up. The hills are lofty, sharply pointed, and capped with snow.

At the head of this gorge I, for the first time, saw an encampment of Digger Indians, and a more famished picture of squalid misery can hardly be imagined. Their wretched comfortless huts are like large molehills; there is a pit sunk in the ground, and a framework of sticks, shaped like a large umbrella arched, over it; old skins and pieces of bark are thrown over this frame, and the whole is covered with earth. The entrance is a hole, into which they creep like animals.

Their food consists principally of esculent roots of various kinds, which they dig during the summer months, and dry in the sun. The field-cricket (*Acheta nigra*) they also dry in large quantities, and eat them just as we do shrimps. Bread made from acorn-flour is also another important article of their diet. They seldom fish or hunt. Their arms are bows and arrows; their clothing, both male and female, simply a bit of skin worn like an apron; they are small in stature; thin, squalid, dirty, and degraded in appearance. In their habits little better than an ourang-outang, they are certainly the lowest type of savage I have ever seen.

We camped in the evening on a large plain called Big Flat.

May 10th.—It was bitterly cold all night, and froze sharply. We got off soon after sun-up, and literally crept along the side of a high range of mountains, densely wooded, and forming one side of the valley of the Sacramento, which has dwindled down into a mere mountain-burn. Here I came suddenly on a little colony of miners, engaged in gold-washing. I discovered the place was named Dogtown—the entire town consisting of a store, a grogshop, and a smithy. I paid twenty-five cents (a shilling) for a mere sip of the vilest poison I ever tasted, libellously called 'Fine Old Monongahela Whisky.' About six miles farther, still on the same trail, I came to another gold-claim, where there were no houses at all, called Portuguese Flat. Passed through some thin timber; camped on a lovely mountain-stream.

May 11*th*.—Shotgun Creek; my camp is on the side of a steep mountain, and, about a mile farther on, is another stream, Mary's Creek. Camped on this stream was a small pack-train, that had been with stores to some mining-station. I heard wolves barking and howling all night, and twice I drove them out of my camp with a fire-log. The next morning, as I passed the camp of the packers, they were in sad grief. The rascally wolves had pulled down one of their mules, and torn it almost to pieces. I rode up in the wood to see its mangled remains. The ravenous beasts must have fixed on its haunches, and ripped it up whilst it lived. I was sadly grieved for the poor beast that had come to so untimely an end, and for the man who had lost him—at least 30*l*. worth.

For two more days I followed up the course of the Sacramento, and crossed it for the last time. Standing at the ford, and looking straight up the valley, the scenery is wild and beautiful in the extreme; on either side sharp pinnacle-like rocks shoot up into all sorts of fantastic shapes, dotted with the sugar-pine, scrub-oak, and manzanata in front; and blocking up, as it were, the end of the valley, stood Mount Shasta, at this time covered to its base with snow.

This vast mountain is a constant landmark to the trappers, for it can be seen from an incredible distance, and stands completely isolated in the midst of the Shasta plains. I camped close to the very snow at its base, in a little dell called 'Strawberry Valley.' The next day reached the Shasta plains, and camped early in the day.

May 15*th*.—As I was to bid goodby to civilisation, and abandon all hopes of seeing aught but savages, after leaving this camp, and being by no means sure of the road, I made up my mind to ride into Yreka and obtain information about the Indians, and the state of the trails, and also (what was of equal importance) obtain a relay of provisions; the distance from my camp to the city was about thirty miles.

Yreka city is a small mining-station, situated on one side of the great Shasta plains; it stands quite away from law, society, and civilisation, gold being the magnet that attracts first the miner, and then the various satellites (jackals would be the more appropriate name) that follow his steps. I left the mules in charge of my packmaster, and started at sun-up. The ride was a most desolate affair, over an interminable sandy plain, without even a shrub or flower, much more a tree, to break the monotony. I reached Yreka about ten, and put up at the 'What Cheer House,' bespoke my bed, and ordered breakfast. The keen morning-air and a thirty-mile ride had made me perfectly ravenous, and I waged alarming havoc on the ham and eggs, fixings, and corn-dodgers, that, I must say, were admirable. The tea was not a success, being a remarkably mild infusion, very hot, and sweetened with brown sugar; but it washed down the solids, and the finest congou could not have done more.

Thus recuperated, I started off to call on Judge——, to whom I had a letter of introduction from my agents in San Francisco. It did not take long to find the Judge's quarters, the lanes, streets, and alleys being distinctions without any material differences. The mansion in which his judgeship 'roomed' was a small shanty, with a porch or verandah round it, to keep off the sun when it happened to be hot, and the wet when it rained. I knocked with my knuckles—no reply; tried again—still silence; resorted to the handle of my hunting-knife, anything but mildly—that did it.

'I raither calkilate, stranger, you'd better jist open that door; *I* ain't agwine to, you bet your boots.'

I opened it, and walked in. There sat Judge

—— in a large armchair, cleverly balanced on the two hind-legs. No, it was not sitting, or lying, or standing, or lounging; it was a posture compounded of all these positions. His (I mean Judge ——'s) legs were extended on a level with his nose, and rested on the square deal table before him. He was smoking an immense cigar, one half of which was stowed away in his cheek, rolled about, and chewed; whilst the other half protruded from the corner of his mouth, and reached nearly to his eye. A little distance from the Judge was an immense spittoon, like a young sponging-bath. He was 'whittling' a piece of stick with a pocket-knife, and looked the embodiment of supreme indifference. The chair he occupied and the table—whose only use, as far as I could see, was to rest his legs on—constituted the entire furniture.

The Judge himself was a long spare man, and gave me the idea of an individual whose great attribute consisted in possessing length without breadth or thickness; everything about him was suggestive of length. Beginning at his head, his hair was long, and his face was long, and his nose was long, and a long goatee-beard terminated the end of his chin; his arms were long, and his legs were long, and his feet were long; he had a long drawling utterance, and was inordinately long at arriving at a moderate pitch of civility. He eyed me over and drawled out, 'W-a-e-l!' I handed my letter, and quietly awaited its effect; as he was long in everything else, he was long in opening it. Having made a minute inspection of the exterior, he slowly took it from its yellow envelope, and gradually seemed to understand from its contents that he was to be civil.

'So you ain't bin long in these parts, Cap'en?' said the Judge, without in the smallest degree shifting his position.

I said I was quite a stranger, and should be glad if he would give me some information about the trails and the Indians, along the route I intended taking.

'Bars and steel traps!' roared the Judge. 'You'll have your har ris, sure as beaver medicine! Why, thar ain't worse redskins in all Oregon than the Klamaths. Jist three months agone come Friday, the darn'd skunks came right slick upon Dick Livingstone and his gang. You've heerd of Dick, I guess?' (I said I had not.) 'Wael, most people has, leastways. They was jist a-washing up a tall day's work, up Rogue river, when the Klamaths swarmed 'em just as thick as mosquitos in a swamp. Several went under, bet your life, for Dick and his boys warn't the ones to cave in. But 'twarn't no use; the reds jist crowded them clean down, and took the har off everyone of 'em. The trails, too, is awful soft. Mose Hart says—and he's now from Bogus Holler, whar you have to go—that a mule is jist sure to mire down a'most any place.'

'Well,' I said, 'your news is not by any means refreshing, Judge; nevertheless, I mean going.'

'Wael, Cap'en, maybe you 're right; makin' back-tracks ain't good, anyway; we are a go-ahead people, we are, and it won't pay to be skeerish, anyway. S'pose we go and take a drink, and I'll jist put you through the city; I guess I'm well posted about most things in these diggins.'

So we did the city, which did not take very much time to do; we did the stores, where every person, from the master to the errand-boy, did nothing but sit on the counter to chew, whittle, and spit. The amount of whittling done in this city is perfectly astounding; every post supporting the verandahs outside the stores and bar-rooms was whittled nearly through; some of them in two or three places. We did the bar-rooms, and did sundry drinks with divers people. I purchased provisions, hired a guide, took leave of the Judge (who was not half a bad fellow when you understood him), and retiring to my inn, determined to enjoy the luxury of a bed and a long night-in, having slept on the ground since leaving Red Bluffs; and if the Judge was right about the redskins, the chances were considerably against my ever stretching my limbs on another. So, to make the most of it—for a start at sun-up and a long ride, added to a tedious day, had pretty well fagged me—I retired very early, and turned in.

It really was a lovely bed, just like bathing in feathers. I stretched out my limbs until they fairly cracked again, and rolled in enjoyment. My thoughts were soon wandering; and visions of home, mixed up with mules falling over precipices, battles with Indians, an ugly feeling round the top of my head, judges, drinks, rowdies, all jumbled together in a ghostly medley—floated off in misty indistinctness, and I subsided into the land of dreams.

I awoke, with an indistinct idea that I was at a ball, with a jiggy kind of tune whirling through my brain. Pish! I must have been dreaming; so I turned over, and tugged the blankets more tightly round my shoulders, vexed that such a stupid dream should have awoke me. Hark! what on earth is that? 'Ladies and gents, take your places, salute your partners,'—then crash went two fiddles, crowding out a break-down. Again the voice—'Half right and left'—and off they went. The sounds of countless feet, scuffling rapidly over a floor, told me, in language not to be mistaken, that a ball was going briskly on very near my head.

I sat up, rubbed my eyes, took a long mournful yawn, and began to consider what had best be done. I discovered that a thin wooden partition only intervened betwixt my head and the ball-room; everything rattled to the jigging tune of the music and the dancers; the windows, the doors, the wash-crockery, the bed, all jigged; and I began to feel myself involuntarily nodding to the same measure, and jigging mentally like the rest. Shades of the departed! I could not stand this. Goodby bed, and feathers, and sleep! I may as well dance in reality as in imagination; and abandoning all my anticipated delights, dressed, and entered the ball-room.

It was a long room, lighted with candles hung against the wall in tin sconces; the company—if variety is charming—was perfect. The costumes, as a rule, were more suggestive of ease than elegance; scarlet shirts and buckskin 'pants' were in the ascendant. The boots as a rule, being of the species known as Wellingtons, were worn outside the trousers, inducing the latter indispensables to assume a bunchiness about the knees, not calculated to display the symmetry of the leg to advantage. Very few had any jackets on, but all, without exception, carried a bowie-knife and six-shooter in their waistbelts. The ladies' costumes were equally varied: most of them wore bright-coloured muslins, of very large patterns, and showy waist-ribbons, tied behind in a large bow, with streamers down to their heels.

The dance was just 'down' when I came into the room. I saw a few citizens I had met in the day, but each one seemed to have his 'fancy gal,' and any chance of getting an introduction was a vain hope. The fashion, I discovered afterwards, is either to bring or meet your partner at the ball-room, and dance with her, and her only, all the evening.

A waltz was called, and I wanted a partner. Looking round, I espied a lady sitting near the end of the room, who evidently had not got one. She was in the same place when I entered the room, and it was clear to me, by her unrumpled appearance, that she had not danced for the evening. 'Faint heart never won fair lady' might, I imagined, apply as forcibly to dancing as to wooing or fighting; if I am snubbed it won't be all the world, and I suppose I shall live it down —so here goes! Walking boldly up to her, I asked coolly, but rather apologetically, if she would try a waltz.

'Guess, stranger, I ain't a-fix'd up for waltzin.'

'Perhaps, madam,' I said, 'you will excuse me, although unknown to you, if I ask you to dance the next cotillon with me?'

Looking into my face with an expression half doubt, half delight, she said: 'Stranger, I'll have the tallest kind of pleasure in puttin' you right slick through a cotillon, for I've sot here, like a blue chicken on a pine-log, till I was like to a-grow'd to the seat.'

This satisfactorily arranged, I sat down by her side until the waltz finished, to have a good look at and trot out my new inamorata. She was a blonde beauty, with fair hair and light-grey eyes, that flashed and twinkled roguishly; and robed in some white material, with blue ribbons in her hair and round her waist—a mountain-sylph, that any wanderer in search of a partner would have deemed himself lucky to have stumbled on. Our conversation was rather discursive, until I discovered that home-politics, or rather the duties and requirements of a *gal t'hum*, was a never-failing spring from which to draw fresh draughts of household knowledge. At last the cotillon was called by the master of the ceremonies, and again I heard—'Take your places, salute your partners;' the fiddles started the same kind of jigging tune, and away we went.

A cotillon is a compound, complicated kind of dance, evidently constructed from the elements and fragments of many other dances: a good deal of quadrille, a strong taste of lancers, a flavour of polka and waltz—the whole highly seasoned with Indian war-dance. You never stand still, neither can you lounge and talk soft nothings to your partner—it is real, *bonâ fide*, downright, honest dancing. I soon discovered why the men left off their jackets: a trained runner could not have stood it in clothing. My jacket and waistcoat soon hung on a peg, and, red-shirted like the rest, I footed it out gallantly.

My partner was a gem, with the endurance of a ballet-girl in pantomime time. How many cotillons we got through I never clearly remembered; but we danced on, till the grey morning light, stealing in through the windows, warned the revellers that Old Sol was creeping from behind the eastern hills, and that the day, with all its cares and toils, was near at hand once more.

My fair partner positively refused to allow me to see her home. Being a casual acquaintance and not a lover, I suppose, of course, that it was highly proper on her part. I thanked her sincerely, for I really felt grateful to her for enabling me to dance away a night that I had destined for a long luxurious repose. With a hearty 'good-night' we parted, never to meet again.

It was a glorious morning—the air cool and fresh, the sky unflecked by a single cloud. The sun was just tipping the hilltops with rosy light, and peeping slily into the valleys, as I wandered out to think over my strange adventure. My way led by chance up the back of the street, and out by a little stream to the gold-washings. Early as it was, all was bustle and activity. Many of my friends of the ball were now wresting the yellow ore from its hiding-places, the anticipation of gold dispelling all sense of fatigue. The want of water is a great drawback to these diggings. So valuable is it, that it has been brought by a small canal a distance of thirty miles, and is rented by the miners at so much a cubic foot.

I lingered here some time, for there is much to see, then turned my steps towards my inn through the city.

'Say—Cap'en—here—hold on!'

I turned, and saw a man in a one-horse dray, whipping up his horse, and violently gesticulating for me to stop. He soon came up, and jumping out of the dray, seized my hand, and shook it with a grip that made my very eyes water.

'Guess you ain't acquainted with this child?'

I said no; I had not the pleasure of knowing him.

'I spotted you, Cap'en, just as soon as ever I seed you making tracks down the street. My gal Car'line told me how she put you through all the dance last night.'

It suddenly flashed upon me that the drayman was my partner's papa. Here's a lively affair! If he does not ask me my intentions, and riddle me with a six-shooter if I refuse to marry his 'gal' at once, I shall deem myself the most fortunate of men. I civilly said, in reply, that I found his daughter a most admirable partner.

'I rather guess you did, Cap'en; she's all watch-spring and whalebone, she is; can't skeer up a smarter gal than "Car" in these parts, if you was to do your darndest. She! why, she's worth her weight in nuggets to the man as gets her.'

I felt cold all over—I thought it was coming. 'You must excuse me,' I said; 'my breakfast is waiting, and I daresay we shall meet again.' (I knew this was an awful twister.)

'I'm sure we shall, Cap'en. Let's licker:' so we adjourned to the nearest bar-room and took an 'eye-opener,' and so I escaped from the drayman. I drew a deep breath, and felt as if I had got clear from the claws of a grisly bear—made for the inn as fast as I could, gobbled up a hasty breakfast, packed up my goods, and with my guide started for my camp.

Often I turned and gazed anxiously over the plain, expecting I should see the drayman, his daughter Caroline, and a priest in hot pursuit; and there and then, on the Shasta plains, I should be, *nolens volens*, linked to my fair-haired partner, for a life's cotillon!

Such was my first, and such was my last, my only night in Yreka! 'All's well that ends well,' and I trust the fair Caroline has as pleasant a remembrance of the Cap'en as he has of her!

I found my camp all right, saddled up, and am off on my perilous journey through the wilds of Oregon. The Shasta plains are vast sandy flats, half prairie, half desert, sparsely covered with withered grass, and not a bush or tree or shrub, as far as the eye could wander, had struggled into life. 'Tis true a stunted artemisia, or wild-sage bush, had fought its way inch by inch in its struggle for existence, and looked so old, dry, and parched, that your idea was, if you laid a finger on it, it would powder up like dried herbs; but whatever had been in shape of grass, or herb, or shrub, was gone, cleared bodily and entirely away by the field-crickets.

Never shall I forget this insect array. On getting well upon the plains, I found every inch of ground covered with field-crickets; they were as thick on the ground as ants on a hill; the mules could not tread without stepping on them; not an atom or vestige of vegetation remained, the ground as clear as a planed floor. It was about twenty good long miles to the next water, and straight across the sand-plains, and, for that entire distance, the crickets were as thick as ever. It is impossible to estimate the quantity; but when you suppose a space of ground twenty-seven miles long, and how wide I know not, but at least twice that, covered with crickets as thick as they could be packed, you can roughly imagine what they would have looked like if swept into a heap.

It was long after sundown when we reached the water, tired, thirsty, and utterly worn-out;

but the stream being wide and swift, the crickets had not crossed it, so our tired animals had a good supper, and we a comfortable camp. I rode off to some farm-enclosures I saw, in search of milk and eggs; and, to my great surprise, I noticed every field had a little tin-fence inside the *snake* or *rail* fence, about six or eight inches wide, nailed along on a piece of lumber, placed edgeways in the ground, so that a good wide ledge of tin projected towards the prairie.

'What,' I said to the first farmer I met, 'induces you to put this tin affair round your field?'

'Why, stranger, I guess you ain't a-travelled this way much, or you'd be pretty tall sure that them darned blackshirts out on the prairie would eat a hoss and chase the rider. But for that bit of a tin-fixin' thar, they'd mighty soon make tracks for my field, and just leave her clean as an axe-blade. These critters come about once in four years, and a mighty tall time they have when they do come!'

It was a most effectual and capital contrivance to keep them out, for if they came underneath the tin they jumped up against it, and it was too wide to leap over. These field-crickets (*Acheta nigra*) are black, and very much larger than the ordinary house-cricket. They eat seeds, grass, fruit, and, when they can get nothing else, they devour each other. I frequently got off my horse to see what a large mob of crickets were about. They had dragged down, perhaps, two or three others, and were one and all deliberately tearing them to pieces. If they meet head to head, they rush at each other and butt like rams, but, backing against each other, they lash out their hind-legs and kick like horses. What becomes of them when they die I cannot imagine; the entire atmosphere for miles must become pestilential. I suppose, from their coming in such vast numbers every fourth year, that the larvæ must take that time ere they assume the perfect shape.

May 16th.—The Californian quail, which I found most plentiful along the course of the Sacramento, ceases at the edge of this great sandy desert; it appears to be the limit to its northern range. I note a singular instance, how curiously and readily birds alter their usual habits under difficulties, in the nesting of Bullock's Oriole. A solitary oak stood by the little patch of water, a spring that oozed, rather than bubbled, through the sandy soil where my camp stood; it was the only water within many miles, and the only tree too; every available branch and spray had one of the woven nests of this brilliant bird hanging from it. I have never seen them colonise elsewhere. The nests are usually some distance from each other, and concealed amidst thick foliage.

CHAPTER XI.

CROSSING THE KLAMATH RIVER—HOW TO SWIM MULES—SIS-KY-OUE INDIANS—EMIGRANT FORD — TROUT BALING — A BEAVER TOWN—BREEDING-GROUNDS OF THE PELICANS AND VARIOUS WATER-BIRDS—PURSUED BY KLAMATH INDIANS—INTERVIEW WITH CHIEF—THE DESERT PRONG-HORNED ANTELOPES—ACORNS AND WOODPECKERS—YELLOW-HEADED BLACKBIRDS—SNAKE SCOUT—ARRIVAL AT CAMP OF COMMISSION—END OF JOURNAL.

May 17th.—Leave this sandy waste, cross over a low divide, and descend into a narrow gulley, named Bogus Hollow. Creep along between high craggy peaks for ten miles to reach the Klamath river, a wide, rapid stream that I have to cross, but how, just now is a puzzler. The banks are high; not a tree grows along its sides, or near by, wherewith to make either canoe or raft. I follow on its course for eight miles; the river makes a sudden bend, and in the angle on the opposite side I can see the charred remains of a log-shanty, amidst a clump of trees, one of which has been felled so as to fall across the river, and forms a rude footbridge. We unpack the mules, carry all the packing-gear and provisions on our own backs to the other side, an operation requiring steady heads and sure feet, the footway a single tree, and not even a handrail to steady the crosser. All safely over, and no mishap.

The next operation is to swim the mules, a very simple process if properly managed; a risky and dangerous one if due precautions are neglected. The strength of the current must be estimated, so that the mules may be driven up-stream far enough, to ensure their not being washed farther down the opposite side, than where you are desirous they should land, and the place selected for them to land should always have a shelving shore. Supposing you have a canoe, the bell-horse, deprived of his bell, is towed by the canoe across the stream; a packer, standing in the canoe, keeps ringing the bell violently; the mules, that have followed their leader to the edge of the stream, are prevented galloping along the river-bank by the packers; at last, in sheer despair, they dash into the water and swim towards the clanging bell; nothing can be seen but long ears and noses, or heard save the tinkling bell, the splashing water, and a medley of snorts, ranging from a shrill whistle to a sound compounded of creak and groan, gasped from the older, asthmatical, short-winded mules. If we have no canoe, the bell-horse is ridden into the water; when the rider feels the horse begins to swim, he grasps the mane with his left hand, floats from off the horse's back, swims with his legs as in ordinary swimming, whilst with the right he splashes the water against the horse's face, thus keeping the animal's head always up-stream. On reaching the opposite side, when the horse's feet touch the ground, the man again drops astride, and rides it out, ringing the all-potent bell with all his might.

I learn from my guide that a settler 'squatted' where we cross about a year before, built the shanty, made the footbridge, and put in some grain-crops; but the Indians discovered, killed, and scalped him, burnt his shanty, and carried his wife away prisoner—not a cheering story, considering I am going through their very strongholds.

May 18th.—A sharp frosty morning; very cold, sleeping in the open air. Get away soon after sun-up. Leave the flat grassy valley, and ascend the timbered slopes of the Sis-ky-oue mountains. Follow a bad Indian trail, through barren gorges, and along rocky ledges, for twenty miles; observe lots of deer-tracks, but no deer. Descend the northern slope, arrive at the Emigrant's Ford, and come plump upon a large encampment of Sis-ky-oue Indians. Fifteen miles to the next water; the sun rapidly sinking; men and mules tired. At all risks, I camp near the redskins.

The Emigrant Ford is a wide lake-like expanse of the Klamath river, that spreads out over a level plateau on emerging from a basaltic gorge, through which the river finds its way for some distance. The walls of rock shutting it in being deep and almost vertical, reaching the water in the cañon is an impossibility. As the river widens out it shallows sufficiently for ox-teams and waggons to get through it; and, being almost the only fordable place, was always chosen by emigrant trains coming to Oregon and California.

The remains of half-burnt waggons and human bones still bleaching in the sun, makes one shudder to think of the terrible fate of the weary wanderer, cut off at this fatal spot by the Indians. Their plan was to remain concealed until the trains were all safely through, then to swoop down upon them, while scattered and disordered by crossing, cut loose the oxen, kill the men, carry off the women and children, if girls, burn the waggons, and secure all that suited them in the shape of plunder.

The Indians near my camp were fishing in a small mountain-stream, if baling out fish by the bucketful could be called fishing. Round-fish (*Coregomis quadrilateralis*) and brook-trout (*Fario stellatus*) were in such masses (I cannot find a better word) that we dipped out, with baskets and our hands, in ten minutes, enough fish to fill two large iron pails that we carried with us. How such hosts of fish obtain food, or where they find room to deposit their ova, are mysteries. The Indians were splitting and drying them in the sun strung on long peeled rods.

May 19*th*.—Had no trouble with these Indians. Hire two of them to aid me in again crossing the Klamath river, where it runs from the upper into the lower Klamath lake. For the first four miles we ascend a steep mountain, rather thickly timbered. Killed a grey deer, and saw a splendid herd of wapiti; but the bell frightened them, so I did not get a shot. Cross the ridge, and descend on an open grassy flat, surrounding the lower Klamath lake, which I should say, at a rough guess, is thirty miles in circumference. It is in reality more like a huge swamp than a lake; simply patches of open water, peeping out from a rank growth of rushes at least twelve feet in height.

I should think this place must be the 'head

centre' of the entire beaver population of Oregon ; in some of the patches of open water, there certainly was not room to jam in even a tiny beaver cottage of the humblest pretensions, although the open space occupied by the town was many acres in extent. The trees, although a good half-mile from the water, were felled in all directions, as if busy emigrants had been making a clearing. The branches, lopped from the fallen trees, had been dragged by these busy animals along the well-beaten roads, that led in all directions, from the timber to the rushes, through which roads were also cut, to gain an easy access to the water.

The branches, many of them large and heavy, are dragged by the beavers—backing along the roads, two or three often assisting in tugging a single branch—until the water is reached ; then they seize it with their chisel-like teeth, and using their powerful tails, both as rudders and screw-propellers, float it out, to be employed in building their dome-shaped residences. But of this more at length, when referring to the habits of the beaver.

Wildfowl too are here, in great variety and abundance. For the first time I see the breeding-ground of the Rough-billed Pelican (*Pelicanus erythrorynchus*). Their nests were on the ground, amidst the rushes, but unluckily I did not succeed in finding an egg. The nest is simply a confused heap of rushes, with a lot of down and feathers in the centre. On the water these huge birds swim as easily, buoyantly, and gracefully as swans; and in fishing, do not swoop down from a height, as does the brown pelican, but thrust their heads under water, and regularly spoon up small fish with their immense pouched beaks.

Where could one find a more enjoyable sight, whether viewed with the eye of a naturalist or lover of the picturesque? Before me is the reedy swamp, with its open patches of water, glittering like mirrors in the bright sunlight, rippled in all directions by busy beavers: some making a hasty retreat to their castles, others swimming craftily along, crawl on to the domes and peep at the intruder. Dozing on the sandbanks round the margin of the pools, or paddling with 'oary feet' on the smooth water, are numbers of snowy pelicans: the bright orange encircling the eyes, and colouring the pouch, legs, and feet, looks like flame, contrasted with the white feathers, so intensified is the color by the brilliancy of the sun-rays. Pintails, shovellers, stockducks, the exquisitely coloured cinnamon teal, the noisy bald-pate, and a host of others, are either floating on the water or circling round in pairs, quacking angry remonstrances at such an unjustifiable prying into their nuptial haunts. Overhead, vieing with the swallows in rapidity and grace of flight, countless Terns (*Sterna Fosteri*) whirl in mazy circles: their black heads, grey and white liveries, and orange-yellow beaks, show to great advantage against the sombre green of the swallows, amid which they wing their way. Behind me, and far to the right, the Sis-ky-oue Mountains, in many a rugged peak, bound the sky-line, their slopes descending in an unbroken surface of pine-trees to the grassy flats at their base. To my left, the river that feeds this rushy lake winds through the green expanse, like a line of twisted silver, far as the eye can scan its course; along its bank my string of mules, in dingy file, pace slowly on: the tinkle of the bell-horse, but faintly audible, bids me hasten after them, and leave a scene the like of which I shall never perhaps gaze on again. I did not see any nests of the Tern, although I have but little doubt they breed about these lakes.

Follow the stream and pass a second kind of rushy lake, not nearly so large as the one behind, and reach the southern end of the great Klamath lake, out of which pours a rapid stream, two hundred yards in width, and very deep; camp on its edge, and set to work to discover some means of crossing.

The smoke of my camp-fire has barely reached above the trees, when Indians are seen coming from all directions, some on horseback, others on foot; and canoes in fleets dot the lake, that stretches away until lost in the distance, like a fresh-water ocean. I feel very uneasy. The two Sis-ky-oues have gone, vanished mysteriously. Hastily collect dry wood and light a circle of fires, within which I enclose my mules. I am mobbed by ugly half-naked demons, who are evidently doubtful whether to be friends or foes. By aid of my guide, I manage to bargain for two canoes.

May 20th.—Never laid down all night. Kept the packers guarding my mules, stationing a man between each of the fires. Indians in full force at sun-up. In two hours cross all my stores in the canoes; swim the mules, and without any accident we are safely over the river.

This tribe, the Klamath Indians—the chief of whom, Le-lake, is a man of considerable influence—number about 2,000, and own large herds of horses and cattle. They are nearly always at war, and are the terror of emigrants. The men are well-grown and muscular; they wear little more than the breech-cloth, and most of them still use the bow and arrow. The squaws are short in comparison with the men, and for Indians have tolerably regular features. The men use no saddles, and a strange sight it is to see a number of these demons nearly naked, painted from their heads to their waists, all colours and patterns, skying and whirling round upon their half-tamed beasts, yelling and shouting, with no apparent object that I could discover but that of exhibiting themselves and trying to frighten me.

The morning is dark and cloudy, with a sharp keen wind. Keep close to the shore of the lake, which for the first fifteen miles is shut in by high mountains. The trail winds along the side of this mountain, in some places over bare rock, at others loose rolling stones render it very dangerous and difficult to get over. Emerging on an open sandy plain, about seven miles in width, we cross it, still close to the lake. Then hill again, but not so steep. Reaching an open prairie covered with grass, camp on a small stream, with decent wood on its banks. During the whole day I was beset and worried by Indians riding in among my mules, galloping forward, then back again, from one end of the train to the other, in a most excited state.

Immediately on camping I am again thronged, so ride on to see the chief at his lodge, about four miles from camp; having first enclosed my mules in a ring of fires, and desired my men, in case I do not return in two hours, to abandon the mules and escape as best they can. I find the chief's lodge, in the centre of a very extensive Indian village, situated on the bank of a swift stream. All the lodges are dome-shaped; like beaver-houses, an arched roof covers a deep pit sunk in the ground, the entrance to which is a round hole; through it I descend into the sable dignitary's presence, his lodge differing from the others only in being rather larger, and having more dogs and children round it.

Face to face I stand alone with the dreaded chief—more like bearding a hog in its stye than the Forest Monarch, or the Scottish Douglas, in his stronghold. On a few filthy skins squats a flabby, red-eyed, dirt-begrimed savage, his regal robe a ragged blanket tied round his waist. Sot and sensualist are legibly written on his face, and greed, cruelty, and cunning visible in every twist of the mouth and twinkle of the piglike eyes. My heart misgives me when I think my men, the government property, and my own life, are entirely in the hands of this degraded beast.

Addressing him in Chinook, which he fortunately understood, I explained what my mission was, asked him what he meant by sending armed braves in full war-paint, without any squaws, amongst my mules and men; that I was a 'King George's' chief, and what was more, that another and a much greater chief was awaiting my arrival on the banks of the Columbia, and if I failed to come when so many suns had set over the hills, he would seek me, and if harm had befallen me, would surely burn up all the lodges, drive off the horses, kill the braves, and perhaps hang the chief.

Handing me the all-potent pipe, he replied—'I am your brother; my heart is good; my people are assembling for a war-trail; I mean you no harm. Give me two bags of flour, to pay me for the grass your mules eat.' This I consent to, bolt through the hole like a fox, and gallop with all speed back to my camp. Not one word of all this do I believe; but take additional precautions to guard my mules, and quietly await the tide of events. About dusk the chief arrives in full war-paint, which consists of alternate stripes of vermilion and white, arranged in all sorts of directions, and extending from his waist to his hair. We smoked together; the pipe passing round the circle of 'braves' (that might have been more justly styled 'ragged ruffians,' if they had worn clothes), the chief's bodyguard.

The chief of course wanted everything he saw, as a present; but this, at all hazards, I sternly refused. Finding nothing more was to be obtained by fair means, on receiving the promised payment, he left for the village.

The lake near which I am camped is a magnificent sheet of water, forty miles in length, with an average breadth of fifteen, shut in by steep hills not very heavily timbered, between which are fine open grassy valleys. Wildfowl in swarms dot its surface, and it abounds with fish—so the Indians tell me.

May 21st.—Another sleepless night, morning dark; a cold icy wind nearly freezes one's blood; start as soon as we can see. The chief tells me I can ford the stream near his lodge, but, doubtful of its truth, canter on ahead of the mules, and try it. Just as I thought, deep water; a ruse to get my mules swimming, and when scattered, to pounce upon and steal them.

Ride back towards my train, puzzled what course to pursue. An Indian gallops from amidst the trees, chasing two horses with a lasso, catches one, and proceeds rapidly down-stream. I follow quietly, about a half-mile; then he rides into the river, and, without wetting his horse's sides, gets on the other side.

This is a grand discovery. Gallop to my train. Ride in triumph through the ford, followed by the bell-horse and mules, and bow impudently to the flabby old deceiver, staring at me wonderingly as I pass up the opposite side of the stream.

Without stopping to rest, I push on over a swampy country, with little clumps of alder and cotton-wood-trees, like islands, here and there, for twenty-four miles; keep as close as possible to the edge of the river, until we reach a large morass, from which it heads. Here I camp. Although I have not seen the trace of an Indian since leaving the village, still I feel sure they will follow up my trail.

Light fires as usual, and keep strict watch over the wearied and hungry mules. The men are tired and sleepy; but, jaded as I am in mind and body, contrive to keep them up to their sentry-duty. They get an alternate sleep—I get none.

May 22nd.—Passed a miserably cold night.

Blowing nearly a gale of wind. Found all right in the morning. At daybreak get the mules together, and begin saddling. Two mules managed to slip off about fifty yards from us, when a sudden yell told me they were gone. The Indians had followed, and been concealed close to me in the bush all night, afraid to make an attack, but waiting a chance to stampede the band; this, from my having lighted fires, and kept watch, they were prevented from doing; however, they made good the two that strayed. I started after them, but deemed it prudent not to go too far. They also managed to steal a coat from my packmaster, with $100 in the pocket.

From the high water the trail through the swamp is impassable, so I have to go round it, keeping along on the small ridges, where birch and alder grow; continuing this for about eighteen miles, and crossing several deep creeks and swamps, through which the poor mules are literally dragged, get on to higher and comparatively dry land, two miles of which brings me to the entrance of what my guide calls the desert. The distance across it, he says, is forty miles, with but one chance of water. Into this barren waste I did not think the Indians would follow, so make up my mind to push on, although my men and mules are fearfully fagged. I thought the Indians intended to pursue us to the edge of this wilderness, and when off our guard, worn-out for want of sleep, killing us, and driving off the band of mules.

I am in the very paradise of the prong-buck (*Antilocapra Americana*). In bands of twenty or thirty they gallop close up to the mules, halt, have a good look, and suddenly scent danger; the leading bucks give a loud whistling snort, then away they all scamper, and rapidly disappear. We shot as many as we needed, but at this time the does we killed were heavy in fawn.

The size of the prong-buck, when fully grown, is somewhat larger than the domestic sheep; but its legs, being proportionably much longer, give it a greater altitude. The neck is also of greater length, and the head carried more erect. The hind-legs are longer than the fore ones; a wise provision, not only tending to give additional fleetness, but materially assisting it in climbing steep precipices and rocky crags, up and down which it bounds with astonishing speed and security.

The back is a pale dun colour; a transverse stripe between the eyes; the lip, and each side the muzzle, and a spot beneath the ear, dark reddish-brown; the entire underparts, the edges of the

Their favourite haunts appear to be the grassy prairies, that extend hundreds of miles without a break through Texas and Oregon, dotted everywhere with small patches of timber. As the eye wanders over the limitless tract of prairie, these small isolated belts and clumps of trees exactly resemble beautifully-wooded islands, studding a sea of waving grass. Here the prong-buck wanders in herds of from sixty to seventy; naturally shy, approaching them is not by any means an easy matter; on the least alarm the males give the shrill whistling snort, toss their graceful heads, sniff the air, stamp with their forefeet, then bound away like the wind; the herd circle round at first, then wheel up again in tolerable line, have another look, and, if apprehensive of danger, dash off, and seldom stop until safe from all risk of harm.

There are two methods of hunting them practised by the Indians, on horseback and on foot. If the former, three or four mounted savages, armed with bows, arrows, and lassos, approach from different points, so as to get a herd of antelopes between them on the open prairie. They then ride slowly round and round the herd, each time diminishing the circle: the terror-stricken beasts huddle closer and closer together, and appear perfectly bewildered. When, by this manœuvre, the Indians have approached sufficiently near, each throws his unerring lasso, then shoots arrows at the flying herd. As many as six are often killed and caught at one circling.

On foot the crafty savage, getting the wind of the herd, crawls along the grass, and every now and then lies on his back, and elevates his two legs into the air. Attached to the heel of each mocassin is a strip of ermine-skin, which floats like a pennant. The antelopes soon notice it, stand, and look; down go the heels, and on the Indian crawls; and if the herd does not come towards him, he gets a little nearer. In a short time their curiosity tempts them to approach slowly and cautiously towards the two feet, which are performing every variety of strange evolution. Near enough, they too soon discover their error; the twang of the string and whistling arrow, that goes up to the feather-end in the chest of the foremost male, warns the others to fly, and leave their leader and king a prey to the wily redskin.

We are on the sandy waste, and right well does it merit its name desert, for a more dismal barren wilderness cannot be imagined; its surface is all pumice and cinders, with nothing growing on it but a few sage-bushes and dwarfed junipers. Every step the animals make is fetlock-deep; and dust, that nearly chokes and blinds us, comes from every direction. On, and on, and on we go, but no change, no hope of water.

Just before dark—when I begin to think I have been guilty of an awful mistake, and brought needless misery on both men and animals—I push ahead of the train, in hope of finding water, for the guide is utterly lost. Suddenly I descry the tracks of the prong-buck in the sand; hope revives, water must be near at hand! Carefully I follow on their tracks, that lead down a sloping bank of scoria, and slags of lava, through a narrow gorge, with rocks on either side that look as if they had been burnt in a limekiln—to come out into a narrow valley, where the sight of trees, grass, and water makes my heart leap with delight.

Back I spur to meet the lagging train, toiling on, parched with thirst, blinded with dust; hungry, weary, and exhausted. I guide them to the valley, and at the sight of water, men and mules seem to gain new life, rush wildly towards it, plunge in, and drink as only the thirst-famished can. Unsaddle and let the mules feed for two hours, then light five fires, and keep them closely herded, although I have but very little dread of farther pursuit. Supped on grilled antelope, and got a few hours' sleep.

May 23rd.—All safe; no sign of being followed. Off at dawn; fifteen miles more of this horrid waste, and we begin ascending a ridge of mountains, which I find is the watershed of the streams flowing into the Columbia on one side and into the Klamath river on the other; strike the head-waters of the Des Chutes or Fall river, and camp in a fine grassy prairie belted with pine—the *Pinus ponderosa*. Here I determine to remain two days, to allow resting-time for men and animals.

May 25th.—All wonderfully recruited; rest and good feeding soon repair a healthy body, be it man's or quadruped's. I stroll off with my gun, and observe that numbers of the pine-trees are completely studded with acorns, just as nails with large heads were driven into doors in olden days. I had seen a piece of the bark filled with acorns in San Francisco, and was there informed it was the work of a woodpecker, but, to tell the truth, thought I was being hoaxed; but here I am in the midst of dozens of trees, with acorns sticking out all over their trunks; it is no hoax, for I saw the birds that did it, and shot two of them. This singular acorn-storer is the Californian woodpecker (*Melanerpes formicivorus*), evidently of very social habits. They assemble in small flocks, climbing rapidly along the rough bark of the pitch-pine, rapping here and there, with their wedgelike beaks, to scare some drowsy insect; inducing it to rush out, to be nipped, or speared, with the barbed tongue, ere half-awake; others, sitting on the topmost branches of the oaks and pines, continually darted off after some fugitive moth or other winged insect, capturing it much in the fashion of the flycatchers. The harsh and discordant voice is made up for in beauty of plumage. A tuft of scarlet feathers crowns the head, and contrasts brilliantly with the glossy bottle-green of the back and neck; a white patch on the forehead joins, by a narrow isthmus of white, with a necklet of golden-yellow; the throat is dark-green, and the under-parts of a pure white.

As I look over these stores of acorns, I am at a loss to think for what purpose the birds place them in the holes. In Cassin's 'Birds of America' he quotes from Dr. Heerman and Mr. Kelly's 'Excursions in California.' Both writers positively state that these birds stow away acorns for winter provisions, and the latter that he has seen them doing it: 'I have frequently paused from my chopping to watch them with the acorns in their bills, and have admired the adroitness with which they tried it at different holes, until they found one of its exact calibre.'

I have seen the acorns in the holes, and the birds that are said to put them there, and have no right to doubt the statements of other observers; but it seems strange to me, that I cannot find a single acorn exhibiting any evidence of being eaten during the winter. These were stored on the previous fall; winter has passed away, and yet not a seed has been eaten, as far as I can see. I opened the stomachs of the two birds I shot, but not a trace of vegetable matter was in either of them. Subsequently I killed and examined the stomachs of a great many specimens, but never detected anything save insect remains.

Does this woodpecker *ever* eat acorns? I think *not.* More than this, when the insects die, or go to sleep during the cold, snowy, biting winter months, the woodpeckers, like all other sensible birds, go southwards, and have no need to store up a winter supply, as do quasi-hybernating mammals. Then it occurred to me, that if they really do take the trouble to bore holes, a work of great time and labour, and into every hole carefully drive a *sound* acorn that they never make any use of, it is simply idle industry. As a rule, birds are not such thriftless creatures. I had no opportunity of watching the birds in acorn-time—hence this storing is still to me a mystery that needs further explanation.

I came suddenly on a flock of yellow-headed blackbirds (*Xanthocephalus icterocephalus*), sitting on a clump of bushes skirting a small pool. As they sit amidst the bright-green foliage, they remind me of blossoms; the intense black of the body-plumage shows out so conspicuously against the orangelike yellow of the head, that the colours seem too defined for a bird's livery, and more like the freaks of colouring Nature indulges in when tinting orchideous flowers. I imagine this to be their utmost range northwards, for I never saw them after, although they are frequent visitors to Texas, Illinois, and Mexico. Strike the trail of a grizzly, follow it for some distance, but fail in coming up with my large-clawed friend.

May 26th.—I find I shall have to ferry the Des Chutes river. Send on four of my men ahead, to collect timber for a raft. Find, on arriving at the river-bank, that a heap of dry timber has been collected. With axes and an augur—and here let me advise all who travel with pack-horses or mules never to go without a three-inch augur—we soon build a raft 12 feet long by 6½ feet wide; the timber is fastened together with wooden trenails.

The stream makes a bend at this spot, and does not run quite so swiftly, about eighty yards wide, with a dry bank on the side we are, but swampy on the opposite. We launch our raft; she floats like a boat, make ropes fast to her, and stow a coil on board; with one man I commence crossing, paddling with rough oars hewn from a pine-branch. They pay-out rope as we near the opposite bank; twice we whirl round, and come very near being a wreck, but right again. We are over. Now we make fast our rope, and the men on the other side haul her back; and thus we tug her from side to side, heavily freighted; we have made a very successful crossing, neither losing nor damaging anything. The mules swam the river, and also got safely over.

May 27th.—Fine morning: made an early start; kept close along on the course of the river for about twenty miles, following a ridge lightly timbered. The opposite or east bank is an enormous mass of black basaltic rock, extending several miles in length. The top is like a table, reaching as far as one could see, quite black, and not the vestige of a plant visible. The black expanse had exactly the appearance of a bed of rocks, over which the tide ebbed and flowed. Crossed a creek fifteen miles from camp, deep and swift, and about fifteen yards wide ; five miles beyond this cross another creek, about half the size. Leave the timber and come out on a wide sandy kind of desert, covered with wild-sage and stunted juniper-trees, frightfully dusty, and most tiresome for the mules; no chance of camping until quite over it, which is twenty miles. After a weary march reach a creek, where I stop; a capital camping-ground, with fine grass and water. Passed close along the bases of the Three Sisters, lofty mountains, at this time covered with snow. Saw a great many abandoned lodges, but no Indians. The sandy places were quite alive with the Oregon horned toad (*Tapaya Douglassii*), which is a lizard really very harmless, and particularly ugly. Every stream too was thronged with beaver.

May 28*th*.—Mules all in at 4 A.M. Got off in good time: weather not nearly so cold. Looked over the creek, but saw no gold, but any quantity of beaver-workings; trees four feet round had been cut down by them. Passed through a tract of lightly-timbered land and open grassy valleys; crossed a small creek about eight miles from camp, descending rapidly all the way for about eighteen miles.

Came on to the top of a high basaltic mountain, that seemed to offer an almost perpendicular descent into a deep gorge or *cañon.* I rode right and left, but discovering no better place, down we went; how the mules managed to scramble to the bottom without falling head over heels I know not, but we got safely down. I believe it would have been utterly impossible to have got up over it a second time. Through the gorge ran a large swift stream, called by the Indians Wychus creek, in which we found a good fording-place and got over it; safely camped about a mile below the place we forded. The camp was completely shut in by almost vertical cliffs of basalt and tuffa, covered thickly with what I take to be ancient river-drift; the cliffs were, I should say, quite 100 feet high.

The great black *butte* down which we scrambled was a volcano, and an active one too, not a very long time ago; streams of lava, just like slag, that had run in a molten state as if from out a huge glass furnace, reached from its summit to its base; and the red cindery earth, on either side this congealed stream, told plainly enough how fearfully hot it must have been. One would imagine this district was entirely volcanic, the great desert-waste we crossed being composed of pumice, scoria, and ashes. Perhaps these lesser hills were safety-valves to the more conspicuous mountains in the coast-range of British Columbia and Washington Territory—Mounts Baker, Reiney, St. Helens, and others.

Several pillars, composed of a kind of conglomerate, quite away from all the surrounding rocks, stand as if man had hewn or rather built them—ghostly obelisks, that have a strange and unusual look. I suppose the portions that once joined them to the mass, from which they were detached, must have been crumbled off by Time's fingers, and these solitary pedestals left as records. Round them, too, were scores of tiny heaps of boulders, built, as I am informed, by the Snake Indians, who suppose these pillars are the remains of spirits that have been turned into stone; but for what object they really pile up these little altars I could never discover, though the Indians tell you as a powerful '*medicine*'; but who can say what that means?

May 29th.—All night it rained in torrents, and I do not think I ever saw so dark a night; the rain put out all our fires, and I could neither see men or mules, although close to them. Got the mules together at 7 A.M., but did not make an early start, in consequence of the men being tired from want of sleep: we managed to start at eight o'clock. Our first task was to get out of the gorge. It was a most tedious and even dangerous job, for the ground was loose, and constantly broke away from under the mules' feet, but at last we managed to scramble to the top.

For twenty miles farther it was a continued series of uphill and downhill, all loose basaltic ground, and very hard to travel over. Descending a long sandy hill we came to an Indian reserve (the Warm Spring reservation); and we encamp. The house is a large quadrangular building of squared blocks, loopholed for shooting through. Six white men live here, and the Indians on the reservation are the Des Chutes tribe; they cultivate a small quantity of ground very badly. All hands are in a great state of ferment. A band of Snake Indians have just made a raid on the reservation, driven off seventeen head of stock, and are hourly expected to return. This is cheering, considering I must pass the night here. But, luckily, no Indians came.

May 30th.—I should be seventy miles from the camp I am to join; start with one man as a companion at three o'clock in the morning. The silver stream of light from the unclouded moon illumines the trail we follow as brightly as sunshine. The mules are to follow. As day dawns an open plain is seen, spreading far away right and left, and along it a horseman gallops towards us.

As he nears I make him out to be an Indian on a skewballed horse. We stop and parley, and I find he is a Snake scout; both horse and rider are splendid specimens of their kind. A circle of eagle's feathers fastened to the skin of the ermine surrounds his head, and long raven black hair covers his neck: a scarlet blanket, elaborately beaded, hangs from his shoulders; a broad wampum-belt contains his knife and powder-horn, and in his right hand he bears a rifle. But very little paint daubs his shining-red skin, through which every muscle stands out as if cast in bronze; he is a handsome savage, if there ever was one. As we ride in opposite directions, I cannot help thinking that men and mules will stand but little chance if all the Snakes are like to this sable warrior. Reached a cabin at the Tye creek after doing forty-five miles, where we remained for the night.

May 31st.—Ride in amidst the tents of the Commission, anxiously awaiting my arrival. The following day men and mules arrive safely. So ended my journey through the wilder part of Oregon, having accomplished a hazardous, wearisome journey, making my way a distance of several hundred miles without any trails, or, if any, simply trails used by Indians to reach their hunting or fishing-grounds; sleeping during the whole time in the open air, a saddle my only pillow. Apart from the anxiety, harass, and want of rest, and the necessity of guarding against the hostile Klamaths, to save the mules and our scalps, we all enjoyed the journey thoroughly, not even a cold resulting from the exposure.

CHAPTER XII.

SHARP-TAILED GROUSE — BALD-HEADED EAGLE — MOSQUITOS — LAGOMYS MINIMUS (NOV. SP.)—HUMMINGBIRDS—UROTRICHUS.

THE SHARP-TAILED GROUSE (*Pediocœtes Phasianellus*, Baird; *Tetrao Phasianellus*, Linn.; *Centrocercus Phasianellus*, Jardine; *Phasianus Columbianus*, Ord.)—*Specific characters*: The tail consists of eighteen feathers—prevailing colours black, white, and umber-yellow; the back marked with transverse bars, the wings with round conspicuous white spots—under pure white; the breast and sides thickly marked with V-shaped blotches of dark-brown; length about 18·00; wing, 8·50; tail, 5·23 inches.

This beautiful bird is alike estimable, whether we consider him in reference to his field qualities (therein being all a grouse ought to be, rising with a loud rattling whirr, and going off straight as an arrow, lying well to dogs, and frequenting open grassy prairies), or viewed as a table dainty,

THE SHARP-TAILED GROUSE

(*Pediocaetes phasianellus*).

when bowled over and grilled. Though his flesh is brown, yet for delicacy of flavour—game in every sense of the word—I'll back him against any other bird in the Western wilds. This grouse appears to replace the Prairie-hen (*Cupidonia cupido*) on all the prairies west of the Rocky Mountains. By the fur-traders it is called the 'spotted chicken'; for all grouse, by the traders and half-breeds, are called chickens! and designated specifically by either habit or colour—such as blue chickens, wood chickens, white chickens (ptarmigan), &c. &c.; the *skis-kin* of the Kootanie Indians.

The tail is cuneate and graduated, and about two-thirds the length of the wing; the central pair, considerably longer than the rest, terminate in a point—hence the name *sharp-tailed*.

The singular mixture of colours (white, black, and brownish-yellow), the dark blotches, transverse bars, and V-shaped marks of dark-brown, exactly resemble the ground on which the bird is destined to pass its life. The ochreish-yellow angular twigs and dead leaves of the Artemisia, or wild-sage; the sandy soil, dried and bleached to a dingy-white; the brown of the withered bunch-grass; the weather-beaten fragments of rock, clad in liveries of sombre-coloured lichens, admirably harmonise with the colours in which Nature has wisely robed this feathered tenant of the wilderness.

Often, when the sharp crack of the gun, and the *ping* of the fatal leaden messengers, has rung the death-peal of one of these prairie-chiefs, I have watched the whirring wing drop powerless, and the arrowy flight stop in mid-career, and, with a heavy thud, the bird come crashing down. Rushing to pick him up, and keeping my eye steadily on the spot where he fell, I have felt a little mystified at not seeing my friend: here he fell, I am quite sure; so I trudge up and down, circle round and round, until a slight movement —an effort to run, or a dying struggle—attracts my attention, and then I find I have been the whole time close to the fallen bird. But so closely do the back and outspread wings resemble the dead foliage and sandy soil, that it is almost impossible for the most practised eye to detect these birds when crouching on the ground; and there can be no doubt that it as effectually conceals them from birds of prey.

This bird is abundantly distributed on the western slope of the Rocky Mountains, ranging right and left of the Boundary-line, the 49th parallel of north latitude. It is particularly abundant on the tobacco-plains near the Kootanie river, round the Osoyoos lakes, and in the valley of the Columbia.

I have never seen this grouse on the western side of the Cascade range. This bird is also found in the Red River settlements, in the north of Minnesota, as well as on the shores of Hudson's Bay, and on the Mackenzie river. Mr. Ross notes it as far north as the Arctic Circle.

Of the different species of grouse I met with in my rambles (described in vol. ii.) not one has come so often under my observation as this, the sharp-tailed grouse. Its favourite haunt is on open grassy plains,—in the morning keeping itself concealed in the thick long grass, but coming in about midday to the streams to drink, and dust itself in the sandy banks; it seldom goes into the timber, and, if it does, always remains close to the prairie, never retiring into the depths of the forest.

They lay their eggs on the open prairie, in a tuft of grass, or by the foot of a small hillock; nesting early in the spring, and laying from twelve to fourteen eggs. The nest is a hole scratched out in the earth, a few grass-stalks and root-fibres laid carelessly and loosely over the bottom; the eggs are of a dark rusty-brown, with small splashes or speckles of darker brown thickly spattered over them.

After nesting-time, they first appear in coveys or broods about the middle of August; the young birds are then about three parts grown, strong on the wing, and afford admirable sport. At this time they live by the margins of small streams, where there is thin timber and underbrush, with plenty of sandy banks to dust in. About the middle of September and on into October they begin to pack; first two or three coveys get together, then flock joins flock, until they gradually accumulate into hundreds. On the first appearance of snow they begin to perch, settling on high dead pine-trees, the *dead* branches being a favourite locality; or, should there be any farms, they pitch round on the top of the snake-fences. At the Hudson's Bay trading-post at Fort Colville there were large wheat-stubbles; in these, after the snow fell, they assembled in vast numbers. Wary and shy they are now, and most difficult to get at; the cause being, I apprehend, the snow rendering every moving thing so conspicuous, it is next to impossible for dogs to hunt them.

Their food in the summer consists principally of berries — the snowberry (*Symphoricarpus racemosus*), and the bearberry (*Arctostaphylos uva-ursi*). The leaves of this latter plant are used to a great extent, both by Indians and traders, to mix with or use instead of tobacco, and called *kini-kinick*; the leaves being dried over the fire, and rubbed up in the hand to powder, and smoked in a pipe. The wild roseberries (*Rosa blanda* and *Rosa mirantha*), and many others, usually designated huckle-berries, constitute the food generally consumed by these birds during summer and autumn; although I have often found quantities of wheat-grains and larvæ of insects, grass-seeds, and small wild flowers in their crops. Their thickly-feathered feet enable them to run upon the snow with ease and celerity, and they dig holes and burrow underneath it much after the fashion of the ptarmigan.

During the two winters we spent at Colville, flocks of these birds congregated about the corn-stacks and hayricks at our mule-camp, and at the Hudson's Bay trading-post, Fort Colville. The temperature at that time was often down to 29° and 30° below zero, and the snow three feet deep; yet these birds did not at all appear to suffer from such intense cold, and were strong, wild, and fat during the entire winter, which lasted from October until near April before the snow entirely cleared.

In this valley (the Colville valley) the Commissioner and myself had, I think, as brisk and nice a bit of shooting as I ever enjoyed. If I remember aright, it was towards the end of September, and the birds had packed. We rode down one clear bright morning, about six miles, to the Horse-Guards. Do not at once hastily imagine any analogy between Colville valley and Whitehall. The heavy man, with his heavy boots, heavy sword, heavy dress, heavy walk, and heaviest of all heavy horses—so conspicuous a feature in our London sights—is represented here by the genuine savage, thin and lissom as an eel; his equipment a whip, a lasso, a scalping-knife, and sometimes a trade-gun; a pad his saddle, and the bands of horses, some two hundred in number, his charge. A stream of cold clear water rambles quietly down the hillside; and as the hills are thickly dotted with bunch-grass, affording most glorious pasturage, the Hudson's Bay fort horses are always pastured here, and guarded by Indians; hence comes the name—'the Horse-Guards.'

The Colville valley is, roughly speaking, about thirty miles long, the hills on one side being densely studded with pine-trees, and on the other quite clear of timber, but thickly clothed up to their rounded summits with the bunch-grass. This is a peculiar kind of grass, that grows in tufts, and its fattening qualities are truly wonderful.

The little stream at the Horse-Guards has on either side of it a belt of thin brush, and in this, and in the long grass close to the stream, we found the sharp-tailed grouse. There were hundreds of them—up they went, and, right and left, down they came again! It might have been the novelty of the scene, causing an undue anxiety and excitement, or perhaps it was the liver, or powder, or something else—who knows what? —but this I do know, that neither of us shot our best, but we made a glorious bag nevertheless. They rise with a loud rattling noise, and utter a peculiar cry, like 'chuck, chuck, chuck,' rapidly and shrilly repeated. On first rising the wings are moved with great rapidity, but after getting some distance off they sail along, the wings being almost quiescent.

They pair very early in the spring, long before the snow has gone off the ground, and their love-meetings are celebrated in a somewhat curious fashion. By the half-breeds and fur-traders these festivities are called chicken or pheasant dances.

I was lucky enough to be present at several of these balls whilst at Fort Colville. Their usual time of assembling is about sunrise, and late in the afternoon; they select a high round-topped mound; and often, ere the fair are wooed and won, and the happy couple start on their domestic cares, the mound is trampled and beaten bare as a road.

I had often longed to be present at one of these chicken-dances; and it so happened that, riding up into the hills early one spring morning, my most ardent wishes were fully realised. The peculiar 'chuck-chuck' came clear and shrill upon the crisp frosty air, and told me a dance was afoot. I tied up my horse and my dog, and crept quietly along towards the knoll from whence the sound appeared to come. Taking advantage of some rocks, I weazled myself along, and, without exciting observation, gained the shelter of an old pine-stump close to the summit of a hillock; and there, sure enough, the ball was at its height.

Reader, can you go back to the days of your first pantomime, your first Punch-and-Judy, or bring to your remembrance the fresh, bounding, joyous delight that you felt in the days of your youth, when you had before your eyes some long and deeply-wished-for novelty? If you can, you will be able to imagine my childish pleasure when looking for the first time on a chicken-dance. There were about eighteen or twenty birds present on this occasion, and it was almost impossible to distinguish the males from the females, the plumage being so nearly alike; but I imagined the females were the passive ones. The four birds nearest to me were head to head, like gamecocks in fighting attitude—the neck-feathers ruffed up, the little sharp tail elevated straight on end, the wings dropped close to the ground, but keeping up by a rapid vibration a continued throbbing or drumming sound.

They circled round and round each other in slow waltzing-time, always maintaining the same attitude, but never striking at or grappling with each other; then the pace increased, and one hotly pursued the other until he faced about, and *tête-à-tête* went waltzing round again; then they did a sort of 'Cure' performance, jumping about two feet into the air until they were winded; and then they strutted about and 'struck an attitude,' like an acrobat after a successful tumble. There were others marching about, with their tails and heads as high as they could stick them up, evidently doing the 'heavy swell;' others, again, did not appear to have any well-defined ideas what they ought to do, and kept flying up and pitching down again, and were manifestly restless and excited—perhaps rejected suitors contemplating something desperate. The music to this eccentric dance was the loud 'chuck-chuck' continuously repeated, and the strange throbbing sound produced by the vibrating wings. I saw several balls after this, but in every one the same series of strange evolutions were carried out.

In reference to this bird's adaptability to acclimatisation in our own country, it appears to me to be most admirably fitted for our hill and moorland districts. It is very hardy, capable of bearing a temperature of 30° to 33° below zero; feeds on seeds, berries, and vegetable matter—in every particular analogous to what it could find in our own hill-country; a good breeder, having usually from twelve to fourteen young at a brood; nests early, and would come to shoot about the same time as our own grouse. Snow does not hurt them in the slightest degree; they burrow into it, and feed on what they can find underneath it. The two specimens in the British Museum I shot in the Colville valley; they are male and female, in winter plumage; and anyone, who may feel an interest in getting these birds brought home, may there see for himself what fine handsome creatures they are.

But then comes the question—how are they to be obtained, and how brought to England? I do not imagine it would be a very difficult or expensive matter; the young birds in May could be easily obtained, at any point up the Columbia river, by employing the Indians to bring them to the riverside; and once on board steamer, they could be as easily fed as fowls. The great difficulty *I* have always had is in bringing the young birds from the interior to a vessel; they always die when transported on the backs of animals, however carefully packed. The continued jerking motion given to birds packed on the back of a mule or horse as he walks along has, according to my experience, been the sole cause of their dying ere you could reach water-carriage; but the fact of their being so close to water as they are along the Columbia river, would render their being brought home a very easy task.

The Bald-headed Eagle (*Haliactus leucocephalus*) is seen but seldom, as during its breeding-time it retires into the hills, and usually chooses a lofty pine as its nesting-place. Two of them had a nest near the Chilukweyuk lake, which was quite inaccessible, of immense size, and built entirely of sticks—the same nest being invariably used year after year by the same pair of birds. Their food consists mainly of fish, and it is a curious sight to watch an eagle plunge into the water, seize a heavy salmon, and rise with it without any apparent difficulty. Both the osprey and bald-headed eagle fish with their claws, never, as far as I have observed them, striking at a fish with the beak; during winter they collect, young and old together, round the Sumass lake; and as the cold becomes intense, they sit three and four on the limb of a pine-tree, or in a semi-stupid state, all their craft and courage gone, blinking and drowsy as an owl in daytime.

I have often, when walking under the trees where these half-torpid monarchs of the air sit side by side, fired and knocked one out from betwixt its neighbours, without causing them the slightest apparent alarm; three I picked up one morning frozen stiff as marble, having fallen dead from off their perch.

Why birds so powerfully winged should prefer to remain where the winters are sufficiently intense to freeze them to death, rather than go southward, where food is equally abundant, is a mystery I am unable to explain. Towards the fall of the year, when the hunting and fishing-grounds of the Old-man (*Sea-la-ca*, as the Indians designate the eagle, on account of its *white head*) grow scant of game, hunger prompts them to be disagreeably bold. Constantly a fat mallard, that I had taken a vast amount of trouble to stalk, was pounced upon by a watchful eagle, and borne off, ere the report of my gun was lost in the hills, or the smoke had cleared away; indeed, I have sometimes given the robber the benefit of a second barrel, as punishment for his thievery. Numberless ducks have been lost to me in this way. This eagle is by far the most abundant of the falcon tribe in British Columbia, and always a conspicuous object in ascending a river; he is seated on the loftiest tree or rocky pinnacle, and soars off circling round, screaming like a tortured demon, as if in remonstrance at such an impudent intrusion into its solitudes. The adult plumage is not attained until the fourth year from the nest.

MOSQUITOS (*Culex pinguis*, nov. sp.)—Reader, if you have never been in British Columbia, then, I say, you do not know anything about insect persecution; neither can you form the faintest idea of the terrible suffering foes so seemingly insignificant as the bloodthirsty horsefly (*Tabanus*), the tiny burning fly (beulot or sand-fly of the trappers), and the well-known and deservedly-hated *mosquito*, are capable of inflicting.

A wanderer from my boyhood, I have met with these pests in various parts of our globe—in the country of Czernomorzi, among the Black Sea Cossacks, on the plains of Troy, up on Mount Olympus, amid the gorgeous growths of a tropical forest, where beauty and malaria, twin brothers, walk hand-in-hand—away in the deep dismal solitudes of the swamps on the banks of the Mississippi, on the wide grassy tracts of the Western prairies, and on the snow-clad summits of the Rocky Mountains.

Widely remote and singularly opposite as to climate as are these varied localities, yet, as these pests are there in legions, I imagined that I had endured the maximum of misery they were capable of producing. I was mistaken; all my experience, all my vaunted knowledge of their numbers, all I had seen and suffered, was as nothing to what I subsequently endured. On the Sumass prairie, and along the banks of the Fraser river, the mosquitos are, as a Yankee would say, 'a caution.'

In the summer our work, that of cutting the

Boundary-line, was along the low and comparatively flat land intervening between the seaboard and the foot of the Cascade Mountains. Our camp was on the Sumass prairie, and was in reality only an open patch of grassy land, through which wind numerous streams from the mountains, emptying themselves into a large shallow lake, the exit of which is into the Fraser by a short stream, the Sumass river.

In May and June this prairie is completely covered with water. The Sumass river, from the rapid rise of the Fraser, reverses its course, and flows back into the lake instead of out of it. The lake fills, overflows, and completely floods the lower lands. On the subsidence of the waters, we pitched our tents on the edge of a lovely stream. Wildfowl were in abundance; the streams were alive with fish; the mules and horses revelling in grass kneedeep—we were in a second Eden!

We had enjoyed about a week at this delightful camp, when the mosquitos began to get rather troublesome. We knew these most unwelcome visitors were to be expected, from Indian information. I must confess I had a vague suspicion that the pests were to be more dreaded than we were willing to believe; for the crafty redskins had stages erected, or rather fastened to stout poles driven like piles into the mud at the bottom of the lake. To these large platforms over the water they all retire, on the first appearance of the mosquitos.

In about four or five days the increase was something beyond all belief, and really terrible. I can convey no idea of the numbers, except by saying they were in dense clouds truly, and not figuratively, a thick fog of mosquitos. Night or day it was just the same; the hum of these bloodthirsty tyrants was incessant. We ate them, drank them, breathed them; nothing but the very thickest leathern clothing was of the slightest use as a protection against their lancets. The trousers had to be tied tightly round the ankle, and the coat-sleeve round the wrist, to prevent their getting in; but if one more crafty than the others found out a needle-hole, or a thin spot, it would have your blood in a second. We lighted huge fires, fumigated the tents, tried every expedient we could think of, but all in vain. They seemed to be quite happy in a smoke that would stifle anything mortal, and, what was worse, they grew thicker every day.

Human endurance has its limits. A man cannot stand being eaten alive. It was utterly impossible to work; one's whole time was occupied in slapping viciously at face, head, and body, stamping, grumbling, and savagely slaughtering hecatombs of mosquitos. Faces rapidly assumed an irregularity of outline anything but consonant with the strict lines of beauty; each one looked as if he had gone in for a heavy fight, and lost. Hands increased in size with *painful* rapidity, and—without intending a slang joke—one was in a *k-nobby* state from head to heel.

The wretched mules and horses were driven wild, racing about like mad animals, dashing into the water and out again, in among the trees; but, go where they would, their persecutors stuck to them in swarms. The poor dogs sat and howled piteously, and, prompted by a wise instinct to avoid their enemies, dug deep holes in the earth; and backing in lay with their heads at the entrance, whining, snapping, and shaking their ears, to prevent the mosquitos from getting in at them.

There was no help for it—our camp had to be abandoned; we were completely vanquished and driven away—the work of about a hundred men stopped by tiny flies. Our only chance of escape was to retire into the hills, and return to complete our work late in the autumn, when they disappear. Hard wind is the only thing that quells them; but it simply drives them into the grass, to return on its lulling, if possible, more savagely hungry. Quaint old Spenser knew this; he says, speaking of gnats:—

> No man nor beast may rest or take repast
> For their sharp sounds and noyous injuries,
> Till the fierce northern wind with blustering blast
> Doth blow them quite away, and in the ocean cast.

My notebook, as I open it now, is a mausoleum of scores of my enemies; there they lay, dry and flat; round some of them a stain of blood tells how richly they merited their untimely end.

One thing has always puzzled me in the history of these ravenous cannibals—what on earth can they get to feed on, when there are no men or animals? I brought home specimens, of course; and I am by no means sure I feel any great pleasure in finding my foe to be a new species, but it is, and named *Culex pinguis*, because it was fatter and rounder than any of its known brethren.

The habits of this new mosquito are, in every detail, the same as all the known species. The female lays her eggs, which are long and oval in shape, in the water; then aided by her hind-legs, she twists about the eggs, and tightly glues them together, into a very beautiful little boat-shaped bundle, that floats and drifts about in the water. In sunny weather the eggs are speedily hatched, and the larvæ lead an aquatic life. They are very active, diving to the bottom with great rapidity, and as quickly ascending to the surface to breathe; the respiratory organs being situated near the tail, on the eighth segment of the abdomen, they hang, as it were, in the water, head downwards. After shifting the skin three or four times, they change into the pupa form, in which state they move about, even more actively than before, aided by the tail, and two organs like paddles, attached to it. In this stage of their existence they never feed (I only wish they would always remain in this harmless condition); and although they still suspend themselves in the water, the position is reversed, the breath ing organs being now placed on the chest.

The final change to the perfect or winged state is most curious, and well worth careful attention. The pupa-case splits from end to end; and, looking moist and miserable, with crumpled wings, the little fly floats on its previous home, an exquisite canoe of Nature's own contriving. A breeze of wind sufficient to ripple the water is fatal to it now, as shipwreck is inevitable; but if all is calm and conducive to safety, the little fly dries, the wings expand, it inhales the air, and along with it strength and power to fly; then bidding goodbye to the frail barque, wings its way to the land, and begins a war of persecution.

Mosquitos never venture far over the water after once quitting their skin-canoe: this fact the wily savage has taken advantage of. During 'the reign of terror' the Indians never come on shore if they can help it; and if they do, they take good care to flog every intruder out of the canoes before reaching the stage.

These stages, each with a family of Indians living on them, have a most picturesque appearance. The little fleet of canoes are moored to the poles, and the platform reached by a ladder made of twisted cedar-bark. Often have I slept on these stages among the savages, to avoid being devoured. But I am not quite sure if one gains very much by the change: in the first place, if you are restless, and roll about in your sleep, you stand a very good chance of finding yourself soused in the lake. The perfumes—varied but abundant—that regale your nose are not such as are wafted from 'tropic isles' or

'Araby the blest.' I shall not shock my fair readers with any comparison—you must imagine it is not agreeable. Dogs also live on these platforms; for the Indian dog is always with his master, sharing bed as well as board. These canine favourites are not exempt from persecutors; like the giant of old, they at once 'smell the blood of an Englishman,' and will have some; but, after all, the night steals away, you know not how, until the dawn, blushing over the eastern hill-tops, rouses all the dreaming world—except mosquitos, that never sleep.

On the eastern side of the Cascades the scenery and general physical condition of the country materially changes, and the *Tabanus* and burning-fly become the ruling persecutors.

Lagomys minimus (Lord, sp. nov.)—The Commissioner, myself, a few men, and a small train of pack-mules, set out to visit some of the stations on the Boundary-line, east of the Cascades. Our route lay along the valley of the Shimilkameen river, to strike Ashtnolow, a tributary that led up into the mountains, the course of which we were to follow as far as practicable. We had a delightful trip, through a district indescribably lovely.

There is a wild and massive grandeur about

the eastern side of the Cascades, unlike the scenery of the west or coast slope, which is densely wooded. Here it was like riding through a succession of parks, covered with grass and flowers of varied species.

We reached the junction of the two streams, and camped, just as the sun, disappearing behind the western hills, tinted with purple twilight the ragged peaks of the rocks that shut us in on every side. Scarce a sound of bird or beast disturbed the silence of the forest, and save the babble of the stream, as it rippled over the shingle, all nature was soon hushed in deathlike sleep. I could dimly make out in the fading light the grim hills we had to climb, towering up like mighty giants; the clear white snow, covering their summits, contrasted strangely with the sombre pine-trees, thickly covering the lower portion of the mountains.

We had a stiff climb before us, and my hopes were high in expectation of bowling over bighorn (*Ovis montana*) and ptarmigan. For some distance we scrambled up the sides of the brawling torrent, whose course, like true love, was none of the smoothest, being over and among vast fragments of rock, that everywhere covered the hillside. From amidst these relics of destruction grew the Douglas pine and ponderous cedar (*Thuja gigantea*). Here the ascent was easy enough, but on reaching a greater altitude, the climbing became anything but a joke.

We at last reached a level plateau near the summit, and lay down on the soft mossy grass, near a stream that came trickling down from the melting snow.

Close to my couch was a talus of broken granite, that Old Time and the Frost King between them had crumbled away from a mass of rocks above. As I contemplated this heap of rocks, a cry like a plaintive whistle suddenly attracted my attention; it evidently came from amongst the stones. I listened and kept quiet. Again and again came the whistle, but nowhere could I see the whistler. A slight movement at length betrayed him, and I could clearly make out a little animal sitting bolt upright, like a begging-dog, his seat a flat stone in the middle of the heap.

I had a load of small-shot in one barrel, intended for ptarmigan; raising my gun slowly and cautiously to my shoulder, I fired as I lay on the ground. The sharp ringing crack as I touched the trigger—the first, perhaps, that had ever awoke the echoes of the mountain—was the death-knell of the poor little musician.

I picked him up, and imagine my delight when for the first time I held a new *Lagomys* in my hand. Having made out what he was, the next thing to be done was to watch for others—to find out what they did, and how they passed the time in their stony citadel. I had not long to wait; they soon came peeping slily out of their hiding-places, and, inferring safety from silence, sat upon the stones and cheerily chorused to each other. The least noise, and the whistle was sounded sharper and more shrill—the danger-signal, when one and all took headers among the stones.

I soon observed they were busy at work, carrying in dry grass, fir-fronds, roots, and moss, and constructing a nest in the clefts between the stones, clearly for winter-quarters. The nests were of large size, some of them consisting of as much material as would fill a good-sized basket. One nest was evidently the combined work of several little labourers, and destined for their joint habitation.

There were no provisions stored away, neither do I think they garner any for winter use, but simply hybernate in the warm nest; which, of course, is thickly covered with snow during the intense cold of these northern latitudes, thus more effectually preventing radiation and waste of animal heat. Their food consists entirely of grass, which they nibble much after the fashion of our common rabbit. They never burrow or dig holes in the ground, but pass their lives among the loose stones. Who can fail to trace the evidence of Divine care in colouring the fur of this defenceless creature in a garb exactly resembling the grey lichen-covered fragments amongst which he is destined to pass his life? So closely does the animal approximate in appearance to an angular piece of rock when sitting up, that unless he moves it takes sharp eyes to see him; and the cry or whistle is so deceptive that I imagined it far distant, when the animal was close to me.

The species described and figured by Sir John Richardson—F.B.A., plate 19, *Lepus* (*Lagomys*) *princeps*, the little Cheif Hare—I first saw at Chilukweyuk lake, and next on the trail leading from Fort Hope, on the Fraser river, to Fort Colville. The little fellows were in a narrow gorge, as well as among loose stones. It was about the same date as in the preceding year that I had seen *Lagomys minimus* making its nest; but here not a trace of nest could I see, nor any evidence of an attempt to make one. I soon after returned again by the same trail. The snow having now fallen to the depth of about six inches, completely covering up the rocks and stones, all the animals had disappeared; and although I searched most carefully, there was not a hole or track in the snow, to show they had ever left their quarters to feed or wander about.

As it was quite impossible a nest could have been made in the interim, it is perfectly certain they hybernate in holes without a nest; whereas *Lagomys minimus*, living at a much greater altitude, makes a nest to sleep through the winter.

Lagomys minimus (Lord, sp. nov.).—Sp. Char.: Differs from *Lepus* (*Lagomys*) *princeps* of Sir J. Richardson (F.B.A., vol. i. p. 227, pl. 19) in being much smaller. Predominant colour of back dark-grey, tinged faintly with umber-yellow, —more vivid about the shoulders, but gradually shading off on the sides and belly to dirty-white; feet white, washed over with yellowish-brown; ears large, black inside, the outer rounded margin edged with white; eye very small, and intensely black; whiskers long, and composed of about an equal number of white and black hairs.

Measurement: Head and body, 6½ inches; head,

2 inches; nose to auditory opening, $1\frac{1}{4}$ inch; height of ear from behind, 1 inch.

The skull differs in being generally smaller; the cranial portion of the skull in its superior outline is much narrower and smoother. The nasal bones are shorter and broader, and rounded at their posterior articulation, instead of being deeply notched, as in *L. princeps*. Distance from anterior molar to incisors much less; auditory bullæ much smaller. Incisors shorter and straighter, and very deeply grooved on the anterior surface. Molars smaller, but otherwise similar in form. Length of skull, $1\frac{1}{4}$ inch.

General differences from *Lagomys princeps*:—First, in being smaller, $1\frac{1}{2}$ inch shorter in total length; the ear, measured from behind, $\frac{1}{4}$ inch shorter; the colour generally darker, especially the lower third of the back. Secondly, in the *structural* differences of the skull; for although these differences are not prominent or well-defined, yet they are unquestionable specific variations. Thirdly, in the habit of constructing a nest of hay for the winter sleep, and in living at a much greater altitude.

There is a strange indescribable delight in discovery, and in finding animals for the first time in their native haunts, animals that before one had vaguely heard or only read of; thus digging, as it were, from Nature's exhaustless mine, fresh wonders of Divine handiwork on which eye had not before gazed.

Hummingbirds. — Hummingbirds, and the wild tangled loveliness of tropical vegetation, appear to be so closely linked together, that we are apt to think the one essential to the existence of the other.

We naturally (at least I did in my earlier days) associate these tiniest gems of the feathered creation with glowing sunshine, gorgeous flowers, grotesque orchids—palms, plaintains, bananas, and blacks. This is all true enough, and if we take that large slice of the American continent betwixt the Amazon, the Rio Grande, and the Gila (embracing Guiana, New Granada, Central America, Mexico, and the West Indian islands), as the home of hummingbirds, we shall pretty truthfully define, what is usually assumed to be, the geographical range of this group—a group entirely confined to America. Within the above limits, the great variety of species, the most singular in form and brilliant in plumage, are met with.

Gazing on these gems of the air, one would suppose that Nature had exhausted all her skill in lavishly distributing the richest profusion of

colours, and in exquisitely mingling every imaginable tint and shade, to adorn these diminutive creatures, in a livery more lustrously brilliant than was ever fabricated by the loom, or metal-worker's handicraft.

But away from the tropics and its feathered wonders, to the wild solitudes of the Rocky Mountains,—it is there I want you in imagination to wander with me, and to picture to yourself, which you can easily do if you possess a naturalist's love of discovery, the delight I experienced when, for the first time, I saw humming-birds up in the very regions of the 'Ice King.'

Early in the month of May, when the sun melts down the doors of snow and ice, and sets free imprisoned nature, I was sent ahead of the astronomical party employed in making the Boundary-line to cut out a trail, and bridge any streams too deep to ford. The first impediment met with was at the Little Spokan river,—little only as compared with the Great Spokan, into which it flows. The larger stream leads from the western slope of the Rocky Mountains, and flows on to join the Columbia.

It was far too deep to be crossed by any expedient short of bridging; so a bridge had to be built, an operation involving quite a week's delay. The place chosen, and the men set to work, my leisure time was devoted to collecting.

The snow still lingered in large patches about the hollows and sheltered spots. Save a modest violet or humble rock-blossom, no flower had ventured to open its petals, except the brilliant pink *Ribes*, or flowering currant, common in every English cottage-garden.

Approaching a large cluster of these gay-looking bushes, my ears were greeted with a sharp thrum—a sound I knew well—from the wings of a hummingbird, as it darted past me. The name by which these birds are commonly known has arisen from the noise produced by the wings (very like the sound of a driving-belt used in machinery, although of course not nearly so loud), whilst the little creature, poised over a flower, darts its slender beak deep amidst the corolla—not to sip nectar, in my humble opinion, but to capture drowsy insect revellers, that assemble in these attractive drinking-shops, and grow tipsy on the sweets gratuitously provided for them. Soon a second whizzed by me, and others followed in rapid succession; and, when near enough to see distinctly, the bushes seemed literally to gleam with the flashing colours of swarms (I know no better word) of hummingbirds surrounding the entire clump of *Ribes*.

> 'From flower to flower, where wild bees flew and sung,
> As countless, small, and musical as they
> Showers of bright hummingbirds came down, and plied
> The same ambrosial task with slender bill,
> Extracting honey hidden in those bells
> Whose richest blossoms grew pale beneath their blaze,
> Of twinkling winglets hov'ring o'er their petals,
> Brilliant as rain-drops when the western sun
> Sees his own miniature beams in each.'

Seating myself on a log, I watched this busy assemblage for some time. They were all male birds, and two species were plainly discernible. Chasing each other in sheer sport, with a rapidity of flight and intricacy of evolution impossible for the eye to follow—through the bushes, and over the water, everywhere—they darted about like meteors. Often meeting in mid-air, a furious battle would ensue; their tiny crests and throat-plumes erect and blazing, they were altogether pictures of the most violent passions. Then one would perch himself on a dead spray, and leisurely smooth his ruffled feathers, to be suddenly rushed at and assaulted by some quarrelsome comrade. Feeding, fighting, and frolicking seemed to occupy their entire time.

I daresay hard epithets will be heaped upon me,—cruel man, hard-hearted savage, miserable destroyer, and similar epithets,—when I confess to shooting numbers of these burnished beauties. Some of them are before me at this moment as I write; but what miserable things are these stuffed remains, as compared to the living bird! The brilliant crests are rigid and immoveable; the throat-feathers, that open and shut with a flash like coloured light, lose in the stillness of death all those charms so beautiful in life; the tail, clumsily spread, or bent similar to the abdomen of a wasp about to sting, no more resembles the same organ in the live bird, than a fan of peacock's feathers is like to the expanded tail of that bird when strutting proudly in the sun.

It is useless pleading excuses; two long days were occupied in shooting and skinning. The two species obtained on this occasion were the Red-backed Hummingbird (*Selasphorus rufus*), often described as the Nootka Hummingbird, because it was first discovered in Nootka Sound, on the west side of Vancouver Island; the other, one of the smallest known species, called Calliope. This exquisite little bird is mainly conspicuous for its frill of minute pinnated feathers encircling the throat, of most delicate magenta tint, which can be raised or depressed at will. Prior to my finding it in this remote region, it was described as being entirely confined to Mexico.

About a week had passed away; the bridge was completed, during which time the female birds had arrived; and, save a stray one now and then, not a single individual of that numerous host that had gathered round the *Ribes* was to be seen. They cared nothing for the gun, and would even dash at a dead companion as it lay on the grass; so I did not drive them away, but left them to scatter of their own free will.

My next camping-place was on the western slope of the Rocky Mountains, near a lake, by the margin of which grew some cottonwood trees (*Salix scouleriana*), together with the alder (*Alnus oregona*), and the sweet or black birch (*Betula leuta*). My attention was called to the latter tree by observing numbers of wasps, bees, and hornets swarming round its trunk. The secret was soon disclosed: a sweet gummy sap was exuding plentifully from splits in the bark, on which hosts of insects, large and small, were regaling themselves. As the sap ran down over the bark, it became very sticky, and numbers of small winged insects, pitching on it, were trapped in a natural 'catch-'em-alive-O.'

Busily occupied in picking off these captives were several very sombre-looking hummingbirds. They poised themselves just as the others did over the flowers, and deftly nipped, as with delicate forceps, the helpless insects. I soon bagged one, and found I had a third species, the Black-throated Hummingbird (*Trochilus Alexandri*). Were any proof needed to establish the fact of hummingbirds being insect-feeders, this should be sufficient. I saw the bird, not only on this occasion but dozens of times afterwards, pick the insect from off the tree, often killing it in the act; and found the stomach, on being opened, filled with various species of winged insects.

The habits of the three species differ widely. The Red-backed Hummingbird loves to flit over the open prairies, stopping at every tempting flower, to catch some idler lurking in its nectar-cells. Building its nest generally in a low shrub, and close to the rippling stream, it finds pleasant music in its ceaseless splash. Minute Calliope, on the other hand, prefers rocky hillsides at great altitudes, where only pine-trees, rock-plants, and an alpine flora 'struggle for existence.' I have frequently killed this bird above the line of perpetual snow. Its favourite resting-place is on the extreme point of a dead pine-tree, where, if undisturbed, it will sit for hours. The site chosen for the nest is usually the branch of a young pine; artfully concealed amidst the fronds at the very end, it is rocked like a cradle by every passing breeze.

The Black-throated Hummingbird lingers around lakes, pools, and swamps where its favourite trapping-tree grows. I have occasionally, though very rarely, seen it hovering over flowers; this, I apprehend, is only when the storehouse is empty, and the sap too dry to capture the insects. They generally build in the birch or alder, selecting the fork of a branch high up.

All hummingbirds, as far as I know, lay only two eggs; the young are so tightly packed into the nest, and fit so exactly, that if once taken out it is impossible to replace them. Several springs succeeding my first discovery that these hummingbirds were regular migrants to boreal regions, I watched their arrival. We were quartered for the winter close to the western slopes of the Rocky Mountains. The winters here vary in length, as well as in depth of snow and intensity of cold, 33° below zero being no unfrequent register. But it did not matter whether we had a late or early spring, the hummingbirds did not come until the *Ribes* opened; and in no single instance did two whole days elapse after the blossoms expanded, but Selasphorus and Calliope arrived to bid them welcome. The males usually preceded the females by four or five days.

The Black-throated Hummingbird arrives about a week or ten days after the other two. Marvellous is the instinct that guides and the power that sustains these birds (not larger than a good sized humblebee) over such an immense tract of country; and even more wonderful still is their arrival, timed so accurately, that the only flower adapted to its wants thus early in the year opens its hoards, ready to supply the wanderer's necessities after so tedious a migration!

It seems to me vastly like design, and Fore-seeing Wisdom, that a shrub indigenous and widely distributed should be so fashioned as to produce its blossoms long before its leaves; and that this very plant alone blooms ere the snow has melted off the land, and that too at the exact period when hummingbirds arrive. It cannot be chance, but the work of the Almighty Architect—who shaped them both, whose handi-work we discover at every step, and of whose sublime conceptions we everywhere observe the manifestations in the admirably-balanced system of creation!

The specific characters of these three species, whose northern range I believe was first defined by myself, are briefly as follows:—

Selasphorus rufus (the Nootka or Red-backed Hummingbird).—Male: tail strong and wedge-shaped; upper parts, lower tail-coverts, and back, cinnamon; throat coppery red, with a well-developed ruff of the same, bordered with a white collar; tail-feathers cinnamon, striped with purplish-brown. Female: plain, cinnamon on the back, replaced with green; traces only of metallic feathers on the throat. Length of male, 3·50; wing, 1·56; tail, 1·31 inches. Habitat: West coast of North America to lat. 53° N., extending its range southward through California, to the Rio Grande.

Stellata Calliope.—Male: back bright-green; wings brownish; neck with a ruff of pinnated magenta-coloured feathers, the lower ones much elongated; abdomen whitish; length, about 2·75 inches. Female, much plainer than the male, with only a trace of the magenta-coloured ruff.

Trochilus Alexandri (Black-throated Hummingbird).—Male: tails lightly forked, the chin and upper part of the throat velvety black without metallic reflections, which are confined to the posterior border of the black, and are violet, changing to steel-blue. Length, 3·30 inches. Female, without the metallic markings; tail-feathers tipped with white. Both have the same northern and southern range as *Selasphorus rufus*.

Urotrichus Gibsii, Baird (Western slope of Cascade Mountains); *Urotrichus Talpoides*, Temminck.—This singular little animal, that appears to be an intermediate link between the shrew and the mole, at present is only known as an inhabitant of two parts of the world, widely removed from each other—the one spot being the western slope of the Cascade Mountains, in North-west America, the other Japan. There are, as far as I know, but two specimens extant from the Cascade Mountains—one in the Smithsonian Museum at Washington, the other a very fine specimen that I have recently brought home, and now in the British Museum.* I have carefully compared the Japanese gentleman with his brother from the Western wilds, and can find no difference whatever, either generically or specifically. In size, colour, shape, and anatomical structure they are precisely alike.

The habits of the little fellow from Japan I

* Vide Illustration.

THE UROTRICHUS

know nothing about, but with my friend from the North-west I am much more familiar; and I shall endeavour to introduce him to you as life-like as I can, from what I have jotted down in my notebook. First, then, the Urotrichus is an insectivorous mammal, its size that of a large shrew, about two-and-a-quarter inches in length, exclusive of tail, which is about an inch and a half. This tail is covered thickly with long hairs, which at the tip end in a tuft like a fine camel's-hair pencil, and from this hairy tail it gets the name, *Urotrichus*.

Its colour is bluish-black when alive, but in the dried specimens changes to sooty-brown. The hair is lustrous, and, where it reflects the light, has a hoary appearance, and, as with the mole, it can be smoothed in either direction; this is a wise and admirable arrangement, as it enables the animal to back through its underground roads, as well as to go through them head-first. Its nose or snout is very curious, and much like that of a pig—only that it is lengthened out into a cylindrical tube, covered with short thick hairs, and terminated in a naked fleshy kind of bulb or gland; and this gland is pierced by two minute holes, which are the nostrils. Each nostril has a little fold of membrane hanging down over it like a shutter, effectually preventing sand and minute particles of dust from getting into the nose whilst digging.

Now this curious nasal appendage is to this miner not only an organ of smell, but also serves the purpose of hands and eyes. His forefeet, as I shall by-and-by show you, are wholly digging implements, and, from their peculiar horny character, not in any way adapted to convey the sense of touch. Eyes he has none, and but a very rudimentary form of ear; his highly sensitive moveable nose serves him admirably in the dark tunnels, in which his time is passed, to feel his way and scent out the lower forms of insect life, on which he principally feeds. Had he eyes he could not see, for the sunlight never peeps in to cheer his subterranean home, and sound reaches not down to him. The busy hum of insect life, and the song of feathered choristers, he hears not, so that highly-developed hearing appendages would have been useless and superfluous.

But his nose in every way compensates for all these apparent deficiencies, and shows us how to be admired is Creative Goodness in shaping and adapting the meanest and humblest of His creatures to its habits and modes of life. His forefeet are, like the mole's, converted into diggers;

the strong scoop-shaped nail, like a small garden-trowel at the end of each toe, enables him to dig with wonderful ease and celerity. The hind-feet are shaped into a kind of scraper by the toe being curiously bent, and the length of the hind-foot is about two-thirds more than the fore or digging hand. When I come to his habits, as differing from the mole, I shall be able to point out the use of this strange scraper-like form of hind-foot.

So far I have endeavoured to give you an outline of his general personal appearance, differing from the shrew in the peculiar arrangement of his feet, and from the mole in having a long hairy tail. His nearest relative (if at all related) is the *Condylura*, or Star-nosed Mole, whose nose has a fringe of star-shaped processes round its outer edge, about twenty-two in number. The first and only place in which I ever met this strange little fellow was on the Chilukweyuk prairies. These large grassy openings, or prairies, are situated near the Fraser river, on the western side of the Cascade Mountains. Small streams wind and twist through these prairies like huge water-snakes, widening out here and there into large glassy pools.

The scenery is romantic and beautiful beyond description. Towering up into the very clouds, as a background, are the mighty hills of the Cascade range, their misty summits capped with perpetual snow—their craggy sides rent into chasms and ravines, whose depths and solitudes no man's foot has ever trodden, and clad up to the very snow-line with mighty pine and cedar-trees. The Chilukweyuk river already referred to washes one side of the prairie. Silvery-green and ever-trembling cotton-wood trees, ruddy black-birch, and hawthorn, like a girdle, encircle the prairie, and form a border, of Nature's own weaving, to the brilliant carpet of emerald grass, patterned with wild flowers of every hue and tint,—all shading pleasantly away, and losing their brilliancy in the dark green pine-trees.

In the sandy banks on the edge of the Chilukweyuk river, and the various little streams winding through the prairie-grass, lives the Urotrichus. His mansion is a large hole, lined with bits of grass, and this hole is his sleeping-room and drawing-room. A genuine bachelor, he never dines at home. He has lots of roads tunnelled away from his central mansion, radiating from it like the spokes of a wheel. His tunnels are not at all like those of the mole; he never throws up mounds or heaps of earth, in order to get rid of the surplus material he digs out, as the mole does, but makes open cuttings at short intervals, about four or five inches long; and now we shall see the use of those curiously-formed scraper-like hind-feet.

As he digs out the tunnel with his trowel-hands, he throws back the earth towards his hind-feet; these, from their peculiar shape, enable him to back this dirt out of the hole, using them like two scrapers—only that he pushes the dirt away, instead of pulling it towards himself. Having backed the dirt clear of the mouth of the hole, he throws it out over the edge of the open cutting; after having dug in some distance—and finding, I daresay, the labour of backing-out rather irk-some—he digs up through the ground to the surface, makes another open cutting, and then begins a new hole or tunnel, and disappears into the earth again. When he has gone as far from his dormitory as he deems wise, he again digs through, and clears away the rubbish. This road is now complete, so he goes back again to his central mansion, to begin others at his leisure.

It is very difficult to watch the movements and discover the feeding-time, or what he feeds on, of an animal which lives almost wholly under-ground in the daytime; but I am pretty sure these tunnels are made for and used as roadways, or underground trails for the purpose of hunting. He is a night-feeder, and exposed to terrible perils from the various small carnivora that prowl about like bandits in the dark—stoats, weasels, martens, and skunks. So, to avoid and escape these enemies, he comes quietly along the subterranean roadways, and cautiously emerging at the open cutting, feels about with his wonderful nose; and I doubt not, guided by an acute sense of smell, pounces upon larvæ, slugs, beetles, or any nocturnal creeping-thing he can catch; and so traversing his different hunting-trails during the night, manages in that way to fare sumptuously, and safe from danger. Turning in, to sleep away his breakfast, dinner, and supper, at the first peep of the grey morning, he dozes on, until hunger again prompts him to make another excursion on the 'hunting-path.'

It is scarcely possible to imagine a more skilfully-contrived hunting-system, to avoid danger and facilitate escape, than are these tunnel-trails with open cuttings; for the sly little hunter has, on the slightest alarm, two means of flight at his disposal—one before and another behind him; and the fur, as I have already mentioned, laying as evenly when smoothed from tail to head as it does when turned in the natural direction, enables him to turn astern, and retreat tail-first into his hole as easily as he could go head-first.

When we contemplate this grotesque and strangely-formed little creature, and see how wisely and wonderfully it is fashioned and adapted to its destined place, supplying another missing link in the great chain of Nature, we cannot but feel God's power and omnipresence. Feeding in the dark and living in the dark, eyes would have been superfluous; sound, save from vibration in the earth, or when hunting at the open cuttings, would seldom reach this tiny *hermit*; hence the hearing organs have no external appendage for catching sounds, and are but in a rudimentary form. Hands fashioned into marvellous digging-tools, and hind-feet turned into scrapers, for getting rid of the rubble dug out with the hands, and nose possessing smell and touch in their most exquisite forms, these serve him for guides of unerring certainty and undeviating precision through his darksome wanderings.

CHAPTER XIII.

THE APLODONTIA LEPORINA. (RICH.)

(*Sewellel or Show'tl of the Nesqually Indians.*)

SYNONYMS.—*Aplodontia leporina*, Rich., F.B.A. i. 211, plate xviii.; Aud. Bach. N.A. Qua. iii., 1853, 99, pl. cxxiii.; *Hoplodon leporinus*, Wagler System, Amh., 1830; *Anisonyx rufa*, Rafinesque, Am. Month. Mag. ii. 1817; *Arctomys rufa*, Harlan, F. Am. 1825, 308; *Sewellel*, Lewis and Clark's Travels, ii. 1815, 176.

General Dimensions.—Nose to ear, 2 in. 7 lines; nose to eyes, 1 in. 5 lines; tail to end of vertebræ, 9 lines; tail to end of hair, 1 in. 2 lines; ear, height, 5 lines; nose to root of tail, 14 in. 6 lines.

I FIRST met with this rare and curious little rodent on the bank of the Chilukweyuk river. My canvas house is pitched in a snug spot, overshadowed by a clump of cottonwood trees, growing close to a stream, that like liquid crystal ripples past in countless channels, finding its way betwixt massive boulders of trap and greenstone, rounded and polished until they look like giant marbles.

Towering up behind me are the Cascade Moun-

OU-KA-LA

tains, with snow-clad summits dim in the haze of distance, their craggy slopes split into chasms and ravines, so deep, dark, and lonesome, that no man's footfall has ever disturbed their solitudes, so densely wooded up to the very snow-line with pine, that a bare rock has hardly a chance to peep out, and break the sombre monotony of the dark-green foliage.

Before me, stretching away for about three miles, is an open grassy prairie, one side of which is bounded by the Chilukweyuk river, the other by the Fraser. At the junction of the two streams, at an angle of the prairie, stands an Indian village: the rude-plank sheds and rush-lodges; the white smoke, curling gracefully up through the still atmosphere from many lodge-fires; the dusky forms of the savages, as they loll or stroll in the fitful night, give life and character to a scene indescribably lovely.

The Indian summer is drawing to a close; the maple, the cottonwood, and the hawthorn, fringing the winding waterways, like silver cords intersecting the prairie, have assumed their autumn tints, and, clad in browns and yellows, stand out in brilliant contrast to the green of the pine-forest. The prairie looks bright and lovely; the grass, as yet untouched by the frost-fairy's fingers, waves lazily; wild flowers, of varied tints, peep out from their hiding-places, enjoying to the last the lingering summer.

I had been for some time sitting on a log, admiring the sublime beauty of the scene, spread out before me like a gorgeous picture; the sun was fast receding behind the hilltops, the lengthening shadows were fading and growing dimly indistinct, the birds had settled down to sleep, and the busy hum of insect life was hushed. A deathlike quiet steals over everything in the wilderness as night comes on—a stillness that is painful from its intensity. The sound of your own breathing, the crack of a branch, a stone suddenly rattling down the hillside, the howl of the coyote, or the whoop of the night-owl, seem all intensified to an unnatural loudness. I know of nothing more appalling to the lonely wanderer camping by himself than this 'jungle silence,' that reigns through the weary hours of night.

This silence was suddenly broken, as was my reverie, by a sharp ringing whistle; it was so piercing and clear, that I could not believe it was produced by an animal. Hardly had it died away, when another whistler took it up, then a third, and so on, until at least a dozen had joined in the chorus. I stole carefully in the direction from which the sound came, but as I neared the spot the whistle ceased, and it was now far too dark to descry any object on the ground. So, in doubt, and sorely puzzled to account for such an unusual sound, and with a firm determination to unravel the mystery in the morning, I returned to my camp. Could it be Indians? No, impossible; there were far too many whistlers, and the tone of each whistle was precisely alike. I was equally sure it was not the cry of the rock-whistler (*Actomys*); that sound I knew too well. What could it be?

As the grey light of morning came peering into my tent, I started off to investigate the secret of the mysterious whistler; but all I could discover, after a long and diligent search, was, that there were numerous runs and burrows excavated in the sandy banks of the river, but by what sort of animal I could not for the life of me guess. Setting a steel-trap at the entrance to one of the holes, I strolled down to the Indian village, thinking I should possibly be able to find out from the redskins what it was that made such shrill sounds. Partly by signs, and by using as much of their language as I knew, I endeavoured to make the old chief comprehend my queries.

After attentively watching my absurd attempts to produce a ringing whistle by placing my fingers in my mouth, and blowing through them until my face was like an apoplectic coachman's, a smile of intelligence lit up his swarthy visage: then I violently dug imaginary holes, and explained that the sounds came about twilight; he nodded his head, dived into the tent, and disappeared in the smoke, to shortly emerge again with a rug or robe, made from the skins of an animal that was quite new to me.

It was beautifully soft, glossy, and brown. The skins were about the size of a large rat's, and about twenty in number. Here, then, was the dawn of a discovery. He called the animal *Ou-ka-la*, and made me understand that it lived on roots and vegetable matter, and burrowed holes in the ground.

As the daylight faded out, I again took my seat; and, just as before, when everything was silent, the woods echoed with the Ou-ka-la's cry. I longed for morning, and hardly waited for light, but hastened off to my trap; and, joy of joys, I had one sure enough, caught by the neck. Poor Ou-ka-la! your friends had heard, and you had given, your 'last whistle.' He was dead and cold—trapped, perhaps, whilst I listened wonderingly, keeping my lonely vigil. A very brief examination revealed the fact that I had caught a magnificent specimen of the Aplodontia leporina, of which I had only read.

Captains Lewis and Clark obtained some vague information about this animal, which is given in their journal of travel across the Rocky Mountains, in 1804. All they say of its habits is, 'that it climbs trees, and digs like a squirrel.' They obtained no specimen of the animal, but saw, probably, robes made of the skins. It was subsequently described by Rafinesque, and by him named *Anysonyx rufa*, and by Harlan *Arctomys rufa*. In 1829 Sir John Richardson obtained a specimen, and, after a careful anatomical examination, this eminent naturalist determined it to be a new genus, and renamed it, generically and specifically. The generic name (*Aplodontia*) is founded on its having rootless molars, or grinding teeth—*aploos*, simple; *odons*, a tooth. It belongs to the sub-family *Castorinæ*, dental formula $\frac{2}{2} \frac{00}{00} \frac{55}{44}$ 22.

Sp. ch.—Size, that of a musk-rat; tail very short, barely visible; colour, glossy blackish-brown. Male, length about 14 inches; female resembling the male, but smaller. The fur is dense and woolly, with long bristly hairs, thickly interspersed; the short fur is bluish-gray at the base, the ends of the hairs being tipped with reddish-brown; the bristles are black, and when smooth give a lustrous appearance to the fur. The eyes are very small, and placed about midway between the nose and the ear. The whiskers, stiff and bristly, are much longer than the head, and dark grey. The ears are covered on both sides with fine soft hair, rounded and very short, and not unlike the human ear.

Skull.—The skull is much like that of the squirrel's, with the marked exception of having rootless molars, and the absence of post-orbital processes; the occipital crest is well-developed, the muzzle large, and nearly round. The bony orbits are largely developed; the auditory bullæ are small, but open at once into wide auditive tubes; the first molar is unusually small, oval, and situated against the antero-internal angle of the second. All the molars are rootless: the lower grinders are much like the upper, but somewhat longer and narrower. The molars in both jaws are situated much farther back than is usual, the centre of the skull being about opposite to the meeting of the second and third. The lower jaw is very singularly shaped, the inner edges of the molars on opposite sides being parallel; the descending ramus is bent, so as to be exactly horizontal behind, the postero-inferior edge being a straight line, nearly perpendicular to the vertical plane of the skull's axis. The conformation of the incisor-teeth is admirably adapted to the purposes they have to fulfil; no carpenter's gouging chisels are more effective tools than are these exquisitely-constructed teeth. It is essential that they should always have a sharp-cutting edge, in order to nip through the tough vegetable fibre on which the animal subsists; at the same time, strength and durability are indispensable. The Aplodontia has no whetstone or razor-grinder, to sharpen his tools when they grow blunt; but an Allwise Providence has so fashioned these wondrous chisels in all rodents, that the more they are used the sharper they keep; the contrivance is simple as it is beautiful. The substance of the tooth itself is composed of tough ivory, but plated on the outer surface with enamel as hard as steel. The ivory, being the softer material, of course wears away faster than the enamel; hence the latter, plating the front of the tooth, is always left with a sharp-cutting edge.

The position this genus should occupy, in a systematic arrangement of the rodents, has always been a stumbling-block and a matter of doubt, in great measure attributable to the fact that but a single species of the genus is known, and very few specimens have hitherto been obtained. A fine male specimen has recently been set up in the British Museum collection, that I caught near my camp on the prairie.

In many particulars the Aplodontia very nearly resembles the Spermophiles, particularly the prairie-dog (*Cynomys Ludovicciana*), but differs, as in the true squirrels, in the rootless molars and absence of post-orbital processes. In this respect it is allied to the beaver. It is quite impossible to assign it a well-defined and settled position, until a greater number of specimens are procured, from which more minute and careful examination of the bony and internal anatomy can be made. At present, however, it would appear to connect the beavers with the squirrels, through the Spermophiles.

The name Lewis and Clark gave this animal, Sewellel, is evidently a corruption of an Indian word. The Chinook Indians, once a powerful tribe, live near the mouth of the Columbia; and from them, in all probability, Lewis and Clark obtained the name, and first heard of the animal. But the Chinook name for the Aplodontia is *Og-*

ool-lal, Shu-wal-lal being the name of the robe made from the skins; and this is unquestionably the word corrupted into Sewellel, and misused as the name of the animal. In Puget's Sound the Nesqually Indians call it *Show'tl*; the Yakama Indians, *Squal-lah*; and the Sumass Indians, *Swok-la*.

A single glance at the conformation of the feet would at once convince the most careless observer that climbing trees was not a habit of the Aplodontia. The feet and claws are digging implements, of the most finished and efficient kind: the long scoop-shaped nails, resembling garden trowels; wide strong foot, almost hand-like in its form; the strong muscular arms, supported by powerful clavicles, proclaim him a miner; his mission is to burrow, and most ably he fulfils his destiny. His haunt is usually by the side of a stream, where the banks are sandy, and the underbrush grows thickly; his favourite food being fine fibrous roots, and the rind of such as are too hard for his teeth. He spends his time in burrowing, not so much for shelter and concealment, as to supply himself with roots. He digs with great ease and rapidity, making a hole large enough for a man's arm to be inserted.

In making the tunnels, he seldom burrows very

far without coming to the surface, and beginning a new one. Like a skilful workman, he knows how to economise labour. Having to back the earth out of the mouth of the hole he is digging, the farther he gets in the harder grows the toil; and so he digs up through, and starts afresh, They seldom come out in the daytime, and I have but rarely heard them whistle until everything was still, and the twilight merged into night.

The female has from four to six young at a birth, and she has about two litters in a year. The nest for the young is much like that of the rabbit, made of grass and leaves, and placed at the end of a deep burrow. In the winter they only partially hybernate, frequently digging through the snow to eat the bark and lichen from the trees. Their gait when on the ground is very awkward; their broad short feet are not fitted for progression, and they shamble rather than run, and can be easily overtaken. Where a colony of them have resided for any time, the ground becomes literally riddled with holes, and the trees and shrubs die for want of roots. I imagine, from having found abandoned villages, that they wisely emigrate when their resources are exhausted. The Indians esteem their flesh a great luxury, and trap them in a kind of figure-of-four trap, set at the mouth of the burrow. I daresay they are as good as a rabbit; still, they have too ratlike an appearance to possess any gastronomic attractions for me. *De gustibus non est disputandum.*

The Aplodontia has a terrible and untiring enemy in the badger (*Taxidea Americana*). He is always on the hunt for the poor little miner, digs him out from his hiding-place, and devours him with as much gusto as the Indian. Its geographical range is not very extended, being, as far as I know, confined to a small section of North-western America. I have seen it on the eastern and western slopes of the Cascades, but not on the Rocky Mountains, although it very probably exists there. It is also found at Puget's Sound, Fort Steilacum, and on the banks of the Sumass and Chilukweyuk rivers, west of the Cascades; on the Nachess Pass, at Astoria and the Dalles, on the Columbia, east of the Cascades.

Feeding entirely on vegetable matter (I never discovered a trace of insect or larvæ remains in the stomach), passing its life principally in dark burrows, and limited, as far as we know at present, to a very narrow section of a barren country, it is hard to imagine what purpose it serves in the great chain of Nature, save it be that of supplying food to the badger, and both food and clothing to the savage; and yet we know that it was fashioned for some specific purpose, if we could but read and rightly interpret the pages of Nature's wondrous book. If we ask ourselves, Why was this or that made? how seldom can we answer the question! Why did He, who made the world, the sun, and the stars, deck the butterfly's wing with tiny scales, that by a simple change in arrangement produce patterns beside which the most finished painting is a bungling daub? Why exist those microscopic wonders, (diatoms and infusoria,) formed with shells of purest flint, and of the quaintest devices? Why were these atomies, that tenant every roadside pool, which dance in the sunbeam, and float on the wings of the breeze? Why all the prodigal variety of strange forms crowding the sea, forms more wonderful than the poet's wildest dreams ever pictured? Who can tell?

END OF THE FIRST VOLUME.

LONDON
PRINTED BY SPOTTISWOODE AND CO.
NEW-STREET SQUARE

Lightning Source UK Ltd.
Milton Keynes UK
UKHW031039210519
343056UK00008B/2628/P